To Brendan
Best regards,

John Eckler

MASTERFUL WORDS

JOHN ESHLEMAN

ROBERT D. REED PUBLISHERS • SAN FRANCISCO, CA

Robert D. Reed Publishers
750 La Playa Street, Suite 647
San Francisco, CA 94121
Phone: 650/994-6570 • Fax: -6579
E-mail: 4bobreed@msn.com
www.rdrpublishers.com

Book Design by Marilyn Yasmine Nadel
Cover Design by Julia Gaskill

ISBN: 1-931741-06-9
Library of Congress Card Number: 20001118494
Produced and Printed in the United States of America

*"Words are, of course,
the most powerful drug used
by mankind."* — Rudyard Kipling

CONTENTS

PREFACE

A t about age eight I received a small dictionary that contained mostly one-word definitions. Coming across the word absurd, I consulted my new dictionary, to discover that it meant preposterous, which was of little or no help. It felt like being squeezed in a steel trap upon finding that preposterous meant absurd, relegating me back to square one. Besides picking up an object lesson in life, namely, that these "closed cycle" situations will recur at unscheduled intervals, my fascination with words probably began with that experience.

As time went on I started to make a note of each new, unfamiliar word. It got to the point that I would underline at least five or six such words a day, finish the reading, then go back and write each underlined word on a special pad, and systematically enter the definitions from a dictionary. I discovered that the reading then made much more sense than it did the first time, especially when putting the words in context.

That procedure, however, was time-consuming, unwieldy, and involved the use of rote. There must be a better way, and there is. Knowing not only what a word means, but why, becomes important. Etymology—the history of a word and its cognates traced back to its origin—is a valuable and exciting study; but it, too, is a lengthy process. I decided to short-cut the etymology to the single word in the history that most closely approaches the meaning of the modern word. Also, the word parts, e.g., the prefixes, roots, and stems, tell a lot about a word.

The reader should enjoy this book on the way to better communication skills as a result of a greatly expanded vocabulary.

INTRODUCTION

This book is well suited for students in high school and beyond, especially those in colleges and universities. Its use will successfully lead to better communication, writing, comprehension, language, and vastly improved conversational skills. This, in turn, will widen the imagination and thought processes, leading to improved creativity potential. A mastery of the book will form a solid matrix for the educated use of English.

This book, however, need not be limited to students in school. Indeed, business and professional people who feel they have received insufficient liberal arts education can make excellent use of this book.

The book can be used as a course in itself or studied on an individual basis.

Masterful Words is divided into two parts. The first deals with word parts, namely, prefixes, roots, stems, suffixes, and examples of each. It also includes a quiz and Latin words, their meanings, and English derivatives. Part II contains the main text, namely, the study of more than 1,400 selected words. These words were culled from several years of reading novels, periodicals, op-ed pages, letters to the editor, think-tank publications, alumni magazines, musical and art reviews, syndicated columnists, political commentaries, and books and articles by university presidents and Nobel laureates. I feel that many more people should know and make use of these words.

Part II is designed to show the relationship between old words, usually Latin or Greek, and their modern counterparts, as well as their respective meanings. Knowing where a present word comes from helps one to understand why it has its meaning. The "etymology" is limited to a single word of origin, or a later word, for the sake of brevity and clarity of understanding.

A list of such word comparisons appear on each page, alphabetically arranged for convenience. Sample sentences for each word appear on the reverse side in the same order to show how they can be used in various circumstances.

Quizzes, which ask the reader to match each word with its meaning, appear periodically. Also included in each quiz are ten multiple choice questions, some of which are rather amusing. There are usually over 150 new words in each segment. Many of the early words appear in later sample sentences, reinforcing what has already been learned. Every ninety pages there is a review quiz, and a final review quiz at the end of the book.

Everyone is encouraged to pronounce each word aloud, spell it, and use it in an original phrase or sentence. A pronunciation guide is provided after the main text. *Masterful Words* is so named, because anyone who finishes it will indeed be a master of words. Enjoy it!

PART ONE

To better understand words, it is a good idea to know their component parts. The first part of this course deals with types of word parts. They are, in order: common prefixes, examples of the same prefixes, numerical prefixes, Latin roots, their meanings and derivatives, and stems and suffixes, with examples of each.

New and unfamiliar words often appear at first as mysterious obstacles. The mystery, however, largely disappears for those well acquainted with word parts. Each word part not only tells a lot about a given word, but also branches out for use in many other words, as the examples illustrate.

Become well versed in these word parts. A thorough knowledge of them will make the recognition and learning of words much easier and more enjoyable.

COMMON PREFIXES

a- = without

ab- = from, away, off

ad- = to, toward, in the direction of

ambi- = both, around

ante- = before (in time and space)

anti- = against

apo- = from, away

arch- = main, chief, principal

astr- astro- = star

auto- = self, by oneself or it

be- = completely

bene- = well

bi- = two

by- = near, extra

chrono- = time

co-, col-, com- = with, together

com- = together (see co- above)

circum- = around, about

contra- = against, contrary

cyclo- = circle

de- = down, from, away

demi- = half; less than usual in size, power, etc.

di- = twice, twofold; double

dia- = through, across

dis- = not, away, apart

dynam- = force, power

dys- = bad, ill, abnormal, impaired

endo- = within

epi- = upon, beside, attached to, over

eso- = within

ex-, e-, ec- = out, from

exo- = outside

eu- = well, good

gyro- = rotating, turning, whirling

hemi- and semi- = half

hetero- = other, different

homo- = same, similar, alike

hyper- = above, beyond, extreme

hypo- = under, beneath, down

il-, im-, in-, ir- = not

infra- = below, beneath

inter- = between, among, during

intra- = within, inside

iso- = equal, homogenous, uniform, same

macro- = large

mal- = bad, ill, faulty, wrong, inadequate

mega- = great, large, powerful; million

meta- = along with, after, between; change

micro- = small

mis- = wrong, ill, bad; badly, wrongly

multi- = many, much, multiple, several

neo- = new, recent

ob- = in the way, against; toward

oligo- = few

omni- = all

ortho- = straight, regular, upright, vertical

para- = at the side of, alongside; subsidiary to

per- = through, throughout, during, by means of,

peri- = all around; about, near, surrounding

philo- = loving, liking; predisposed to

poly- = many; several, much

post- = after, later, subsequent

pre- = before; earlier than, prior to

pro- (1) = before in place or time

pro- (2) = moving forward; for, in favor of

proto- = first in time, original; principal, chief

pseud- or pseudo- = false, fake

quasi- = in some sense or degree; somewhat

re- = back, again; against

retro- = backwards, back; in the past

rheo- = flow

sub- = under, up towards, beneath, below

super- = over, above, on top of; extra

supra- above, over, akin to super

tele- = afar, from a distance

trans- = across, through; on the other side

ultra- = farther on, beyond; on the farthest side

un- = not, non- thoroughly; to destruction

vice- = a substitute; subordinate, deputy

xeno- = strange, foreign; stranger, foreigner

QUIZ

1. Match each prefix in the left-hand column with its *opposite* in the right-hand column:

ad-	___	(a)	mal-, male-	macro- ___	(a)	mis-
uni-	___	(b)	post	hypo- ___	(b)	mono-
bene-	___	(c)	infra-	supra- ___	(c)	endo-
pro-(2)	___	(d)	exo-	hetero- ___	(d)	micro-
ante-	___	(e)	multi-	poly- ___	(e)	hyper-
super-	___	(f)	ab-	eu- ___	(f)	sub-
eso-	___	(g)	anti-	ec-, ex-- ___	(g)	homo-

2. Select the prefix which is *closest in meaning* to the one in the left-hand column:

dia-	___	(a) meta-	(b) omni-	(c) trans-	(d) supra-
arch-	___	(a) hyper-	(b) quasi-	(c) oligo-	(d) proto-
mega-	___	(a) super-	(b) macro-	(c) rheo-	(d) para-
endo-	___	(a) hypo-	(b) ortho-	(c) intra-	(d) ob-
peri-	___	(a) circum-	(b) tele-	(c) micro-	(d) philo-
anti-	___	(a) retro-	(b) meta-	(c) contra-	(d) hetero-
ante-	___	(a) ultra-	(b) pre-	(c) endo-	(d) dynam-
apo-	___	(a) hypo-	(b) ab-	(c) post-	(d) infra-
mal-	___	(a) mis-	(b) epi-	(c) dis-	(d) exo-
sub-	___	(a) ambi-	(b) supra-	(c) infra-	(d) iso-

3. Select the word which best defines the prefix:

retro- ____	(a) above	(b) after	(c) backwards	(d) under
quasi- ____	(a) chief	(b) upon	(c) across	(d) somewhat
pseud- ____	(a) apart	(b) afar	(c) false	(d) bad
ortho- ____	(a) near	(b) straight	(c) around	(d) alongside
trans- ____	(a) toward	(b) before	(c) across	(d) within
hetero- ____	(a) different	(b) rotating	(c) beyond	(d) extreme
xeno- ____	(a) same	(b) foreign	(c) against	(d) few
mega- ____	(a) wrong	(b) between	(c) large	(d) along with
auto- ____	(a) eso-	(b) self	(c) through	(d) force

4. Select the prefix which best describes the word:

new ____	(a) tele-	(b) neo-	(c) peri-	(d) exo-
time ____	(a) post-	(b) circum-	(c) chrono-	(d) proto-
loving ____	(a) para-	(b) philo-	(c) com-	(d) sym-
same ____	(a) hetero-	(b) iso-	(c) trans-	(d) oligo-
all ____	(a) quasi-	(b) endo-	(c) omni-	(d) poly-
well ____	(a) bene-	(b) intra-	(c) super-	(d) meta-
after ____	(a) trans-	(b) proto-	(c) post-	(d) ante-
to ____	(a) epi-	(b) ad-	(c) ab-	(d) syn-
among ____	(a) endo-	(b) pro-(1)	(c) exo-	(d) inter-
bad ____	(a) hypo-	(b) dys-	(c) eu-	(d) retro-

PREFIX EXAMPLES

a- = un-, not, without

a-moral	= being *neither* moral *nor* immoral; incapable of distinguishing between right and wrong
a-pathy	= *without* feeling or emotion; lack of interest or concern
a-political	= having *no* interest in politics
a-tonal	= *without* a tonal center or key, in music
a-typical	= *not* typical; irregular, unusual

ab- = from, away, off

ab-duct	= to carry *off* (as a person) by force
ab-errant	= straying *from* the right or normal way; deviating *from* the usual or normal type; atypical
ab-normal	= deviating *from* the normal or average

ad- = to, toward, in the direction of

ad-here	= to stick *to*
ad-journ	= to suspend a session; to move *to* another place
ad-junct	= something joined or added to another thing
ad-nauseam	= to a sickening degree

ambi- = both; around

ambi-dextrous	= using both hands with equal ease
ambi-ance	= a surrounding or pervading atmosphere; environment
ambi-guous	= capable of being understood in two or more ways
ambi-t	= *circuit*, compass; a *sphere* of action or influence
ambi-vert	= a person like *both* an extrovert and introvert

ante- = before (in time and place); prior, earlier, prior to

ante-bellum	= *before* a war, esp. *before* the Civil War
ante-meridian	= being *before* noon (abbr.: A.M.)

anti- = against, opposed to

anti-bacterial	= that *checks* the growth or effects of bacteria
anti-smoking	= 1. one who *opposes* smoking

apo- = from, away, off; detached, separate

apo-siopesis	= the *leaving* of a thought incomplete by a sudden breaking *off*
apo-stasy	= *renunciation* of a religion; *abandonment* of a previous loyalty
apo-cope	= the cutting *off* or the *dropping* of the last sound of a word (Ex. mos' for most)

arch- = main, chief, principal
arch-enemy	= a *chief* enemy
arch-rival	= a *main* rival
arch-etype	= 1 the *original* pattern or model from which all other things of the same type are made; prototype
	2. a perfect example of a type or group

aster-, astro = star
aster-isk	= a star-like sign (*) used in printing for footnote references
aster-oid	= *star*-like; shaped like a star or starfish
astro-nomy	= the science of the universe in which the stars, planets, etc., are studied

auto- = self; by oneself or itself
auto-biography	= the story of one's own life written *by oneself*
auto-didact	= a person who is *self*-educated; a *self*-taught person
auto-matic	= moving, operating, etc., *by itself*
auto-maton	= anything that can move or act *by itself*

be- = completely, thoroughly; on, around, over; make, cause to be
be-draggle	= to wet *thoroughly*
be-fuddle	= to muddle or stupefy as if with drink; confuse, perplex
be-little	= to *cause* a person or thing to seem little or less
be-friend	= to act as a friend to

bene- = well
bene-diction	= expression of *good* wishes
bene-fit	= anything contributing to an *improvement* in condition; help
bene-volent	= disposed to doing *good; kindly; charitable*

bi- = two
bi-cycle	= a vehicle with *two* wheels
bi-sect	= to divide into *two* parts, usually equal parts
bi-ennial	= occurring every *two* years
bi-monthly	= 1 occurring every *two* months, and
	2. occurring *twice* a month (be sure you know *which* bimonthly is being referred to, e.g., pay ments, paychecks, events etc.)

by- = near, extra
by-stander	= a person who stands *near* but does not participate; a mere onlooker
by-product	= anything produced in the course of making another thing; secondary or incidental product or result, thus *extra*

chron, chrono- = time
  chrono-logical = arranged in the order of occurrence or *time* sequence
  chron-ic   = marked by long *duration* or frequent recurrence

circum- = around, about
  circa   = *about*, used before an approximate date or figure
  circum-ference = the *peri*meter (line *around*) of a circle
  circum-navigate = to go completely *around* instead of through; bypass
  circum-scribe = to draw a line *around*
  circum-stances = conditions *surrounding* and affecting a person
  circum-spect = careful to consider all related *circum*stances before
           acting, judging, or deciding; cautious, careful

co-, col-, com-, con- = with, together
  co-alesce   = to grow *together*; to unite into a whole; fuse
  co-exist   = to exist *together* or at the same time
  co-here   = to hold *together*; stick, adhere
  co-habit   = to live *together*
  col-lide   = to come *together* with solid impact; clash
  com-bine   = to merge; become one; to act *together*
  co-operate = to act or work *with* another or others; act *together*

contra- = against, contrary
  contra-band = illegal traffic; smuggled goods (illegal = *against* the law)
  contra-dict = to *resist* or *oppose* in argument; be *contrary* to
  contra-vene = to go or act *contrary* to; to oppose in argument
  contra-ry   = opposite

cyclo- = circle
  cyclo-ne   = a storm that spins clockwise in a *circular*
           motion in the Northern Hemisphere and
           counter-clockwise in the Southern Hemisphere
  en*cyclo*-pedia = a work that contains information on all branches of
           knowledge

de- = down, from, away: used in doing the opposite or reverse of, or
  the removal of
  de-activate = to make *in*active or *in*effective
  de-bilitate = to impair the strength of; enfeeble; weaken
  de-emphasize = to play *down*
  de-bug   = 1. to *eliminate* errors or malfunctions of
           2. to *remove* a concealed microphone or wiretaping device

demi- = half; less than usual in size, power, etc.
  demi-god   = a mythological being having more powers than a
           mortal but *less* than a god
  demi-tasse = a *small* cup for serving coffee

di- = twice, twofold; double
di-chotomy	= a division into *two* parts
di-midiate	= divided into *two* equal parts; *halved;* cut in *two*
di-plopia	= a visual disorder of seeing *two* images of a single object; *double* vision

dia- = through, across
dia-gonal	= *across* a polyhedron, connection opposite angles
dia-meter	= a chord passing *through* the center of a figure or body
dia-phanous	= having such fineness of texture as to permit seeing *through*

dis- = not, away, apart; do the opposite of; deprive of; exclude or expel from; opposite or absence of
dis-able	= *deprive of* strength; cripple; weaken
dis-abuse	= to *free from* error or fallacy
dis-agree	= to *fail* to agree; to *differ* in opinion
dis-bar	= to *expel from* the bar or the legal profession; *deprive* (an attorney) *of* legal status and privileges

dynam- = force, power
dynam-ic	= 1. relating to objects in motion; opposed to *static* 2. energetic; vigorous; forceful
dynam-o	= a forceful, *dynamic* person
dynam-ite	= a powerful explosive

dys- = bad, ill, abnormal, impaired, difficult, etc.
dys-function	= *abnormal, impaired,* or incomplete functioning, as of a body, organ, or part
dys-pepsia	= *impaired* digestion; indigestion
dys-pnea	= *shortness* of breath
dys-topia	= a hypothetical place, society, or situation in which conditions and the quality of life are *dreadful*
dys-trophy	= *faulty* development, or degeneration (muscular *dystrophy*)

endo- = within
endo-skeleton	= an *internal* skeleton (as in mammals as opposed to *exo*skeleton, as in snails, shellfish, turtles, etc.
endo-scope	= an instrument for viewing the *interior* of an organ

epi- = upon, beside, attached to; over, outer, after
epi-center	= the part of the earth's surface directly *above* the focus of an earthquake
epi-dermis	= the *outer (top)* layer of the skin
epi-dural	= located or administered *outside* the dura mater (brain membrane)
epi-logue	= *concluding* section that rounds out the design of a literary work

eso- = within
    eso-teric   = limited to (*within*) a small circle; understood only by a select few

eu- = well, good
    eu-logy   = high praise; commendation
    *eu*phemism   = the use of an *agreeable* expression for one that may offend or suggest something unpleasant

ex-, e-, ec- = out, from
    ec-centric   = 1. *off* center
                        2. deviating *from* the norm (conduct); *out* of the ordinary; odd
                        3. an odd or unconventional person
    ex-cavate   = to dig *out* (earth, soil, etc.); hollow *out*
    ex-pel   = 1. to drive *out* by force; eject
                        2. to dismiss or send away by authority
    e-vaporate   = to remove moisture *from* in the form of vapor; vanish

exo- = outside
    exo-dus   = a mass *departure*
    exo-genous   = produced or originating from *without*
    exo-tic   = *out of* the ordinary; excitingly strange

gyro- = ring, circle, spiral
    gyr-ate   = to move in a *circular* or *spiral* path; rotate on an axis; whirl
    gyro-scope   = a wheel that rotates so as to keep ships or planes level

hemi- and **semi-** = half
    hemi-sphere   = *half* a sphere, in this case, half of the world
    semi-annual   = *half* yearly, or every six months
    semi-circle   = *half* a circle

hetero- = other, different
    hetero- chromatic = having *different* colors
    hetero-dox   = *contrary to* or *different* from an acknowledged standard; holding *un*orthodox opinions or doctrines
    hetero-geneous = consisting of *dissimilar* ingredients; mixed
    hetero-morphic = *deviating from* the usual form; exhibiting *diversity* of form

homo- = same, similar, alike
    homo-chromatic = of or relating to *one* (the *same*) color
    homo-genous   = of the *same* kind or nature
    homo-logous   = having the *same* relative position, value, or structure
    homo-nym   = a word with the *same* pronunciation as another but with a different meaning and, usually, spelling (Ex., boar and bore)

hyper- = above, beyond, super; extreme, overly, excessively, too
   hyper-active   = *excessively* active
   hyper-bole   = *extravagant* exaggeration
   hyper-critical   = *too* critical
   hyper-glycemia = *abnormally high* concentration of sugar in the blood

hypo- = under, beneath, down
   hypo-dermic   = of or relating to parts *beneath* the skin
   hypo-tension   = abnormally *low* blood pressure
   hypo-thalamus = a part of the brain *beneath* the thalamus
   hypo-xia   = condition resulting from a *decrease* in oxygen to
                  body tissue

il-, im-, in-, ir- = not
   il-legal, *im*possible, *in*capable
                  = *not* legal, *not* possible, *not* capable
   ir-recoverable = that cannot be recovered, rectified, or remedied
   ir-revocable   = that cannot be revoked, recalled, or undone;
                  *un*alterable

infra- = below, beneath
   infra-dig   = being *beneath* one's dignity; undignified
   infra-human   = *less* or *lower* than human, esp. anthropoid
   infra-red   = designating those invisible rays just *beyond* the red
                  end of the visible spectrum
   infra-sonic   = having a frequency *below* the audibility range of
                  the human ear
   infra-structure = the *underlying* foundation or *sub*structure; also,
                  the basic installations and facilities on which a
                  community depends, as roads, schools, power
                  plants, transportation, and communication systems

inter- = between, among, during
   inter-collegiate = refers to relations *between* colleges and universities,
                  such as intercollegiate sports, debates, etc.
   inter-im   = the period of time *between*; meantime
   inter-lude   = anything that fills time *between* two events
   inter-mission = an interval of time *between* periods of activity;
                  pause, as *between* acts of a play
   inter-national = refers to relations *between* and/or *among* nations
   inter-state   = *between* states, e.g., *inter*state commerce, *inter*state
                  highways

intra- = within, inside
   intra-mural   = 1. (lit.) *within* or *inside* the walls or limits of
                    2. *inside* the same school; i.e., between or among members of the same school (e.g., intramural athletics)
   intra-vascular = situated *within* a vessel and esp. a blood vessel
   intra-venous = situated *within* or entering by way of a vein (IV injection)

iso- = equal, homogenous, uniform, same
   iso-bar   = a line on a map showing the *same* barometric pressure
   iso-chronal = *uniform* in time; having *equal* duration
   iso-morphic = having the *same* shape or form
   iso-thermal = having the *same* temperature
   iso-tonic   = having *equal* tension

macro- = large
   macro-cosm = the *great* world: universe
   macro-scopic = *large* enough to be seen by the naked eye

mal- = bad, ill, faulty, wrong, inadequate
   mal-content = a *dis*contented (unhappy) person
   mal-evolent = having or showing *ill* will; wishing *evil* or *harm* to others
   mal-function = to *fail* to function as it should

mega- = great, large, powerful; million
   mega-byte   = a *million* bytes
   mega-lith   = a *huge* stone, esp. one used in construction in ancient times
   mega-lopolis = a very *large* city
   mega-phone = a cone-shaped device used to *intensify* or direct a voice

meta- = along with, after, between, among; change; situated behind or beyond
   meta-plasia = *transformation (change)* of one tissue into another
   meta-chromatic = referring to a *change* or *changes* in color
   meta- morphosis = a *change* in form, shape, or structure
   meta-phor   = a word or phrase in place of another showing a likeness *between* them

micro- = small
   micro-climate = the fairly uniform climate of a small site or habitat
   micro-cosm   = a *little* world
   micro-gram   = one *millionth* of a gram
   micro-scope = an optical instrument for making enlarged images of *minute* objects

mis- = wrong, ill, bad; badly, wrongly
mis-behave   = to act *improperly*
mis-calculate = to calculate *wrongly*
mis-deed   = a *wrong* deed; offense
mis-use   = *incorrect* or *improper* use

multi- = many, much, multiple, several, many times over
multi-lateral = having *many* sides
multi-lingual = using or capable of using *several* languages
multi-millionaire = one who has *many* millions of dollars
multi-vitamin = a tablet or capsule that contains *several* vitamins

neo- = new, recent
*neo*genesis = *new* formation; regeneration
*neo*logy   = use of a *new* word, or a *new* use of an established
               word
*neo*phyte   = a *new* convert; *novice*
*neo*plasm   = an abnormal *new* grow

ob- = in the way, against, toward
*ob*stacle   = something that stands *in the way* or *opposes*
*ob*streperous = unruly; stubbornly *defiant*
*ob*struct   = to *block* or *close up; hinder;* be *in the way; impede*
*ob*trude   = to thrust *forward* without request, calling attention
                 to oneself

oligo- = few
*olig*archy   = government by the *few*
*oligo*phagous = eating only a *few* special kinds of food
*oligo*poly   = a situation in which a *few* producers can affect the
                 market

omni- = all
omni-potent = *all* powerful
omni-present = present in *all* places and at *all* times; ubiquitous
omni-vore   = one that eats *all* types of food
omni-scient = *all* knowing

ortho- = straight, regular, upright, vertical, at right angles
ortho-dontics = *straight*ening of the teeth
ortho-gnathous = having *straight* jaws
ortho-gonal   = mutually *perpendicular*
ortho-grade   = walking with the body *upright* or *vertical*
ortho-graphic = characterized by *perpendicular* lines or *right angles*

para- = at the side of; alongside; beyond, aside from, to one side, by, subsidiary to

para-llel	= extending in the same direction, never meeting; *side-by-side*
para-legal	= a person trained to do *subsidiary* work for lawyers
para-medical	= designating *auxiliary* medical personnel
para-military	= formed on a military pattern, working *alongside* a regular military organization, often as a potential, semi-official, or secret *auxiliary* military force
para-ite	= a person, plant, or animal that lives at the expense of another without making any useful contribu tion to the host with often harmful effects

per- = through, throughout, during, by means of

per-ambulat	= to travel over or *through*, esp. on foot; traverse
per-colate	= to cause to pass *through* a permeable substance; to ooze or trickle *through*; to be diffused *through*; penetrate
per-meate	= to spread or diffuse *through* (a room)
per-vade	= to become diffused *throughout* every part of

peri- = all around; about; near; surrounding; enclosing

peri-cardium	= the membrane that *encloses* the heart
peri-meter	= the boundary of a *closed* plane figure
peri-neurium	= the connective-tissue sheath that *surrounds* a bundle of nerve fibers
peri-scope	= a tubular optical instrument, usually for use on submarines, that provides a view *all around* or on all sides

phil- *or* **philo-** = loving, liking, predisposed to

phil-anthropy	= *goodwill* to fellowmen
philo-gyny	= fondness for women
philo-logy	= the study of literature; linguistics
philo-sopher	= one who *seeks* wisdom or enlightenment; scholar, thinker
philo-sophy	= orig., *love of* wisdom or knowledge

poly- = many, several, much

poly-chromatic	= showing *several* colors; *multi*colored
poly-gamy	= marriage to *more than one* person at the same time
poly-gon	= a figure of *many* angles = a *many*-sided figure
poly-morphic	= having *several* forms or shapes
poly-syllabic	= having *more than three* syllables

post- = after, later, subsequent
    post-graduate = one who continues study *after* graduation from college
    post-meridian = being *after* noon (abbr.: P.M.)
    post-pone = to put off until *later*; defer; delay
    post-prandial = *after* a meal (a *postprandial* stroll, conversation, etc.)

pre- = before, earlier than, prior to
    pre-amble = an *introductory* statement
    pre-dict = to *fore*tell, to state or indicate *beforehand*
    pre-fix = an affix attached to the *beginning* of a word (com
        pare *suffix*)
    pre-historic = of the period *before* recorded history
    pre-requisite = something required *beforehand*, esp. as a necessary
        condition for something following (Econ 1 is a
        prerequisite for Econ 101)

pro- (1) = before in place or time; prior to; in front of
    pro-em = a *preliminary* comment; *pre*face; *pre*lude
    pro-genitor = a *fore*father; an ancestor in the direct line
    pro-gnosis = a *fore*cast
    pro-logue = the *preface* or *introduction* to a literary work

pro- (2) = moving forward or ahead of; defending; supporting, for, in
    favor of
    pro-ceed = to *advance* or go *on*; to move along
    pro-mote = to *advance* to a higher position; to *further* the
        popularity of
    pro-pel = to drive *forward* or *onward*
    pro- choice = *defending* or *supporting* choice of schools, etc.

proto- = first in time, original; principal, chief
    proto-type = 1.the *first* thing or being of its kind; *original;*
        model; pattern.
        2. a person or thing that serves as a model for one
        of a later period

pseud-, pseudo- = false, fake, feigned, spurious
    *pseudo*nym = a *false* name; a "pen" name, often used by authors
    pseudo-sophistication = *false* or *feigned* sophistication

quasi- = seemingly, almost, somewhat, having some resemblance; apparent;
    partly
    quasi-official = *not exactly* official but *seemingly* so; *somewhat* official

re- = back, again; against

re-bound	= to bounce *back*
re-sist	= to exert force *against*
re-build	= to build *again*
re-naissance	= *re*birth

retro- = backwards, back in the past

retro-active = 1. having application to things *prior to* (*back in the past*) its enactment (a *retro*active law, tax, rule, etc.)
2. going into effect as of a specified date *in the past* (a *retro*active pay increase)

rheo- = flow

rheo-meter = an instrument for measuring the *flow* of viscous substances

rheo-phile = preferring or living in *flow*ing water (*rheo*phile fauna)

rheo-stat = a resistor for regulating the *current* (*flow*) of electricity by means of variable resistances

sub- = under, up towards, beneath, below

sub-cutaneous =	*under* the skin (a *sub*cutaneous injection)
sub-marine =	an *under*water boat
sub-terranean =	*below* ground
sub-way =	an *under*ground train

super- = over, above, on top of; extra; greater in amount, quality, or degree than

super-abundant = being *more than* is usual or needed; *surplus, excess*

super-structure = a structure built *on top of* another; that part of a building *above* the foundation; that part of a ship *above* the main deck

supra- = above, over, *akin to* **super-,** transcending

supra-liminal = existing *above* the threshold of consciousness

supra -renal = situated *above* or anterior to the kidney(s)

sym-, syn- = with, together; at the same time

sym-biosis = the living *together* of two dissimilar organisms in a mutually beneficial relationship

syn-chronous = happening or occurring *at exactly the same time*

syn-ergism = *cooperative* action such that the total effect is greater than the sum of the effects taken independently (2 + 2 = 5)

syn-thesis = the *com*bination of parts or elements so as to form a whole

tele- = afar; from a distance
tele-communication = communication *at a distance*
tele-photography = the photography of *distant* objects
tele-scope = a tubular optical instrument for viewing *distant* objects

trans- = across, through; on the other side; beyond; so as to change
trans-cend = to rise above or go *beyond* the limits of
trans-continental = that *crosses* a continent, *on the other side* of a continent
trans-gress = to go *beyond* the limits set; violate; to go *across* a boundary
trans-it = an act or process of passing *through* or over
trans-parent = fine or sheer enough to be seen *through;* easily seen *hrough*

ultra- = farther on; beyond the ordinary; on the farthest side of; extreme
ultra-modern = having the *very latest* ideas, styles, or tendencies
ultra-secret = *highly* secret
ultra-sophisticated = *extremely* sophisticated

un- = non, non-, opposite of or contrary to
un-able = *not* able; *in*capable; *in*competent
un-conscious = *not* conscious
un-constitutional = *not* according to or consistent with the constitution

vice- = one who acts in the place of; subordinate; deputy; substitute
vice-mayor = one who acts *in the place of the* mayor when necessary
vice-chancellor = a person who *substitutes* for the regular chancellor or acts as his assistant
vice-president = the officer next in rank to the president, who *acts in the place of* the president when necessary

xeno- = strange, foreign; stranger, foreigner
xeno-phile = one attracted to *foreign* things (as manners, styles, or people)
xeno-phobia = fear or hatred of *strangers, foreigners,* or anything *foreign*

QUIZ

1. Select the prefix which is closest in meaning to the one in the left-hand column:

co-	(a) dia-	(b) syn-	(c) ad-	(d) epi-
pro-(1)	(a) homo-	(b) ambi-	(c) ante-	(d) supra-
di-	(a) un-	(b) demi-	(c) eu-	(d) bi-
homo-	(a) iso-	(b) quasi-	(c) ortho-	(d) com-
im-	(a) sym-	(b) ob-	(c) un-	(d) re-
per-	(a) mal-	(b) trans-	(c) apo-	(d) para-
hemi-	(a) semi-	(b) ambi-	(c) omni-	(d) peri-
a-	(a) retro-	(b) exo-	(c) un-	(d) hypo-

2. Select the word which best defines the prefix:

aster-	(a) flow	(b) across	(c) star	(d) upright
be-	(a) again	(b) wrong	(c) with	(d) completely
cyclo-	(a) below	(b) circle	(c) down	(d) during
de-	(a) many	(b) few	(c) down	(d) together
ultra-	(a) near	(b) against	(c) extreme	(d) strange

3. Select the prefix which best describes the word:

near	(a) by-	(b) oligo-	(c) trans-	(d) eso-
together	(a) inter-	(b) para-	(c) com-	(d) apo
rotating	(a) super-	(b) meta-	(c) cyclo-	(d) gyro-
out, from	(a) ultra-	(b) ec-	(c) xeno-	(d) dys-
deputy	(a) para-	(b) meta-	(c) vice-	(d) sub-
half	(a) micro-	(b) demi-	(c) mega-	(d) infra-

4. Select the prefix which is *opposite* in meaning to the one in the left-hand column:

a-	(a) dys-	(b) sym-	(c) de-	(d) tele-
by-	(a) bene-	(b) proto-	(c) tele-	(d) poly-
demi-	(a) micro-	(b) mega-	(c) meta-	(d) peri-
exo-	(a) inter-	(b) ab-	(c) super-	(d) eso-
pro-(1)	(a) ante-	(b) post-	(c) homo-	(d) philo-
pro-(2)	(a) contra-	(b) com-	(c) auto-	(d) iso-
multi-	(a) meta-	(b) oligo-	(c) macro-	(d) hyper-
super-	(a) infra-	(b) epi-	(c) intra-	(d) para-
sub-	(a) ob-	(b) trans-	(c) epi-	(d) ortho-
hetero-	(a) ultra-	(b) retro-	(c) circum-	(d) iso-

What two prefixes mean *bad, ill*?   (1)_____   (2)_____
What two prefixes mean *from, away*?   (1)_____   (2)_____
What three prefixes mean *under, beneath*? (1)_____   (2)_____
                                             and   (3)_____
What three prefixes mean *within*?   (1)_____   (2)_____
                                             and   (3)_____

The opposite of *proceed* is:
    (a) digress   (b) transgress   (c) retrogress   (d) progress

An all-powerful person is:
    (a) a dynamo   (b) omnipotent (c) omniscient (d) an ambivert

A change of shape is: (a) isomorphic   (b) amorphous (c) a metamorphosis

Define *inter*collegiate   _____

Define *intra*mural   _____

NUMERICAL PREFIXES

LATIN	GREEK

uni- = one
uni-cycle = *one* wheel
uni-form = *one* form, same form
uni-lateral = *one*-sided
uni-que = being the only *one*

mono- = one
mono-chrome = *one* color
mono-cle = an eyeglass for *one* eye
mono-lingual = using *one* language
mono-lith = a *single* great stone

bi- = two
bi-cycle = a vehicle with *two* wheels
bi-ennial = occurring every *two* years
bi-sect = to divide into *two* parts

di- = twice, double, twofold
di-chotomy = division into 2 parts
di-midiate = cut in *two*; *halved*
di-plopia = "*double* vision"

tri- = three
tri-ple = *three*fold; three times as much
tri-angle = a polygon with *three* sides

tri- = three
tri-ad = a group of *three*
tri-archy = government by *three*

quadr- = four
quadr-uple = four times as much
quadr-angle = a *four*-sided figure

tetra- = four
tetra-d = a group of *four*
tetra-gonal = *four* angles and sides

quinque-, quinqu- = five
quinque-nnium =
a period of *five* years
quin-tet = a group of *five;* basketball team

penta-, pent- = five
penta-gon = a *five*-sided figure
penta-thlon = contest of 5 events

sex- = six
sex-tet = a group of *six* persons
sex-tuple = *six* times as much

hex- = six
hex-agon = a *six*-sided figure
hex-apod = having *six* legs (insects)

sept- = seven
sept-ennial = of or every *seven* years
sept-et = a group of *seven*

hepta-, hept- = seven
hept-ad = a group of *seven*
hept-agon = a *seven*-sided figure

octo-, oct- = eight
oct-et = a musical composition for *eight* instruments or voices

nona- = nine
nona-gon = a polygon of *nine* angles and *nine* sides

deca-, dec-, deka-, dek- = ten
de-cade = 1) a group or set of *ten* 2) a period of *ten* years
deca-gon = a plane polygon of *ten* angles and *ten* sides
dec-imal = numbered or proceeding by *tens*; based on the number *ten*

undec- = eleven
undec-ylenic acid = an organic acid of *eleven* carbon atoms (C11H20O2)

triskaideka- = thirteen
triskaideka-phobia = fear of the number *thirteen*

icosa-, icosi- = twenty
icosa-fold = times *twenty*; *twenty* times more, as many, as much
icosa-hedron = a solid figure having *twenty* plane surfaces

centi- = hundred; hundredth part
cent-ury = one *hundred* years
centi-meter = one *hundredth* part of a meter

hect-, hecto- = hundred
hect-are = *one hundred* ares, or 10,000 sq. meters, or 2.47 acres

kilo- = thousand
kilo-gram = a metric unit of weight equal to 1,000 grams (2.2046 pounds)
kilo-meter = a metric unit of linear measure equal to 1,000 meters
(3,280.8 ft. or about 5/8 mile; more specifically, 23/37 mile)

milli- = thousandth (mille- = thousand)
mille-nnium = a period of 1,000 years
milli-meter = one *thousandth* of a meter (0.03937 inch)
milli-second = one *thousandth* of a second

NUMERICAL PREFIXES

nano-	one billionth	0.000000001
micro-	one millionth	0.000001
milli-	one thousandth	0.001
centi-	one hundredth	0.01
deci-	one tenth	0.1
uni-, mono-	one	1.0
sesqui-	one and a half, half again	1.5
bi-, di-	two	
tri-	three	
quadr-, tetra-	four	
quinque-, penta-	five	
sex-, hex-	six	
sept-, hepta, hept-	seven	
oct-, octo-	eight	
nona-	nine	
dec-, deca-	ten	
undec-	eleven	
triskaideka-	thirteen	
icosa-, icosi-	twenty	
centi-, hect-, hecto-	hundred	
kilo-, mille-	thousand	

SOME "QUICKIE" LATIN

LATIN WORD	MEANING	DERIVATIVE(S)
abscondere	to hide; leave behind	abscond
abtrahere	to drag away, draw away	abstract
acuere	to sharpen	acumen, acute
adamas	steel; diamond	adamant
agere	to drive, do, act	agenda, agile, agility
alter	another	alter, alteration, altruism, alternative
altercatio	dispute, debate, quarrel	altercate, altercation
ambigere	to wander around	ambiguous
amicus	friend	amiable, amicable
anculus	servant	ancillary
arbitrium	judgment	arbiter, arbitrate, arbitrary
asinus	ass	asinine
astus	craft, cunning	astute
audere	to dare, be bold	audacious, audacity
ceder	to go	cede, accede, recede, secede
clamare	to shout	acclaim, clamor, claim
cor	heart	accord, cordial, coronary
dicere	to say, tell, speak	dictate, dictum, predict, diction, edict
ducere	to lead	abduct, conducive, conduct, deduce
erudire	to educate, instruct	erudite, erudition
frater	brother	fraternity, fraternal, fraternize

LATIN WORD	MEANING	DERIVATIVE(S)
insidiae	ambush	insidious
jacere	to throw	abject, dejected, inject, interject, object, project, subject
magnus	great, large	magnificent, magnify, magnitude
manus	hand, handiwork	manual, manuscript, manufacture
mater	mother	maternal, maternity, matriarchy
maximus	greatest, largest	maxi, maximal, maximum
minimus	smallest, least	mini, minimum, minimize, minuscule
nomen	name	nomenclature, nominal, nominate
novellus, novus	new, young, fresh	innovate, novel, novelty, novice
pater	father	paternal, paternity
pes, pedis	foot	pedal, pedestrian
pello, pellere	to push, drive	compel, expel, propel, repel
peto, petere	go to, seek, look for, ask	compete, petition
ponere, posit	to put, lay down, place	apposite, depose, deposit, position
porto, portere	to carry	deport, export, import, portable
scio, scire	to know	conscious, omniscient, science
scribo, scribere	to write	prescribe, proscribe, scribe, script

LATIN WORD	MEANING	DERIVATIVE(S)
solver	to release, loosen, free	absolve, dissolve, resolve
soror	sister	sororal, sorority
spectare	look at, observe, watch	inspect, retrospect, spectator
stringere	to draw tight	astringent, strict, stringent
subtilis	fine, slender, delicate	subtle
summa, summus	highest, the top of	summit, summa cum laude
surdus	deaf; stupid	absurd
tenere	to hold	abstain, contain, maintain, tenacious, tenable, tenant, tenet
urbs, urbis	city	exurbanite, suburb, urban
venio, venire	come	advent, circumvent, convention
veritas	truth	veracity, verify, veritable
video, videre	to see	visible, vision, visual, visibility
vinco, vincere	to conquer, defeat	convict, convince, invincible, victorious
vita	life	convivial, survive, vital, vitality, vitamin, vivacious
voco, vocare	to call, summon	convoke, evoke, vocation, vocal

SUFFIXES

-ac =
1. characteristic of
elegi*ac* = sad; mournful; plaintive
2. of, related to
cardi*ac* = of, near, or affecting the heart
3. affected by or having
mani*ac* = a) a wildly or violently insane person
b) a person who has an excessive or persistent enthusiasm or desire for

-aceous = of the nature of, like, belonging to, producing, or characterized by
cret*aceous* = characteristic of chalk; chalky
herb*aceous* = 1. having the nature of herbs, as distinguished from woody plants
2. like a green leaf in texture, color, shape, etc.
seb*aceous* = relating to fatty material; fatty

-acious = characterized by, inclined to, full of
ten*acious* = holding firmly (a ten*acious* grip);
retentive (ten*acious* memory);
persistent; stubborn; (ten*acious* courage)
fall*acious* = erroneous (fall*acious* reasoning); misleading or deceptive

-acity = a characteristic, quality, or tendency
cap*acity* = the ability to hold or store; ability, caliber; potentiality
mend*acity* = a lie; falsehood; quality or state of being untruthful
sag*acity* = the quality of being shrewd and discerning

-acy = quality, condition, position, etc.
contum*acy* = stubborn resistance to authority, willful contempt of court
suprem*acy* = state or quality of being supreme

-ade =
1. the act of --ing
block*ade* = a blocking action designed to prevent passage in or out
2. result or product
arc*ade* = a passage having an arched roof
3. participant(s) in an action
brig*ade* = a group of people organized to function in some work (a fire brig*ade*)
4. drink made from
lime*ade* = a drink made from lime juice

-age =
  1. act, condition, or result of (marri*age*, us*age*)
  2. amount or number of (acre*age*)
  3. cost of (post*age*)
  4. home of (hermit*age*)
  The suffix *-age* appears in many words borrowed from French into Middle English, e.g., sav*age*, voy*age*

-ance =
  1. the act or process of --ing
  discounten*ance* = showing disapproval
  2. the quality or state of being
  forbear*ance*   = self control; patience
  3. a thing that ---s
  hindr*ance*   = obstacle, obstruction; impediment
  4. a thing that is --ed
  utter*ance*   = something said
  remitt*ance*   = sending money; money sent

-ant =
  1. that has, shows, or does
  defi*ant*   = openly and boldly resisting
  radi*ant*   = shining brightly; beaming
  2. a person or thing that
  occup*ant*   = one who occupies a house
  account*ant*   = one who inspects, keeps, or adjusts accounts

-ar =
  1. of, relating to, like
  singul*ar*   = one, oneness, only; unique
  pol*ar*   = of the North or South pole; also, directly
                       opposite in direction or nature
  2. the agent of an action
  registr*ar*   = a university official responsible for registering
                       students, maintaining their records, etc.

-ard = one that carries some action, or possesses some quality, to excess
  slugg*ard*   = a habitually lazy or idle person
  drunk*ard*   = a person who often gets drunk; inebriate

-arian =
  1. (one) characterized by or having (octogen*arian* = a person 80
  years old, between 80 and 90); (centen*arian* = a person at least 100
  years old)
  2. a) (one) believing in (Unit*arian*) b) (one) advocating
  (disciplin*arian* = a person who believes in strict discipline)
  3. (one) associated with (antiqu*arian* = a person who collects or
  studies relics and ancient works of art) (agr*arian* = relating to land)

-arious = relating to, connected with
    hil*arious*   = noisily merry; very funny
    vic*arious*   = taking the place of another thing or person;
                             substitute; deputy;

-ary =
    1. relating to, connected with
    urin*ary*   = relating to urine
    eleemosyn*ary* = charitable
    2. a) a thing connected with
        diction*ary*
        b) a place for
        gran*ary*, libr*ary*

-ate (I) =
    1. forming verbs - evapor*ate*, invalid*ate*, rejuven*ate*, vaccin*ate*,
    orchestr*ate*
    2. forming adjectives - collegi*ate*, rose*ate*, passion*ate*

-ate (II) =
    3. forming nouns:
        a) an office, function, agent, official, or group of officials
        potent*ate*   = a person having great power; ruler; monarch
        director*ate* = the position of director; a board of directors
        b) the land, territory, or dominion of (a person or office); e.g.,
        sultan*ate*   = the land ruled by a sultan; the authority, office,
        or reign of a sultan
        c) a person or thing that is the object of (an action); e.g.,
        leg*ate*   = an envoy or ambassador
        mand*ate*   = an authoritative order, esp. a written one;
                     the wishes of constituents expressed to a legislature
                     as through an election and regarded as an order
        d) salt made from any of certain acids with names ending in -ic;
        its metal or non-metal in its highest oxidation state (ammonium
        nitr*ate*)
        e) a result of some process (distill*ate*)

-athon = an event marked by length or endurance: used freely to form
    nonce compounds (walk*athon*, drink*athon*; sale-*a-thon*

-ative = of or relating to, serving to, tending to (demonstr*ative*,
    inform*ative*, talk*ative*)

-cidal =
    1. of a killer or killing (homi*cidal*)
    2. that can kill (fungi*cidal*)

-cide =
    1. a killer (pesti*cide*)
    2. a killing (homi*cide* = any killing of a human being by another)

-cracy = form of government
    demo*cracy*   = government of the people; rule of the majority
    mobo*cracy*   = a social or political class of powerful persons
    techno*cracy*   = theory of social organization

-cy =
    1. quality, condition, state, or fact of being (idio*cy*)
    2. position, rank, or office of (captain*cy*)

-dom =
    1. rank or position of, domain or dominion of (king*dom*)
    2. fact or state of being (wis*dom*, martyr*dom*)
    3. a total of all who are (official*dom*)

-ean = of, belonging to, like (Europ*ean*, Aeg*ean*)

-ectomy = a surgical excision of
    append*ectomy* = surgical removal of the vermiform
                      [shaped like a worm] appendix
    tonsill*ectomy* = surgical removal of the tonsils

-ee =
    1. the recipient of an action, grant, or benefit
    appoint*ee*   =   one who receives an appointment)
    pay*ee*   = the one who is paid) (select*ee* = the one selected
    2. a person in a specified condition
    absent*ee*   =   one who is absent
    employ*ee*   = one who is employed
    [as opposed to *employer* = one who employs])

-eer =
    1. a) a person or thing that has to do with (auction*eer*, mountain*eer*)
       b) a person who writes, makes (pamphlet*eer*, profit*eer*)
    2. to have to do with
    election*eer*   = one who works for a candidate or party in an election

-escent =
    1. in the process of --ing; starting to be, being or becoming
    obsol*escent*   = in the process of becoming obsolete)
    cal*escent*   = becoming warm
    2. giving off or reflecting light, or showing a play of color
    phosphor*escent*

-ese =
    1. forming adjectives a) of a country or place (Javan*ese*) b) in the
    language of (Canton*ese*)
    2. forming nouns
       a) a native or inhabitant of (Portug*uese*, Japan*ese*)
       b) the language or dialect of (Brooklyn*ese*) c) the style
       of or the jargon associated with [often used to form nonce
       words] (journal*ese*, bureaucrat*ese*)

-esque =
   1. in the state or manner of (Roman*esque*)
   2. having the quality of; like (statu*esque*

-facient = making or causing to become
   lique*facient*   = causing to liquefy
   rube*facient*   = causing redness, as of the skin

-fication = a making, creating, causing (calci*fication*, glori*fication*)

-fold =
   1. having a number of parts (a ten*fold* division)
   2. times as many, as much, as large (to profit ten*fold*)

-gen =
   something produced in a specified way
   patho*gen*   = any agent, esp. a micro-organism, able to cause disease
   pyro*gen*   = *Med.* a substance that causes fever)

-genic = pertaining to production or generation
   carcino*genic*   = producing cancer
   crypto*genic*   = idiopathic = of a disease whose cause is unknown
                     or uncertain
   iatro*genic*   = caused by medical treatment
   lacto*genic*   = milk producing
   pyro*genic*   = producing heat or fever
   toxico*genic*   = producing toxic substances

-gnosis = knowledge, recognition
   dia*gnosis*   = 1. the act of deciding the nature of a disease by
                     examination of the symptoms
                     2. a careful examination and analysis of the facts in
                     an attempt to understand or explain something
                     (a *diagnosis* of the economy)
   pro*gnosis*   = a forecast; esp. a prediction of the probable cause
                     of a disease and the chances of recovery

-gon = a figure having (a specified number of) angles
   tetra*gonal*   = having four angles and four sides

-graph =
   1. something that *writes* or records
   tele*graph*   = an apparatus that sends a message by electric
   impulses to a distant receiver (long-distance *"writing"*)

-hood =
   1. state, quality, condition (child*hood*)
   2. the whole group of [a specified class, profession, etc.]
   (priest*hood*, mother*hood*, neighbor*hood*)

-ism = act (critic*ism*); condition (alcohol*ism*); doctrine, theory (Buddh*ism*); belief in a system or set of principles (individual*ism*, conservat*ism*, egalitarian*ism*)

-itis = inflammation of

arthr*itis*	= inflammation of a joint; hepat*itis* = inflammation of the liver
gingiv*itis*	= inflammation of the gums
burs*itis*	= inflamed bursa

-logy = science, doctrine, or theory of

bio*logy*	= science of *life, living* things
theo*logy*	= study of God

-oid =

1. forming adjectives : like or resembling (crystall*oid*)
2. forming nouns : something resembling (cellul*oid*)

andr*oid*	= in science fiction, an automaton made to resemble a human being
aster*oid*	= starlike

-oma = tumor

lymph*oma*	= progressive enlargement of lymphoid tissue resulting from the proliferation of malignant lymphoid cells
sarc*oma*	= malignant tumor that begins in connective tissue

-ose = full of, having the qualities of, like

comat*ose*	= in a coma or stupor; lethargic; torpid
bellic*ose*	= of a quarrelsome or hostile nature; eager to fight or quarrel; warlike **Syn.** belligerent

-osis =

1. state, condition, action (hypn*osis*)
2. pathological (abnormal or diseased) condition of

psych*osis*	= abnormal mental condition)
tubercul*osis*	= a disease affecting various tissues of the body, but most often the lungs
leukocyt*osis*	= an increase in the number of leukocytes [tiny white blood cells] in the blood

-pathy =

1. feeling, suffering

sym*pathy*	= sameness of *feeling*
anti*pathy*	= a strong and deep-rooted dislike; aversion
a*pathy*	= lack of emotion; lack of interest; unconcern; indifference

2. disease

neuro*pathy*	= any disease of the nervous system
psycho*pathy*	= mental disorder

-phagous = that eats (something specified)
   ichthyo*phagous* = fish-eating

-phile = one who loves, likes, or is attracted to
   Franco*phile* = one who *likes* France, the people, customs, culture, etc.
   cine*phile* = one who *is attracted to* movies; a *devotee* of films

-phobe = one who *fears or hates*
   xeno*phobe* = one who fears or hates strangers or foreigners or anything foreign or strange

-phobia = fear, dread, hatred
   photo*phobia* = an abnormal fear or sensitivity to *light*
   acro*phobia* = an abnormal fear of being in *high places*
   ophidia*phobia* = fear of *snakes*

-ship =
   1. quality, condition, state of being (hard*ship*, friend*ship*)
   2. the rank or office of (professor*ship*, lord*ship*, dictator*ship*)
   3. ability or skill as (statesman*ship*, penman*ship*, sportsman*ship*)
   4. all individuals of the specified class collectively (reader*ship*)

-some =
   1. like, tending to be (toil*some*, tire*some*, lone*some*)
   2. a group of a specified number of members (two*some*, three*some*, four*some*)

-tomy =
   1. a dividing
   dicho*tomy* = *division* into two parts
   2. an incision, a surgical operation
   lobo*tomy* = a cutting into the frontal lobe of the cerebrum

-ulent = full of, abounding in
   corp*ulent* = having a *large bulky* body; obese
   flat*ulent* = 1. having or causing gas in the stomach or intestines (*full of*)
                2. vain; empty; pompous in speech or behavior (*full of*)
   floc*culent* = like bits of wool
   suc*culent* = juicy; *full of* vitality, freshness, or richness
   vir*ulent* = 1. a) marked by a rapid, severe, and malignant course (a *virulent* infection)
                  b) able to overcome bodily defense mechanisms a *virulent* pathogen)
                2. *extremely* poisonous or venomous
                3. obj*ectionably* harsh and strong

-valent = quantity, value, force, meaning; feeling toward

    equi*valent*   = equal in *quantity, value, force, meaning, etc.*

    ambi*valent*   = simultaneous conflicting *feelings toward* a person or thing, as love and hate

-vorous = feeding on, eating

    omni*vorous*   = *eating* any sort of food, both animal and vegetable food

-wise = in a specified direction, position, or manner

    length*wise*   = *in the direction of* the length

    clock*wise*   = *in the direction in* which the hands of the clock move

    other*wise*   = 1. *in* another *manner;* differently (to believe *otherwise*)

                        2. in all other points or respects (an *otherwise* intelligent person)

QUIZ

1. How many chlorine atoms are in carbon *tetra*chloride? _____
2. How many carbon atoms are in *oct*ane? _____
3. What does *uni*lateral mean? _____
4. The Pentagon has how many sides? _____
5. A *deca*thlon consists of how many events? _____
6. A *quad*rangle on campus is surrounded on how many sides by buildings? _____
7. The Latin root *scrib* and the Greek root *graph* both mean to

_____

8. Fill in the meanings of the following roots: naut _____;
     nomen _____; spec _____; urb _____;
     nov _____; vis _____; vita _____;
     aud _____; corpor _____; cent _____;
     fort _____; liter _____; rupt _____;
     vent _____

9. Name the suffix referring to:

a surgical excision	(a) –fication	(b) –ectomy	(c) –pathy	(d) –oma
science, doctrine	(a) –acity	(b) –dom	(c) –ship	(d) –logy-
form of government	(a) –phobia	(b) –tomy	(c) –cracy	(d) –hood
knowledge, recognition	(a) –osis	(b) – phile	(c) –gnosis	(d) –gen
inflammation	(a) –pathy	(b) –itis	(c) –athon	(d) –cide-
production	(a) –esque	(b) –genic	(c) –ative	(d) –ose-
feeling, suffering	(a) –pathy	(b) –osis	(c) –ulent	(d) – ary
full of, abounding in	(a) –some	(b) –ulent	(c) –phile	(d) –wise
eating (select two)	(a) –vorous	(b) –escent	(c) –phagous	(d) –tomy
attracted to	(a) –ship	(b) –phobia	(c) –phil	(d) –fold

PART TWO

This section is designed to show the relationships between old words, usually Latin or Greek, and their modern counterparts, as well as comparisons between their respective meanings.

Knowing where a present word comes from helps one to understand why it has its meaning. The "etymology" is limited to a single word of origin, or later in its history, for the sake of brevity and clarity of understanding. The abbreviations of the languages of origin are defined on the next page.

Usually thirteen such word comparisons, arranged alphabetically for convenience, appear on each page, and sample sentences for each word are on the reverse side, in the same order.

Quizzes, which match the words with their meanings, along with ten multiple choice questions, are provided periodically. Another feature is the appearance of words learned early in the text in the sample sentences for words encountered later. The words are arranged in alphabetical order for easy reference. There are approximately 150 new words in each segment. It is therefore necessary to learn them as they come in alphabetical order, in order to pass the quizzes. It is also strongly recommended to say each word aloud several times, as well as to spell it. There is a pronunciation guide for selected words at the end of the text.

Try to use each word in an original phrase or sentence, and, of course, examine the sample sentences. Recognize and understand the words as you encounter them in reading.

LANGUAGE ABBREVIATIONS

AF, AFr	Anglo-French
Ar	Arabic
Brit	British
Chin	Chinese
Dan	Danish
Du	Dutch
E	English
Fr	French
Ger	German
Gmc	Germanic
Gk	Greek
It	Italian
L	Latin
LL	Late Latin
LG	Low German
ML	Medieval Latin
MDu	Middle Dutch
ME	Middle English
MFr	Middle French
MGk	Middle Greek
NL	New Latin
OE	Old English
OFr	Old French
OHG	Old High German
OIt	Old Italian
OL	Old Latin
ON	Old Norse
ONF	Old North French
OPer	Old Persian
Pg, Port	Portuguese
Russ	Russian
Skt	Sanskrit
Sp	Spanish
Sw	Swedish

SEGMENT ONE

ETYMOLOGY	OLD MEANING
WORD	**NEW MEANING**

L abassiare	to lower, bring down
abase	**to humble, lower in esteem**

MF abair	to astonish
abash	**to disconcert, embarrass, put to shame**

OF abbatre	to knock, beat down
abate	**make less in amount, degree, or force**

L aberrare	to wander, go astray
aberrant	**straying from the normal or usual way; one whose behavior is odd**

MF abeter	to incite
abet	**to help in a purpose, esp. in wrongdoing**

OF abeance	desire, expectation
abeyance	**temporary suspension of activity**

L abhorrere	to shudder (from)
abhor	**to detest, loathe, shirk from, hate**

OE abidan	to bide, wait
abide	**withstand; accept without objection**

L abjectus	thrown away
abject	**down in spirit; hopeless, wretched**

L ab- + jurare	to swear
abjure	**renounce; reject; ; give up; avoid**

L abolescere	to disappear, vanish
abolish	**do away with wholly; annul; destroy**

L abominari	to disapprove as an ill omen
abominate	**to hate or loathe intensely**

L ab- + origine	from the beginning
aborigine	**first inhabitant; native**

Sample Sentences

abase It's a bad idea to *abase* people, to *humble* them, or to *lower* them *in esteem.*

abash Casey must have felt *abashed* for striking out. That it *put him to shame,* or *embarrassed* him, was evident to the crowd.

abate The heavy storm finally *abated* by evening; it *eased up* considerably. The *abatement* was a big relief to many.

aberrant His *aberrant* behavior annoyed others in the library. His *unusual straying from the normal* got him expelled from the study hall.

abet He *abetted* his pals in the bank robbery by driving the getaway car. He *helped* them escape.

abeyance The plan was put *in abeyance* until all the details were agreed upon. Thus, the group agreed to a *temporary suspension* of the idea, to put it *on hold.*

abhor Many people *abhor* certain habits of others—line-crashing, standing in front of others seated at an event, pushing and shoving, etc. They *detest* or *loathe* such behavior.

abide It is hard to *abide* by some rules that seem unreasonable or irrational, but it is important to *accept without objection* or *go along with* most rules in order to avoid chaos.

abject The citizens of countries without education generally live in *abject* poverty; they have *hopeless, wretched* living conditions.

abjure He tried very hard to *abjure* cigarette smoking, to *give up* or *avoid* the habit.

abolish Some people would like to *abolish* certain laws or government agencies, that is, to *do away with* them *totally,* to *get rid of* them *entirely,* to *annul* them.

abominate The abolition of cigarette smoking on airplanes came about because most people *abominate* it. They *hated* it *intensely.*

aborigine A person who had no ancestors born outside his or her native territory is an *aborigine,* or *native.* An *aboriginal* family is *native* to the area, where all of the ancestors were born.

ETYMOLOGY	OLD MEANING
WORD	**NEW MEANING**

L aboriri	to miscarry
abort	**stop in early stages; cut short a mission**
L abradere	to scrape off
abrade	**erode; irritate; roughen**
L abscondere	to hide from
abscond	**go away secretly and hide**
L absolvere	to loosen from
absolve	**to free from guilt; acquit**
L abstinere	to hold back
abstain	**to do without; refrain from**
L abstrahere	to draw away; withdraw
abstract	**detached from specifics; not real**
L abstrudere	push away; conceal
abstruse	**hard to understand; recondite**
L absurdus	not to be heard of
absurd	**untrue; ridiculous; laughable**
OF abouter	to join end to end
abut	**to border on; touch**
Gk abyssos	bottomless
abysmal	**immeasurably low or wretched**
L acclamare	to shout at; cry out
acclaim	**praise, applause**
L accrescere	to increase. grow
accrue	**to collect; accumulate by addition**
L acquiescere	to rest; die; become quiet
acquiesce	**agree without protest or enthusiasm**

SAMPLE SENTENCES

abort The storm did not abate; in fact, it got worse, so they had to *abort* their golf match, i.e. *cut* it *short*.

abrade The long, steady flow of water gradually *abraded* the rocks to smooth stones. This type of *abrasion* is called *erosion*. *Abrasive* manners can *irritate* people. Certain *roughened* areas of the skin are called skin *abrasions*.

abscond The assistant bank teller got fed up one day and *absconded* with the money—over a million in twenties, fifties, and C-notes packed in a suitcase—on a Friday after closing. She *fled secretly and hid* somewhere in Brazil, many believe.

absolve The defense attorney convinced the jury to *absolve* his client of any wrong- doing, to *free* him *from guilt*, to *acquit* him.

abstain The doctor told his obese patient to *abstain* from desserts, to *do without* them, to *refrain from* them. // There were 7 "yes" votes, 6 "no's," and one *abstention*. that is, one person who *refrained from voting* on the matter at hand.

abstract Interpretations of *abstract* art are opinions based on *detachment from reality*.

abstruse The professor's lectures on metaphysics were *abstruse,* according to many students. They found them *hard to understand*, or *recondite*.

absurd It is *absurd* to think a pick-up squad from a local club could beat the NFL champions. The idea is *ridiculous* or *laughable*.

abut Your property *abuts* that of your neighbor; it *borders on* his. California *touches* Nevada. The boundaries of lands with respect to adjacent lands are called *abuttals*.

abysmal The *abysmal* poverty found in other parts of the world is far worse than any poverty in the US; it is immeasurably *low or wretched*.

acclaim The coach was greeted by loud, enthusiastic, and prolonged *acclaim* as he went to the podium; the large crowd gave him *loud, eager praise* and *applause* for winning the national championship.

accrue He built his wealth by setting out to *accrue* shares of stock through dividend reinvestment programs. He set out to *accumulate by addition* more of what he already had.

acquiesce Some men *acquiesce* in their wives' decision to attend the opera; they *agree quietly without protest or enthusiasm* to go.

ETYMOLOGY	OLD MEANING
WORD	**NEW MEANING**

L acumen
point, sharp point
acumen
quickness of mind; shrewdness

L aio
I say!
adage
a common saying about observations

L adamas
hardest metal; diamond
adamant
unshakable; inflexible in opinion

OF a jorn
at the specified day
adjourn
to put off until a future time

L adjungere
to add, join
adjunct
something added, joined or attached to

NL ad libitum
in accordance with one's wishes
ad lib
make up as one goes along; improvise

L admonere
to warn
admonish
**to advise; caution against faults;
indicate duties; express disapproval**

Ladornare
to get ready
adorn
to add beauty, splendor; to decorate

L adulare, adulari
to flatter, kowtow, fawn upon; "wag the tail"
adulation
excessive flattery or admiration

L adultare
to falsify
adulterate
to corrupt; make impure or inferior

L advocare
to summon, call upon to come
advocate
to plead in favor of; to support

Gk aigis
goatskin; shield of Zeus
aegis
protection; sponsorship; auspices

Gk aer
air
aerobic
taking place in the presence of oxygen

SAMPLE SENTENCES

acumen He handles problems with *acumen*; he shows *quickness of mind* and *shrewdness*.

adage "What goes around, comes around," "What goes up must come down," and "Haste makes waste." are *adages*, or *common sayings about observations*.

adamant One who is *adamant* in his opinions is *unshakable*; he is *inflexible* in his beliefs.

adjourn Owing to the tie vote at such a late hour, the club decided to *adjourn* the meeting, to *put it off until a future time*.

adjunct They built a new *adjunct*. It was a *tool shed added to*, or *joined to,* the garage.

ad lib Without her notes, she had to *ad lib* her speech, that is, had to *make up her own words as she went along*. She had to *speak spontaneously.*

admonish She *admonished* him about going with the wrong crowd; she *warned* and *cautioned* him *against* it.

adorn She wanted to *adorn* the big room for the party, to *decorate* or *add beauty* to it.

adulation The subordinate official thought he could win favors by showing *adulation* for those above him, but his co-workers were aware of his *excessive flattery* or *admiration* toward his superiors.

adulterate She thought she bought a pure cashmere sweater, but found out later it was *adulterated* with nylon. The sweater was thus *made impure* or *inferior*.

advocate It was natural that the lions would *advocate* complete integration of all the animals in the zoo and that the antelopes would oppose the idea. The lions would *plead in favor of* or *support* the plan, but the deer voted "no" on it.

aegis The young heiress was under the *aegis* of her aunt until she reached adulthood. The aunt provided *protection* and *sponsorship* for the young girl.

aerobic Mammals need an *aerobic* atmosphere to survive, that is, one *in the presence of oxygen*. *Anaerobic* organisms live in the *absence of oxygen*.

ETYMOLOGY	OLD MEANING
WORD	**NEW MEANING**

Gk aisthetikos
aesthetic

perceptible by the senses
relating to the beautiful; artistic

L aestivus
aestivate

summer
to spend the summer

L affari
affable

to speak to
pleasant; at ease in talking to others

L affectatio
affectation

act of striving; conceit
artificial behavior not natural to self

ML affiliare
affiliate

to adopt as a son
have close connection; associate with

L affinis
affinity

bordering on
attraction to or liking for

L affigere
affix

to fasten to
attach physically; attach to; append

L affligere
afflict

to cast down
to distress severely; to trouble, injure

L affluere
affluence

to flow abundantly
influx; abundance of property; wealth

VL affrontare
affront

to the forehead
offense, insult, indignity

L agendum
agenda

come on! well then
list of things to be done or considered

L grandis
aggrandize

great, large, tall; strong
**to make great or greater; increase;
enhance wealth, power, or position of**

L aggravare
aggravate

to make heavier
make worse; arouse the anger of; annoy; irritate

SAMPLE SENTENCES

aesthetic The works of Leonardo da Vinci, Rembrandt, Holbein, Vermeer, Delacroix, Renoir, and many others are *aesthetic* masterpieces, *artistic* treasures.

aestivate Some prefer to *aestivate* on a tropical island, while others like to *spend the summer* by a lake in the mountains.

affable She is generally *affable* at social gatherings; she is very *pleasant* and *at ease in talking to others.*

affectation She is known for her *affectations* at parties; people are wise to her *artificial* and *unnatural behavior.*

affiliate "He is *affiliated* with the police department." One of the funniest euphemisms of all time, meaning "he is in jail." He was *associated with* the police, indeed.

affinity They have a strong *affinity* for football, a true *attraction* to the game, a genuine *liking* for it.

affix At functions where most people don't know each other it helps to *affix* a name tag, that is, to *attach* it to your shirt or jacket so people can call you by name.

afflict Acne *afflicts* many high school students; they are *distressed severely* and *troubled* by this temporary skin problem.

affluence A well-planned investment program can bring great *affluence* to anyone with enough patience; it can result in great *wealth* and *abundance of property.*

affront The big star considered a secondary role an *affront* to his abilities and talents. He regarded it as a real *insult*, an *indignity* to his pride.

agenda Many clubs and other organizations hold scheduled meetings for which an *agenda* is provided, that is, a *list of things to be done or considered.*

aggrandize With each new level of achievement, most people seek to *aggrandize* that which they have gained, whether it be to *enhance wealth, power, or position.*

aggravate Continuing to play after an injury can *aggravate* the situation, *make it worse.* Sometimes a pest can *aggravate* another; i.e., *annoy* or *irritate* that person.

ETYMOLOGY	OLD MEANING
WORD	NEW MEANING

L agere
agility
to act
nimbleness; quick, graceful movement

L ager
agrarian
a field
relating to land or farmers

ME in kenebowe
akimbo
in a sharp curve; bow-bent
with hands on hips, elbows bent outward

L alacritas
alacrity
liveliness
promptness in response; eager readiness

Fr à la carte
a la carte
lit. by the bill of fare
with a separate price for each menu item

It a il + fresco
alfresco
in the cool
in the open air; outdoors

L alienus
alienate
strange; unsuited to; different from
make hostile where earlier relationship existed

OE a- + lecgen
allay
to lay
reduce in intensity; to calm, make quiet

L allegare
allege
to dispatch; cite
to assert without proof; adduce

L ad- = to + levis
alleviate
light
to relieve, lessen; ease pain or suffering

ML allocare
allocate
to place to
to apportion; earmark; set apart

OFr aloter < Gmc lot
allot
lot
to assign as a portion or lot; parcel out

L alludare, *lit.*
allude
to play with
to make indirect reference; refer

L altercatio
altercation
dispute; debate, quarrel
an angry or heated argument

SAMPLE SENTENCES

agility Gymnasts and synchronized swimmers perform with much *agility*, with a lot of *quick, graceful movements.*

agrarian His *agrarian* outlook and values are very different from those of city people, whose views and attitudes are not characteristic *of the land* or *farming.*

akimbo The confident coach stood *akimbo* on the sidelines during the pre-game warm-ups; that is, *with hands on hips and elbows extended outward.*

alacrity The new employee responded to the company president's party invitation with *alacrity*, i.e. with *promptness* and an *eager readiness.*

a la carte The nervous young student, out on his first date, couldn't decide whether to order the fixed dinner or *a la carte*, i.e., *with a separate price for each menu item.*

alfresco They chose to dine *alfresco* on the warm summer evening, i.e., to eat *outdoors.*

alienate In some operas an evil schemer will try to *alienate* two lovers through trickery. He will try to *make* them *unfriendly or hostile where earlier love existed.*

allay It took great news from Wall Street to *allay* his bitter feelings about the traffic ticket. It served to *calm* him down, to *reduce in intensity* his stress.

allege Too many people actually believe what anyone will *allege*. They will swallow what some self-styled authority will *assert without proof.*

alleviate The drug, combined with physical therapy, *alleviated* the pain of the shoulder injury. The treatment *eased* the *suffering*, or *relieved* it considerably.

allocate The booster club, including a few high-rollers, voted to *allocate* funds to build a new basketball arena and refurbish the football stadium. The group planned to *armark, or set apart*, the money for those purposes.

allot The captain had to *allot* each man a cup of water per day, i.e. to *parcel out* each share.

allude He was abashed to hear anyone *allude* to his prison time at social gatherings. It upset him when anyone *made indirect reference* to it.

altercation An *altercation* over politics between two of the guests disrupted the dinner party. It was an *angry, heated argument* over certain issues.

ETYMOLOGY	OLD MEANING
WORD	**NEW MEANING**

L alter
another
altruism
selfless concern for others' welfare

Ar aljama'ah
the assembly
amalgamate
mix together; unite; become one

L ambigere
to wander about; to be in doubt
ambiguous
having two or more meanings; vague

L ambire
to go round; encircle
ambit
bounds, limits; sphere of action; scope

L ambulare
to walk
ambulatory
of walking; able to walk; not confined

L melior
better
ameliorate
to make better; grow better; improve

OFr amener
to bring about; lead in
amenable
responsive; submissive; obedient

OFr a merci
at one's mercy
amerce
to punish by fine

L amicus
friend
amiable
friendly; good-natured

Gk amnestia
forgetfulness
amnesty
a pardon for a large group of persons

Gk ana- + chronos
against time
anachronism
anything out of its proper time

Gk analogos
proportionate; in due ratio
analogous
comparable; similar; like

Gk anarchos
without a leader or ruler
anarchy
absence of government; disorder

SAMPLE SENTENCES

altruism One of the great human virtues is *altruism*, which is far more likely under the aegis of a free society than a captive one, where *concern for others* is rare.

amalgamate It is often beneficial to *amalgamate* two corporations, to *merge* or *unite* them, to cut overlapping costs, operate more efficiently, and increase value.

ambiguous The politician's answers to the questions were *ambiguous*, that is, they were *vague, unclear, uncertain,* or *had two or more meanings.*

ambit The candidate covered his *ambit* in his quest for votes. He went to the *limits,* or *scope,* of his district. *Ambit* also means *a sphere of action, expression, or influence.*

ambulatory He is now *ambulatory* after recovering from an ankle operation;. He is now past needing crutches and is *able to walk.*

ameliorate The tourist's French was terrible, but a determined effort and an excellent teacher greatly *ameliorated* the situation, *improved* it hugely.

amenable Appointed or unelected officials are not *amenable* to the people's wishes, not *responsive* nor *accountable* to them.

amerce He pleaded to the traffic court not to *amerce* him for speeding. The judge said that to *punish* him by *fine* was reasonable.

amiable Even when things were not going very smoothly, e.g., a low grade on a quiz, a flat tire, a broken date, or a dip in the market, he was *amiable,* nearly always *friendly* and *good- natured.*

amnesty The governor proposed *amnesty* for late taxpayers, a *pardon*, if they pay up.

anachronism A Civil War uniform is an *anachronism* in today's army, just as a wooden sailing vessel in today's navy is far *out of date.*

analogous The wings of a bird are *analogous* to those of an airplane. Although different in structure and origin, they are *similar* and *comparable* in function.

anarchy When the unstable, interim oligarchy toppled, *anarchy* followed. There was *absence of government* and *disorder.*

ETYMOLOGY	OLD MEANING
WORD	**NEW MEANING**

Gk anathema
anathema
thing devoted to evil; curse
something detested or disliked

L ancilla
ancillary
servant
subordinate, subsidiary; auxiliary

L angustiae
anguish
difficulty; distress; narrowness
extreme pain, suffering; agony; sorrow

L animadvertere
animadversion
to notice; censure, punish
adverse, often unfair criticism,

L animus
animus
spirit, mind, soul; opinion, feelings
attitude; hostility; malevolent ill will

L annectare
annex
to bind to
to attach; add to, append; take for oneself

L ad- + nihil
annihilate
to nothing
destroy; vanquish totally

L ad- + nullus
annul
to none, not any
reduce to nothing; make legally void

Gk anomalos
anomalous
uneven
abnormal; irregular; not expected

Gk anthologos
anthology
gathering flowers
a collection of poems, stories, etc.

Gk anthropos
anthropology
man
the study of humans and humanity

Gk antipathes
antipathy
of opposite feelings
strong dislike, aversion; distaste

Gk antitithenai
antithesis
to place against
contrast, opposition; direct opposite

SAMPLE SENTENCES

anathema Cigarette smoke and listening to long cell-phone conversations are *anathema* to many people. Each is *something detested or disliked*.

ancillary Volunteer groups often provide *ancillary* help to nurses and other health professionals; they perform *subsidiary* or *auxiliary* duties and functions.

anguish The team felt mental *anguish* as their lead was slipping away with the change in momentum; it had to face the *agony* and *sorrow* of the possibility of losing.

animadversion Mental errors, not physical ones, will sometimes elicit *animadversions* from the coach; *adverse criticism* can be forthcoming.

animus The crowd's *animus* towards the referee after an unpopular call often lasts awhile, but the *hostility* disappears completely with a favorable decision.

annex Although the price was high, they decided to *annex* the lot next door, to *attach* it to their property.

annihilate The basketball team *annihilated* the visitors 109 to 61, a school record score against them; the locals *totally vanquished* the other team.

annul The popular couple decided to *annul* their marriage, to *make* it *legally void*, to the surprise of their many friends.

anomalous Her *anomalous* actions and behavior at the formal dinner party surprised many of the guests, who did not understand her *abnormal* mannerisms.

anthology He likes reading from his *anthologies*, because he learns something new each time he turns to his *collection of literary selections*.

anthropology One of the most popular courses at the university is *anthropology*, because students enjoy the *study of mankind*.

antipathy Most people have an *antipathy* for rude, coarse, crass, or inconsiderate behavior in public; they have a *strong dislike, aversion,* and *distaste* for it.

antithesis The newspaper editor says taxes should be raised, but the business man favors the *antithesis*, lower taxes. Each opinion is the *exact opposite* of the other, or *antithetical*.

Etymology	Old Meaning
Word	**New Meaning**

Gk apathea
apathy
without emotion
no interest, unconcern, indifference

Fr aplomb
aplomb
lit. perpendicularity, equilibrium
self-possession, confidence, poise

Gk apokryptein
apocryphal
to hide away
fictitious, untrustworthy, counterfeit

Gk apogaios
apogee
far from the earth
the highest or farthest point

Gk apo- + stasis
apostasy
from a standing
defection, desertion of a cause

L pallere
appall
to be pale; to fade; to be anxious
to overcome with shock or dismay

OF (L ad-) + pais
appease
to peace
to calm, pacify; to buy off an aggressor

L appendere
append
to weigh, to pay
attach, affix; add as a supplement

L apprehendere
apprehension
to understand (ad- + prehendere = to take)
arrest; mental grasp; anxiety; dread

Fr appris
apprise
learned, taught
give notice to; tell; inform

L ad- + propriare
appropriate (verb)
to take
set apart for; take without authority

Fr à propos
apropos
to the purpose
at the right time; apt; by the way

L arbiter
arbitrary
a witness; judge; umpire
**left to one's whim; selected at random
and without reason**

SAMPLE SENTENCES

apathy He is enthusiastic about fishing and duck-hunting but shows *apathy* for opera, symphony, and other cultural arts; he has a *lack of interest* in them.

aplomb By greatly increasing her vocabulary, she has much more *aplomb* in speaking with highly educated people; she has greater *poise* and *self-confidence*.

apocryphal His argument was based on *apocryphal* data, often found on the op-ed pages, where *fictitious, untrustworthy,* and *spurious* opinions abound.

apogee She began investing as the stock market reached its *apogee* and was upset when it tapered off; but one year later it reached a new *highest point* and all was well.

apostasy The *apostasy* of communism on the part of many refugees from captive societies, their *defection* from it, should come as no surprise.

appall The guests were *appalled* by his aberrant, anomalous behavior at the reception; they were *overcome with shock* and *dismay*.

appease The unarmed home owner was in no position to take a stand against the armed robber, so he tried to *appease* him, tried to *buy him off* on his terms.

append It is very convenient to *append* name tags on garments at class reunions. It helps to *affix* or *attach* the name tags so others can identify you after 20 years.

apprehension Badly unprepared for the big mid-term because of too much TV, he entered the exam hall with *apprehension*, a *dread,* an *anxious feeling.*

apprise A coach, a general, or a C.E.O., will want his aides or assistants to *apprise* him of developments in a changing situation, to *inform* him or *give notice* of them.

appropriate While we were working on the barbecue, some strangers *appropriated* the table we had reserved, *took* it *without authority* for their use.

apropos An alfresco dinner seemed *apropos* on the warm, early fall evening; everyone agreed it was *apt* and *fitting the occasion.*

arbitrary Parking in one of many available spaces is a harmless *arbitrary* decision, but placing a bet on a number at a roulette table, *chosen at random and without reason,* can be bad since the bettor has no clue as to the outcome.

ETYMOLOGY	OLD MEANING
WORD	**NEW MEANING**

L arbiter
arbitrator
a judge
one who settles differences; judge

L arboreus
arboreal
of a tree
like a tree; living in trees

L arcanus
arcane
secret; able to keep secrets
understood by only a few; mysterious

L ardere
ardor
to be on fire; burn, shine
passion; eagerness; enthusiasm; zeal

OF a- (L ad-) + raisnier
arraign
to speak
to call a prisoner to answer to charges

ML arredare
array
to put in order
orderly grouping; impressive display

L arrogare
arrogate
to appropriate to oneself
to claim or seize without justification

L articulare
articulate (adj.)
to separate into joints; to utter distinctly
jointed; able to speak easily, clearly

L artifex
artifice
skilled craftsman; artist
trick; false behavior; clever skill

Gk asketikos
ascetic
laborious
a self-denying person

L ad- + scribere
ascribe
to add in writing
to refer to a cause; attribute; credit

L asinus
asinine
ass; fool
stupid; silly; of unsound judgment

ME ascaunce
askance
as though, as if
with a side glance of suspicion, distrust

L asper
asperity
rough; bitter; harsh; severe; rugged
roughness of surface or manner; rigor

SAMPLE SENTENCES

arbitrator Being the *arbitrator* in a contested will settlement is difficult, but someone had to be the *one who settles difference,* or the *judge.*

arboreal She was surprised that her son, now 16, suddenly showed a renewed interest in spending time in his *arboreal* domicile, known as his *tree* house years earlier.

arcane The sociology major felt left out among the engineers and physicists when they discussed *arcane* theories, ideas *understood by only a few* and *mysterious* to her.

ardor Most successful people pursue their aims, goals, and ambitions with *ardor,* that is, they are driven by *passion, eagerness, enthusiasm, and zeal.*

arraign The parents were nervous, embarrassed, and frightened when the court was about to *arraign* their son, to *call him to answer to charges* of drunken assault.

array Arrivals at the pre-game tailgate party were elated with her *array* of foods and other goodies. It was a truly *impressive display.*

arrogate A few wise guys tried to *arrogate* one of our picnic tables just as we were about to use it; they tried to *take* it *without justification.*

articulate The board members were very impressed by her *articulate* presentation of the report. She was *able to speak easily*; the report was *clearly presented.*

artifice The assistant shipping clerk used *artifice to* convince strangers at the party that he was a rising executive; his *false behavior* and *clever skill* fooled them.

ascetic He prefers the severe life of an *ascetic,* one who is austere in appearance, manner, and attitude, and who avoids any luxuries, i.e., a *self-denying person.*

ascribe She *ascribed* her success to good coaching and conditioning. She also *attributed* and *credited* good advice to her success.

asinine The notion that chickens can swim and ducks can't is as *asinine* as the idea that the sun goes around the earth—absolutely *stupid, silly.*

askance After he made the asinine claim that oil is heavier than water, people looked *askance* at him. They looked *with a side glance of suspicion, disapproval,* and *distrust.*

asperity After experiencing the *asperity* of wintry, rocky terrain for some time, the idea of going to warm beaches won out over more *harshness* and *severity* of winter.

ETYMOLOGY	OLD MEANING
WORD	**NEW MEANING**

L assilire
assail

to leap upon
to attack with blows or words

OF assai
assay

test, effort
try; analyze; judge the worth of

L ad- + sentire
assent

to feel; think
to agree to something; concur

L assere
assert

lay claim to
state positively; show existence of

L assidere
assiduous

to assist
done with constant attention; diligent

L assignare
assignation

to assign
agreement to meet; meeting place

L assimulare
assimilate

to make similar
take in; absorb into a system or group

L ad- = suavis
assuage

sweet
to quiet, pacify; satisfy, relieve

L ad- + stringere
astringent

to draw tight
having a biting quality; puckery

L astus
astute

craft, cunning
having a clever mind; wily; shrewd

OE on + sundor
asunder

away from
into parts and pieces; separate

L atavus
atavism

great-great-great grandfather; ancestor
a throwback; primitive, ancestral type

Gk atrophos
atrophy

ill fed
wasting away; halt of development

SAMPLE SENTENCES

assail In the closing moments of a close game it is a bad idea for the coach to *assail* the referee. To *attack* him *violently with words* will result in a technical foul.

assay The miner, applying for a loan, asked the bank to *assay* his ore, which he hoped to use as collateral. The bank agreed to *analyze* it, *judge the worth of* it.

assent He hoped that the membership committee would *assent* to admit him to the club; he wished it would *agree after thoughtful consideration* to accept him.

assert The defense attorney *asserted* that his client was not at the scene of the crime; he *stated positively* that she was not there.

assiduous Although it was a very tough project, he completed it through *assiduous* effort. It involved *diligent* work, the kind *done with constant attention.*

assignation Their offices being far apart, an *assignation* somewhere between them was planned for lunch. They made an *agreement to meet* there; the secluded restaurant was an ideal *meeting place.*

assimilate The freshman wondered how well he would *assimilate* into the fraternity, and the members wondered how well he would *absorb into the group.*

assuage Several members came to *assuage* him that the chapter assented to assimilate him. They sought to *calm* and *pacify* him, to *relieve* his nerves.

astringent Certain fruits, such as pineapples and persimmons, and many mouthwashes, are *astringent*, that is, *having a biting quality.* They are *puckery.*

astute By *astute* maneuvering he avoided detection and escaped from many agents in the airport. By *having a clever mind*, he made several *wily* and *shrewd* moves.

asunder At the pick-up football game in the park, quite a few shirts were ripped *asunder*, torn *into bits and pieces.*

atavism The new offensive tackle is a rare *atavism*, who required a specially fit uniform and had to be weighed at the freight scales at Ypsilanti; he is a true *throwback.*

atrophy Poor blood supply or nerve damage can cause *atrophy* of muscles, which is a *wasting away, halt of development*, or *degeneration* of tissue.

| ETYMOLOGY | OLD MEANING |
WORD	NEW MEANING
L attenuare	to make thin
attenuate	**to weaken; lessen the force or severity**
L ad- + testari	to be a witness
attest	**authenticate; be proof of; to testify**
L attere	to rub against
attrition	**a wearing down; reduction of personnel**
L audacis	bold, daring; rash
audacious	**rudely bold; unrestrained, brazen**
L audire	to hear, learn; be told; listen
audit	**examine (accounts); attend a course**
L augere	to increase; enrich
augment	**to make greater, more numerous; add to**
L augur	a prophet, seer
augury	**sign of things to come; portent; omen**
L aura, *lit.*	air, breeze
aura	**distinctive atmosphere; impression**
L auspicium	augury, omen
auspicious	**boding well; favorable; successful**
Gk austeros	harsh; severe
austere	**stern; forbidding; somber; ascetic**
Gk autokrates	ruling by oneself
autocracy	**government with one person in charge**
Gk autodidaktos	self-taught
autodidact	**a self-taught person**
Gk autonomos	independent (auto- + nomos = law)
autonomy	**state of self-governing; freedom**

SAMPLE SENTENCES

attenuate Closing a window will *attenuate* a loud noise from outside, such as a buzz-saw, jack hammer, or leaf blower. It will *lessen the severity* of it.

attest After he assayed the sample of ore, the chemist *attested* to its purity, i.e., he*authenticated* it, *verified* its degree of purity.

attrition The team with the larger number of capable substitutes won the game by *attrition;* it won by *a wearing down* of the other team, which was fatigued.

audacious The ushers at the opera escorted the drunk out because of his *audacious* behavior; his *brazen, unrestrained* actions disturbed many.

audit The IRS agent came to *audit* the farmer's tax returns, that is, to *examine, go over* his accounts. The student *audited* an art class, i.e., *attended the course for no credit.*

augment A person can *augment* his income in a variety of ways, e.g., *make it greater* by working a second job, interest, dividends from investment, or renting property.

augury The stone faces of the jurors as they filed in meant an unwelcome *augury* for the defendant and his attorney; it was a bad *sign of things to come.*

aura His acumen in solving problems and his aplomb in speaking to strangers show an *aura* of leadership qualities, a *distinctive impression* of a "take charge" type.

auspicious High scores and good time management suggest an *auspicious* beginning for future academic success, that is, a *promising, favorable* indication.

austere The *austere* expressions on the jurors' faces were not at all auspicious for the defense attorney. Their *stern, forbidding* looks worried him greatly.

autocracy In an *autocracy* a single individual makes all the decisions for everyone else. It is a *government having one person in charge.*

autodidact Years after graduation, many people become *autodidacts,* because their formal educations are long past and they are now *self-taught persons.*

autonomy States and local governments seek more *autonomy* from distant, centralized governments, that is, *freedom* and *conditions of self-governing.*

ETYMOLOGY	OLD MEANING
WORD	**NEW MEANING**

L auxilium
auxiliary
help
assisting; subsidiary; ancillary

OF valoir
avail
to be of worth
to be of use; be present, obtainable

L avarus
avarice
greedy
greediness; huge desire for wealth

ME a- + vengen
avenge
to punish for a wrong done
to get revenge, get even

L avertere
averse
to turn away (from); avoid
not willing; opposed to; disinclined

L avertere
avert
to turn from, away from
turn aside (as eyes) in avoidance; avoid

L avidus
avid
eager, covetous; avaricious, greedy; hungry
urgently eager; vigorously enthusiastic

L avocare
avocation
to call away
a subordinate occupation; hobby

L advocare
avow
to summon; call to one's aid
to declare openly, bluntly without shame

Gk achos
awe
pain
emotion of dread, respect, and wonder

Gk axioun
axiom
to think worthy
a proposition seen as self-evident truth

SAMPLE SENTENCES

auxiliary Volunteers in *auxiliary* roles are valuable, because they provide *ancillary, helpful* work, allowing the paid professionals to pursue their roles.

avail Protesting his low grade *availed* him nothing. His plea *was of no use* to him.

avarice After attending several parties with a few affluent people who worked hard, the daydreamer developed an *avarice*, a *greediness for wealth*.

avenge To *avenge* a hard pitch aimed at him, the batter flung his bat at the pitcher. This seemed to him as a way to *get even*.

averse Some people are *averse* to eating broccoli; they are *disinclined* to tasting it, indeed, *opposed to* consuming the vegetable.

avert The new bride tried to *avert* eye contact with her former boyfriend, who showed up unexpectedly at the party; she *turned* her eyes *aside in avoidance*.

avid She is an *avid* opera patron and collector of oil paintings, while her husband is an *eager* and *enthusiastic* golfer and fisherman.

avocation He claimed that waiting tables at night was merely an *avocation*, that his main occupation is that of financial advisor. Being a waiter was his "*side job*."

avow The freshmen *avowed* they would not lose to USC during their careers at Stanford; they declared so *openly and bluntly, unabashedly*.

awe He stood in *awe* of the scene of his bungee jump. He was in a state of *dread, respect, and wonder*.

axiom The idea that 2 + 2 equals 4 is an *axiom*, whereas "the sun is shining in the quad" is not; the former is a *proposition seen as self-evident truth*, not so the latter.

ETYMOLOGY	OLD MEANING
WORD	**NEW MEANING**

ME baillif + wik
bailiwick
dwelling place
domain of expertise or authority

OHG balo
baleful
evil
harmful; ominous; sinister

OFr banal
banal
of objects owned by feudal serfs
dull; stale; unoriginal; trite

OHG bano
bane
death
source of harm or ruin; woe; curse

Port barroco
baroque
imperfect pearl
ornamentally curved; ornate

ME be- + gilen
beguile
to deceive
to divert; hoodwink; cheat; charm

Du be- + legeren
beleaguered
around + to camp
**besieged, surrounded; harassed;
beset with difficulties**

L bellicus
bellicose
of war; military
inclined to start quarrels or fights

MFr muser
bemuse
to idle, loiter; *prob.*, to gape, stare
confuse, bewilder; cause to be lost in thought

L bene + gigni
benign
well + to be born
gentle; of a mild character; kind

ME be- + sechen
beseech
to seek
to beg for; request earnestly

L blandus
blandish
smooth-tongued, fawning, flattering
coax with flattery; cajole

F blasé
blasé
apathetic from too much enjoyment
sophisticated, worldly-wise

SAMPLE SENTENCES

bailiwick Most universities do not have two *bailiwicks* for the same individual: football coach and dean of admissions, two *domains of authority.*

baleful The *baleful* threat of an audit by the dreaded IRS worried the honest taxpayer; to him it was *foreboding evil, ominous,* and *sinister.*

banal A badly limited vocabulary can lead to *banal* speech and writing, to expressions that are *dull, stale from overuse,* and *lacking originality.*

bane Apathy is a *bane* of serious endeavor, just as fatigue is a *bane* for a team during a game; each is a *source of ruin,* a *woe,* a *curse.*

baroque The interior designer converted the plain foyer to a *baroque* style, one *having curved ornamentation, over-decorated,* and *ornate.*

beguile The main skill of a good poker player is to *beguile* the others into thinking he has a much better hand than he has, that is, to *hoodwink* or *charm* them.

beleaguered The clerk was *beleaguered* all day during the sale by phone calls, other departments, and shoppers; then, he was *besieged, surrounded,* and *harassed* from all sides, everyone demanding his attention at the same time.

bellicose The police restrained some *bellicose* fans of the losing team after the game; they were *inclined* to *start fights* with the happier fans.

bemuse While waiting in the hotel lobby, tourists were *bemused* by the sudden entry of the university band. They were *confused, bewildered* and *lost in thought* by the band's appearance and antics.

benign At first everyone was afraid of the fierce-looking dog, but he turned out to be quite *benign* around people; fortunately, he was *harmless* and *gentle.*

beseech She went to the police station to *beseech* the captain to release her boy-friend, saying he didn't do it. "I *beg* of you to let him go," she said.

blandish The teen-age girl tried to *coax* her parents *with flattery* for more money and use of the car; she tried to *blandish* them.

blasé He was so used to his team winning all the time that he felt rather *blasé* when it won yet another championship; he was almost *apathetic* and *worldly-wise* about it.

Etymology	Old Meaning
Word	**New Meaning**

L blatire
blatant
to babble, to chatter
noisy; completely forward and showy

OHG blidi
blithe
joyous
glad; light-minded, casual; heedless

OE bealluc
bollix
ball
perform badly; botch (used with *up*)

Gk bombyx
bombast
silk garment
pretentious speech; self-importance

E *dialect* bosk
bosky
bush
having many trees or shrubs; wooded

Charles Boycott,
Eng. agent
boycott
refused to lower rents in Ireland

refusal to have dealings with

OIt bravare
bravado
to challenge; show off
swaggering conduct; pretense of bravery

OE brase
brazen
brass
harsh; loud; contemptuously bold

Gk boukolos
bucolic
cowherd
of shepherds; typical of rural life; rural

It buffone
buffoon
jester
clown; a gross, ill-educated person

F bureau + Gk kratos
bureaucracy
desk + power
unelected officialdom; red tape

ME burjon
burgeon
bud
sprout; grow, expand rapidly; flourish

SAMPLE SENTENCES

blatant The unruly fan was escorted from the arena because of his *blatant* behavior. His *forward, noisy* actions got him ejected.

blithe After successfully blandishing her parents for money and favors, the teenager was *blithe* about spending the money; she was *light-minded, casual,* and *heedless* about it.

bollix By ordering the wrong merchandise he *bollixed up* the promotional sale. He *performed badly, botched it, threw* the store *into disorder.*

bombast One candidate turned off the crowd with too much *bombast.* He gave a *pretentious speech*, a *pompous show of self-importance.*

bosky After long periods of work or study it is pleasant to hike in *bosky* areas, places which are *wooded, with plenty of trees or shrubs.*

boycott People or groups will sometimes *boycott* an establishment if they disagree strongly with its policy; they will *refuse to have dealings* with it.

bravado Rarely will a meek or staid person show much *bravado.* If anything, they tend to shy away from *blustering, swaggering conduct.*

brazen One sometimes sees *brazen* behavior in heavy traffic congestion e.g., *harsh and loud* honking and *bold and contemptuous* actions toward others.

bucolic "Getting away from it all" often involves a *bucolic* experience, one *typical of rural life*, e.g., visiting a farm, or out in the country.

buffoon It is best not to make eye contact with a *buffoon* if you wish to avoid involvement with such a *gross, ill-educated person.*

bureaucracy That part of the government known as the *bureaucracy* is the *unelected officialdom* and is also known as *red tape*, which means that ideas and actions get tied up and move very slowly if at all.

burgeon The small company started in a garage, but success enabled it to *burgeon;* it *grew, expanded rapidly*, and *flourished.*

QUIZ

Match the following words with their meanings:

(1) abide   [   ] to give aid or help, often in wrongdoing
(2) abolish   [   ] to hate or loathe intensely
(3) abject   [   ] straying from the normal or usual way
(4) aborigine   [   ] temporary suspension of activity
(5) abet   [   ] to make less in degree, force, or intensity
(6) abominate   [   ] to disconcert or embarrass; put to shame
(7) aberrant   [   ] down in spirits; hopeless, wretched
(8) abeyance   [   ] first inhabitant; a native
(9) abate   [   ] to withstand; accept without objection; tolerate
(10) abash   [   ] to do away with wholly; destroy; annul

(1) absolve   [   ] to agree without protest or enthusiasm
(2) acclaim   [   ] to do without; refrain from
(3) abstract   [   ] unshakable; inflexible in opinion
(4) acquiesce   [   ] to cut short a term or mission
(5) abscond   [   ] to collect; accumulate by addition
(6) absurd   [   ] hard to understand; recondite, deep
(7) abstain   [   ] to free from guilt; acquit
(8) accrue   [   ] to applaud, praise; shout praise
(9) abstruse   [   ] detached from specifics or reality; not reality
(10) abort   [   ] to go away secretly and hide
(11) adamant   [   ] untrue; ridiculous; laughable

(1) admonish   [   ] make up as one goes along; improvise
(2) adjourn   [   ] to corrupt; make impure or inferior
(3) acumen   [   ] excessive flattery or admiration
(4) ad lib   [   ] to plead in favor of; support
(5) adorn   [   ] to put off until a future time; suspend a session
(6) aegis   [   ] quickness of mind; shrewdness
(7) adulterate   [   ] advise; caution against faults; show disapproval
(8) adulation   [   ] protection; sponsorship; auspices
(9) advocate   [   ] to add beauty or splendor; to decorate

(1) affluence   [   ] artificial behavior not natural to oneself
(2) aggrandize   [   ] cause to be estranged; create hostile relationship
(3) agenda   [   ] offense, insult, indignity
(4) affable   [   ] relating to the beautiful; artistic
(5) afflict   [   ] to have a close connection; associate with
(6) affinity   [   ] influx; abundance of property; wealth
(7) aesthetic   [   ] pleasant; at ease in talking to others
(8) alienate   [   ] to distress severely; to trouble; injure
(9) affront   [   ] attraction to or liking for
(10) affiliate   [   ] to make greater; enhance, wealth or power,
(11) affectation   [   ] a list of things to be done or considered

(1) allay   [   ] to apportion; earmark; set apart
(2) alfresco   [   ] relating to land or farmers
(3) altercation   [   ] promptness in response; eager readiness
(4) alleviate   [   ] to assert without proof; adduce
(5) akimbo   [   ] with a separate price for each menu item
(6) agility   [   ] a noisy heated angry dispute or argument; quarrel
(7) allege   [   ] to assign as a portion; parcel out
(8) allocate   [   ] to relieve, lessen; ease pain or suffering
(9) a la carte   [   ] in the open air; outdoors
(10) allude   [   ] to reduce in intensity; to calm, make quiet
(11) agrarian   [   ] with hands on hips, elbows bent outward
(12) alacrity   [   ] nimbleness; quick, graceful movement
(13) allot   [   ] to make indirect reference to; refer

(1) amnesty   [   ] absence of government; disorder
(2) analogous   [   ] having two or more meanings; vague
(3) amalgamate   [   ] make better; grow better; improve
(4) anachronism   [   ] selfless concern for the welfare of others
(5) amenable   [   ] of walking; able to walk
(6) ameliorate   [   ] to mix together; unite; become one
(7) altruism   [   ] a pardon for a large group of persons
(8) ambiguous   [   ] comparable; similar, like
(9) anarchy   [   ] anything out of its proper time
(10) ambulatory   [   ] responsive; submissive, obedient

(1) anathema   [   ] strong dislike, aversion; dislike
(2) ancillary   [   ] abnormal; irregular; not expected
(3) annul   [   ] to destroy; to defeat totally
(4) anguish   [   ] the direct opposite; contrast
(5) anthropology [   ] something that is intensely disliked; a curse
(6) anomalous   [   ] subordinate, subsidiary; auxiliary
(7) annex   [   ] reduce to nothing; make legally void
(8) antipathy   [   ] extreme pain; suffering; agony; sorrow
(9) antithesis   [   ] the study of humans and humanity
(10) annihilate   [   ] to attach; add to; take for oneself

(1) apathy   [   ] defection; desertion of a cause
(2) appease   [   ] attach, affix; add as a supplement
(3) apropos   [   ] fictitious, untrustworthy; counterfeit
(4) apprehension [   ] self-possession, confidence, poise
(5) apprise   [   ] to take without authority; to set apart for
(6) arbitrary   [   ] at the right time; apt; "by the way"
(7) append   [   ] to calm, pacify, conciliate; buy off an aggressor
(8) apostasy   [   ] the highest or farthest point
(9) appropriate   [   ] to overcome with shock or dismay
(10) aplomb   [   ] no interest, unconcern, indifference
(11) appall   [   ] give notice to; to tell, inform
(12) apocryphal   [   ] selected at random without reason; whimsical
(13) apogee   [   ] arrest; mental grasp; anxiety; dread

(1) ascetic   [   ] passion; eagerness, enthusiasm; zeal
(2) arcane   [   ] able to speak easily and clearly; jointed
(3) array   [   ] harshness; roughness of sound, or manner
(4) arraign   [   ] to refer to a cause; to attribute; to credit
(5) ardor   [   ] a trick; false behavior; clever skill
(6) askance   [   ] stupid; silly; of unsound judgment
(7) asperity   [   ] a self-denying person
(8) ascribe   [   ] to call a prisoner to answer charges
(9) articulate   [   ] with a side glance; with disapproval or distrust
(10) artifice   [   ] orderly grouping; impressive display
(11) asinine   [   ] understood by only a few; mysterious

(1) assimilate   [   ] to try, test; analyze; judge the worth of
(2) astringent   [   ] having a clever mind; wily; shrewd
(3) assuage   [   ] to state positively; show existence of
(4) asunder   [   ] done with constant attention; diligent
(5) atrophy   [   ] a throwback; a primitive, ancestral type
(6) assent   [   ] to attack with blows or words
(7) assay   [   ] to quiet, pacify; satisfy; ease the distress of
(8) astute   [   ] having a biting quality; puckery
(9) assignation   [   ] a wasting away; a halt of development
(10) assiduous   [   ] into parts and pieces; separate
(11) assail   [   ] to take in; absorb into a system or group
(12) assert   [   ] to agree to something; concur
(13) atavism   [   ] agreement to meet; meeting place; tryst

(1) audacious   [   ] boding well, favorable; successful
(2) augury   [   ] distinctive atmosphere; a sense
(3) attenuate   [   ] to make greater, more numerous; add to
(4) attest   [   ] examine (accounts); attend a course for no credit
(5) attrition   [   ] a state of self-governing; freedom
(6) auspicious   [   ] stern; forbidding; somber; ascetic
(7) augment   [   ] to authenticate; be proof of; to testi
(8) austere   [   ] rudely bold; unrestrained, brazen
(9) aura   [   ] a wearing down; reduction in personnel
(10) autonomy   [   ] sign of things to come; portent, omen
(11) audit   [   ] to weaken; lessen the force or severity of

(1) avocation   [   ] greediness; excessive desire for wealth; cupidity
(2) avow   [   ] to be of use; be present, at hand; obtainable
(3) averse   [   ] assisting; subsidiary; ancillary
(4) auxiliary   [   ] urgently eager; vigorously enthusiastic
(5) awe   [   ] a proposition seen as self-evident truth
(6) avenge   [   ] to declare openly, bluntly, and without shame; assert
(7) avid   [   ] not willing; opposed to; disinclined
(8) avarice   [   ] emotion of dread, respect, and wonder
(9) axiom   [   ] a subordinate occupation; hobby
(10) avail   [   ] turn aside to avoid; see coming and ward off
(11) avert   [   ] to get revenge, get even

(1) beguile   [ ] to beg for; request earnestly
(2) baleful   [ ] gentle; of a mild character; kind
(3) bailiwick   [ ] source of harm or ruin; woe; curse
(4) beleaguered [ ] glad; light-minded; casual; heedless
(5) baroque   [ ] dull; stale; unoriginal; trite
(6) bemuse   [ ] to divert; hoodwink; cheat; charm
(7) bellicose   [ ] apathetic to excitement; worldly-wise
(8) bane   [ ] domain of expertise or authority
(9) benign   [ ] harmful; ominous; sinister
(10) blithe   [ ] besieged; harassed; beset with difficulties
(11) beseech   [ ] confuse, bewilder; cause to be lost in thought
(12) blasé   [ ] ornamentally curved; overly decorated; ornate
(13) banal   [ ] inclined to start quarrels or fights

(1) blandish   [ ] to claim or seize without justification
(2) bureaucracy [ ] swaggering conduct; pretense of bravery
(3) bucolic   [ ] noisy; completely forward and showy
(4) arbitrator   [ ] clown; a gross, ill-educated person
(5) boycott   [ ] pretentious speech; self-importance
(6) bollix (up) [ ] to sprout; grow; expand rapidly; flourish
(7) arrogate   [ ] to coax with flattery; to cajole
(8) brazen   [ ] having many trees or shrubs; wooded
(9) bravado   [ ] unelected officialdom; red tape
(10) burgeon   [ ] perform badly; botch
(11) blatant   [ ] of shepherds; typical of rural life; rural
(12) bombast   [ ] refusal to have dealings with
(13) buffoon   [ ] one who settles differences; a judge
(14) bosky   [ ] harsh; loud; contemptuously bold

QUIZ

1. If someone makes an absurd statement, the usual reaction is to:
(a) abide it   (b) look askance   (c) acclaim it   (d) assay it

2. The best professor is:
(a) abstruse   (b) ambiguous   (c) articulate   (d) arcane

3. You would choose a neighbor who is:
(a) adamant   (b) apocryphal   (c) amicable   (d) apathetic

4. The dentist you would prefer is:
(a) affable   (b) blithe   (c) adroit   (d) arbitrary

5. A buffoon is most likely to be:
(a) amenable   (b) aesthetic   (c) articulate   (d) audacious

6. You prefer dealing with a salesman who shows:
(a) aplomb   (b) adulation   (c) affectation   (d) animus

7. You prefer dealing with an advisor who is:
(a) beleaguered   (b) astute   c) brazen   (d) bellicose

8. Which of the following are the LEAST astringent?
(a) persimmons   (b) pineapples   (c) vegetable oils   (d) mouth-washes

9. A self-governing body or group is:
(a) an autonomy   (b) a bureaucracy   (c) an autocracy   (d) a bailiwick

10. Severe pain is something you want to:
(a) allot   (b) aggravate   (c) alleviate   (d) advocate

SEGMENT TWO

ETYMOLOGY	OLD MEANING
WORD	**NEW MEANING**
Fr cabale	intrigue
cabal	**group joined in a secret plot**
MF cacher	to press, hide
cachet	**approved great prestige, status**
Gk kakophonia	kak = bad + phonia = sound
cacophony	**harsh or discordant sound**
Fr cajoler	to chatter like a jay in a cage
cajole	**to persuade with flattery**
L callosus	hard-skinned; solid
callous	**feeling no emotion or sympathy**
ME calu	not yet enough feathers to fly
callow	**lacking adult sophistication**
L capax	capable of holding; roomy
capacious	**able to contain much; spacious**
It capriccio	head with hair standing on end
caprice	**sudden change of mind; whim**
L captiosus	deceptive; dangerous
captious	**quick to find fault; critical**
L castigare	to correct; punish
castigate	**to punish; criticize severely**
MD cater	tomcat + wrauwen = to wail
caterwaul	**to cry harshly; quarrel noisily**
Fr causer	to chat
causerie	**informal conversation; chat**
L caballus	horse
cavalier	**given to offhand dismissal of important matters; debonair**

SAMPLE SENTENCES

cabal Several people in the office formed a *cabal* because they disliked the new boss. They were a *group plotting to undermine* her.

cachet A major prize or award usually brings *cachet* to the winner, a *sign of approval conferring great prestige* or *high status.*

cacophony Many basketball fans disliked the *cacophony* resulting from both bands playing at the same time. The *harsh, discordant noise* was very unpleasant.

cajole Her date's car broke down, so she had to *cajole* her dad for the use of his car in order to go out. She *persuaded* him *with flattery* to gain use of the car.

callous He thought himself *callous* for passing the hitch-hiker, but he knew that giving a stranger a lift is often unsafe, so he felt less *unsympathetic* about it.

callow The *callow* small-town freshman, seated at the crowded banquet table, didn't know which cup was his- the one on the left or the right. He was *unsophisticated, immature.*

capacious It is wise to take *capacious* luggage on long trips for the many items you may wish to bring home. Take *spacious* suitcases, those *able to hold a great deal.*

caprice While shopping for crystal and fine china, she bought a tool kit on a *caprice*. This *sudden, impulsive change of mind*, this *whim*, surprised her friends.

captious Her mother-in-law became rather *captious* upon viewing the thick layer of dust during the white glove test; she was *quick to find fault* with her housekeeping.

castigate She *castigated* her husband for falling asleep and snoring at the opera; she *subjected* him *to harsh criticism, read* him *the riot act.*

caterwaul The new neighbors down the street began to *caterwaul*, breaking the stillness of the night. One could hear them *quarrel noisily.*

causerie What many thought to be a formal discussion turned out to be a *causerie*, an *informal conversation*, or *chat.*

cavalier When informed that his house was on fire, he was very *cavalier* about it. He was *light-hearted in his dismissal* of the matter, saying, "These things will happen."

ETYMOLOGY	OLD MEANING
WORD	**NEW MEANING**

| L cavillor | to jeer, scoff; to quibble |
| **cavil** | **to raise trivial objections to** |

| L censura | censorship; criticism |
| **censure** | **blame; find fault with; criticize** |

| Gk charisma | favor, gift |
| **charisma** | **magnetic charm or appeal** |

| It ciarlatano | a quack |
| **charlatan** | **a pretender to expertise; fake** |

| ME charry, chary | sorrowful; dear |
| **chary** | **cautious, hesitant, vigilant about dangers or risks** |

| ME chastisen | to punish |
| **chastise** | **inflict punishment; scold** |

| L chimaera | fire-breathing monster, part lion, goat, serpent |
| **chimerical** | **unreal, improbable; imaginary** |

| Gk chole | bile |
| **choleric** | **easily angered; hot-tempered** |

| L circumlocutio | circum- = around + locutio = speech |
| **circumlocution** | **use of too many words to say something; evasion in speech** |

| L circumspicere | to look around; be cautious |
| **circumspect** | **careful; on the lookout** |

| L clarus + Fr voir | clarus = clear, bright + voir = to see |
| **clairvoyant** | **unusually perceptive; clear-sighted** |

| L clandestimus | secret |
| **clandestine** | **held in or conducted in secrecy** |

| L cauda | tail |
| **coda** | **conclusion of a musical; finale** |

SAMPLE SENTENCES

cavil Regardless of how high the quality of anything may be, there are those who will *cavil* about it; they will *raise trivial objections to* it, *find fault with* it.

censure The fans *censured* the two drunks who spoiled their enjoyment of the game; they *blamed* and *criticized* them as the security guards ushered them out.

charisma Although he had less substance to offer, he was elected because he had more *charisma*, that is, a *special magnetic charm* about him.

charlatan At parties strangers gathered around him until they found out he was a *charlatan*; he was a *fake*, a *pretender to expert knowledge*.

chary He is *chary* about everything from crossing the street to investment decisions; he was always *cautious, hesitant,* and *vigilant about dangers and risks*.

chastise The host *chastised* his dog for absconding with the steak while his boss was on the way over for the barbecue; he *scolded* the dog, *censured* him *severely*.

chimerical Some things once thought to be *chimerical* turned out to be realistic or feasible. What was considered *unreal, improbable,* or *imaginary* was actually achieved, like landing on the moon.

choleric The coach became *choleric* after the official's third straight bad call against his team; it made him *hot tempered, irate,* and *easily moved to anger*.

circumlocution Why do so many politicians – and others – fall back on *circumlocution* to answer a simple question, *the use of too many words to say something?*

circumspect Lost in the jungle, they were *circumspect* with every step, very *careful to consider circumstances and consequences* with all the dangers lurking.

clairvoyant Many people thought him to be *clairvoyant* after his many accurate predictions. He seemed *unusually perceptive* and *clear-sighted*.

clandestine A cabal arranged a *clandestine* meeting to plot against someone in the main office. It was to be a meeting *conducted in secrecy*.

coda The noted conductor received thunderous accolades after the *coda*, which is the *concluding part* of the symphony, or the *finale*.

Etymology	Old Meaning
Word	**New Meaning**
L coercere	to enclose, confine, repress, control
coerce	**to dominate; compel; enforce**
L cogere	to drive together; collect
cogent	**powerful; convincing; valid**
L cogitare	to think; ponder; imagine
cogitate	**ponder with intentness; plan, plot; think deeply**
L co- + gnaatus, natus, nasci	to be born
cognate	**related; generally alike**
L cognoscere	to know; to get to know; recognize
cognizant	**aware; having special knowledge**
L collatio	bringing together; comparison, analogy
collate	**compare; put in proper order**
L colloquium< colloqui	to converse; to talk to; speak with
colloquial	**used in informal conversation**
L colludere	to play together or with
collusion	**secret agreement for illegal plot**
Gk komat, koma	deep sleep
comatose	**lethargic; drowsy; dull, inactive**
L comis	courteous; friendly
comity	**friendly quality; social harmony**
L commetior	to measure
commensurate	**equal in extent; proportionate**
L commodum	convenience
commodious	**conveniently spacious; roomy**
L compellere	to drive, bring together
compel	**to cause to do by pressure; force**

SAMPLE SENTENCES

coerce Fearing a riot, the police tried to *coerce* the fans to stay off the field after the game; they tried to *enforce by threat,* to *compel* everyone to not come onto the field.

cogent In his introductory remarks to the incoming freshman class the president made a *cogent* argument in favor of time-budgeting, a *powerful, convincing.* and *valid* one.

cogitate There are times when a person must *cogitate* about serious matters; one must not be blithe about them, but should *meditate* or *think deeply* in each case.

cognate French and Spanish are *cognate* languages, as are English and German; that is, *related, generally alike.*

cognizant It is advantageous to be *cognizant* of events and situations that concern you. To be *aware* and *have specific knowledge* of what's going on is very helpful.

collate The student was asked to *collate* the changes in the trend in Greek art with the downfall of the Roman Empire, to *compare critically* the two developments.

colloquial Two people from the same region usually converse in *colloquial* verbal communication. It is *familiar, informal* conversation.

collusion They were in *collusion* to give false testimony at the trial, that is, were in *secret cooperation for an illegal purpose.*

comatose At the end of the workout on the first day of practice the players were *comatose.* They became *lethargic, drowsy,* and *dull.*

comity There was general *comity* between the two groups of fans before and after the Rose Bowl Game, a *friendly social atmosphere* and *harmony.*

commensurate It is generally felt that one's pay should be *commensurate* with the quality and quantity of his work; it should be *proportionate* to his value to the firm.

commodious Wall Street was very kind to him, and as a result he built a new house far more *commodious* than his first one. It was very *comfortably spacious,* more *roomy.*

compel Foul weather and darkness *compelled* the hikers to turn back; the circumstances *forced* them to go back, *caused* them to do so *by overwhelming pressure.*

ETYMOLOGY	OLD MEANING
WORD	**NEW MEANING**

L complacere	to please very much
complacent	**self-satisfied; smug; unconcerned**

L complere	to fill up; complete, fulfill, finish
complement	**component that completes**

L comprehendere	to grasp, catch; comprise
comprehensive	**covering broadly; inclusive**

MFr compte	account, count
comptroller	**official who audits accounts**

L compellere	to drive; bring together; compel
compulsive	**driven by force, or necessity**

L compellere	to drive, bring together, compel
compulsory	**demanded by authority; required**

L compungere	to prick; to sting
compunction	**anxiety from guilt; misgiving**

L conatus	effort; inclination
conation	**instinct; a wish or craving**

L conservus	fellow slave
concierge	**all-purpose hotel desk manager**

L conciliare	to unite; win over; bring together
conciliate	**gain favor by pleasing acts; appease; pacify; be friendly**

L concomitari	to accompany
concomitant	**occurring along with; at the same time**

L com- + descendere	go down; stoop; lower oneself
condescending	**having air of superiority**

L condignus	very worthy
condign	**deserved; appropriate; merited**

SAMPLE SENTENCES

complacent When things go well for a long time, some people tend to become *complacent*. They become *smug* and *self-satisfied*.

complement The team has its full *complement* of players, the *component that completes* the roster.

comprehensive The history professor promised the class a *comprehensive* mid-term, one *covering broadly* the subject, and *inclusive*.

comptroller The business partners decided to call in a *comptroller* to go over the books, an *official who audits or supervises accounts*.

compulsive The tennis player had a *compulsive* urge to practice more and harder, an urge *driven by necessity* to win more often.

compulsory School attendance is *compulsory* in the state; it is *required* by law, *mandatory, demanded by authority*.

compunction The inconsiderate man in a crowded gathering had no *compunctions* about coughing in the faces of others, no *qualms* or *feeling of guilt*.

conation Even after several speeding tickets, he still had a *conation* to drive fast, a strong *inclination*, a *craving* or *impulse* to do so.

concierge Tourists ask the *concierge* for all kinds of things; he is the *hotel attendant who makes reservations, handles mail, arranges tours, etc.*

conciliate The person in the weaker bargaining position will try to *conciliate* the the stronger foe, to *pacify* or *appease* him, or *gain favor by pleasing acts*.

concomitant Roses are beautiful, but the *concomitant* thorns warn everyone to handle them with care; the thorns are *occurring along with* the roses. "Every rose has its thorns."

condescending An All-American senior should never be *condescending* toward a freshman recruit; he should not be *having an air of superiority* toward him.

condign Fines or penalties should be *condign* for what was done wrong, neither too light nor excessive, but justly *deserved, appropriate,* or *fitting*.

ETYMOLOGY WORD	OLD MEANING NEW MEANING
L condolescere **condolence**	to begin to ache, feel very sore **sympathy with one in sorrow**
L confluere **confluence**	to flow together **a coming together; meeting**
OFr com- + frere **confrere**	with + brother **colleague; fellow worker**
L confutare **confute**	keep from boiling over; repress; silence **overwhelm in argument; disprove**
L com- + genius **congenial**	one's disposition or inclination **agreeable; pleasant; attractive**
L com- + gignere **congenital**	to beget; produce; bring forth **existing at birth; inherent; innate**
L congruere **congruent**	to coincide; correspond; agree, suit **in agreement; coinciding**
L conjicere **conjecture**	to throw together; infer; interpret **an uncertain inference; a guess**
L conjurare **conjure**	to take an oath; to conspire, plot **create as if by magic; invent**
L conivere **connive**	shut the eyes; blink; be asleep **pretend ignorance of wrongdoing; cooperate secretly; conspire**
L cognoscere **connoisseur**	to get to know; learn; identify **an expert; critical judge**
L com- + notare **connote**	to mark; write; note **to imply more than exact meaning**
L consentire **consensus**	to agree; determine together; plot **opinion held by all or most; general agreement**

SAMPLE SENTENCES

condolence Many friends expressed their *condolences* to the family of the deceased at the funeral. They expressed *sympathy* with those in sorrow.

confluence There was a *confluence* of great minds at the seminar, a *coming together* of brilliant thinkers.

confrere The two *confreres* were also close friends who hung out a lot together; in the shop they were *colleagues*, or *fellow workers*.

confute Two other confreres, not the best of friends, were always trying to *confute* the assertions of each other, to *overwhelm in argument*, or *disprove*, the other's claims.

congenial The *congenial* members of the club made the guest feel welcome. The guest in turn found the members very *agreeable* and *pleasant*.

congenital Although he made lots of money, he was often broke because of debts to bookies and casinos; he seemed to be a *congenital* gambler, an *inherent* risk taker.

congruent His opinions were *congruent* with those of the professor, especially when the latter declared him the best student in the class. He was completely *in agreement*.

conjecture The professor gave a very tough, comprehensive examination. Many students had to rely on *conjectures* for their answers, pure *guesswork*.

conjure The class thanked the student who *conjured* up a clever scheme to block the glare from a windshield of a parked car; he *created as if by magic* his idea.

connive The students *connived* when asked by the principal the identity of the one who let the air out of his tire. They *pretended ignorance of wrongdoing*.

connoisseur When uncertain about the quality of an artwork or a fine wine, people seek the opinion of a *connoisseur* before buying. They seek a *critical judge*, an *expert*.

connote A college education *connotes* many things, such as making lifelong friends, fun, and learning how to think; it *implies more* than classes, libraries, and labs.

consensus At the sorority's annual spring dance party it was the *consensus* that one sister's date was the ugliest man there. That *general agreement* among the members won her the "Ugly Drake" award.

ETYMOLOGY	OLD MEANING
WORD	**NEW MEANING**
L consignare	to seal, sign; attest, vouch for
consign	**transfer to another's care**
L consors	sharing in common
consort	**an associate; spouse; companion**
L consternare	startle; stampede; throw into confusion
consternation	**confused and distressing excitement**
L consummare	to sum up, finish, complete; perfect
consummate	**very skilled; of the highest degree**
L contemnare	think light of; have no fear of; despise
contemn	**treat, view with contempt; scorn**
L contentus	strained, tense
contentious	**likely to argue, quarrelsome**
L contiguus	adjoining; near; within reach
contiguous	**in actual contact; adjacent**
L contingere	to touch, affect, concern
contingent	**possible; likely but not certain; dependent on something else**
L contritus	bruised; worn out
contrite	**grieving for sin; remorseful**
LL contropare	to compare
contrive	**devise; fabricate; invent; concoct**
L convertere	to turn around; turn back
converse	**something reversed in relation**
L convivium	banquet, entertainment; guests
convivial	**fond of feasting and good company**
L convocare	to call a meeting of; muster
convoke	**to call together to a meeting**

SAMPLE SENTENCES

consign He absconded to South America with the goods *consigned* to him, and as a result is now a fugitive. He stole the shipment *transferred to his care* and fled.

consort She rarely goes anywhere without her *consort*, but once in a while travels with a friend. In any event her *spouse* usually tags along.

consternation Two former confreres, each thinking the other dead, eyed each other in *consternation* at a party. They met in utter *amazement* and *dismay*.

consummate He is the *consummate* golfer – *complete in every detail, perfect*. He is a *consummate* liar – *extremely skilled and accomplished*.

contemn Many people in the restaurant seemed to *contemn* the man holding a long and loud conversation over his cell phone; they appeared to *view* him *with scorn*.

contentious Many baseball games feature an encounter between a *contentious* manager and an umpire; the manager is *likely to cause an argument* after a "bad" call.

contiguous Forty-eight of our states are *contiguous* and two are not. The forty-eight are *in actual contact*, each *touching others along common boundaries*.

contingent The couple knew that buying the new house was *contingent* upon selling their present one. Getting the new one was *conditioned by*, or *dependent on* the sale.

contrite Having borrowed some money from a close friend, he felt very *contrite* about not paying it back before his friend died. He was *grieving for this*, and *remorseful*.

contrive Some students try to *contrive* ways to break the rules, e.g., to sneak alcoholic beverages into the stadium. They *devise. invent*, or *concoct* such schemes.

converse A dog is not a cat, and the *converse* is true: a cat is not a dog. A rainy day and a clear night is the *converse* of a clear day and a rainy night; no P is S is the *converse* of no S is P. Each example shows what is meant by *converse*, or *reversal in relation*.

convivial The couple really likes to live it up; they are *convivial*; that is, they are *fond of parties, great dining, fine wines*, and *good company*.

convoke After winning several consecutive games, the coach *convoked* the team to warn against a letdown. He *called* the players *together to a meeting, summoned* them.

ETYMOLOGY	OLD MEANING
WORD	**NEW MEANING**

L convolvere
convoluted

roll up; coil up; intertwine
twisted, coiled; involved, intricate

L copia
copious

abundance; plenty
in large quantity; profuse in words

L cornu copiae
cornucopia

horn of plenty
inexhaustible store; abundance

L corollarium
corollary

garland; present; gratuity
something that naturally follows, accompanies, or parallels

L corpus
corpulent

body
having a large bulky body; fat

L com- + relatio
correlate

with relation
show relationship of or between

L corrigere
corrigible

make straight; put right; to correct
can be set straight; correctable

L corroborare
corroborate

to make strong; invigorate
support with evidence; confirm

Gk kosmos
cosmopolitan

world
having worldwide sophistication

MFr coterie
coterie

association of peasant tenants
an intimate, exclusive group

L continere
countenance

to hold together; restrain; contain
calm expression; composure; look

Fr coup
coup

blow, stroke
brilliant, sudden stroke or act

Fr coup de grace
coup de grace

a stroke of mercy
decisive finishing blow, act, or event

SAMPLE SENTENCES

convoluted She wrote a novel very *convoluted* in form. The story was *twisted* in many ways and *involved* and *intricate* in details.

copious In the doubles match she expressed *copious* praise for her partner's play; she was *profuse in words* of praise after they won the match.

cornucopia The sea provides a seeming *cornucopia* of fish, which means an *inexhaustible store*, or an *abundance* of fish.

corollary The *corollary* to a bigger income is higher taxes; the higher tax is *something that naturally follows or parallels* the bigger income.

corpulent During the off season the coaches don't want the players to become *corpulent* from inactivity and overeating; they don't want them too *fat* or *heavy*.

correlate It is probable that one can *correlate* vocabulary and success; it is likely that one can *establish a relationship* between them.

corrigible There are many mistakes, habits, behavioral patterns, and common errors that are *corrigible*; they are *capable of being set right,* are *correctable* and *reparable*.

corroborate The district attorney was seeking an eye-witness who could *corroborate* the unusual story, one who was able to *support* it *with evidence,* or to *confirm* it.

cosmopolitan The couple appeared to be very *cosmopolitan*, judging from their interests, manners, and tastes; they were *marked by worldwide bearing and sophistication.*

coterie She was the only one in the elegant room who was not a member of an elitist *coterie,* but being cosmopolitan, she fared well with the *exclusive, intimate group.*

countenance He awaited the opinion of the wine he brought, and the connoisseur's *countenance* assuaged his anxiety; his *look* of approval upon tasting it pleased him.

coup The cleanup hitter's surprise squeeze bunt was the *coup* of the game. It was a truly *brilliant, successful move* which caught the other team off guard.

coup de grace The blocked punt recovered in the end zone with less than two minutes to play was the *coup de grace*, the *decisive, finishing blow* of the game.

ETYMOLOGY	OLD MEANING
WORD	**NEW MEANING**
Fr coup d'état	stroke of state
coup d'état	**sudden overthrow of government**
L convenire	to meet; agree; to be suitable
covenant	**a formal, binding agreement**
L cooperire	to cover over, overwhelm
covert	**kept private; hidden; veiled**
L cupidus	desirous; eager; loving; greedy
covet	**to desire what belongs to another**
L crassus	thick; gross; dense; dull; stupid
crass	**lacking delicacy or refinement; insensitive; stupid**
L crepare	to crack; creak; rattle; chatter
craven	**lacking courage; fainthearted**
L credere	to entrust; believe; think; suppose
credible	**worthy of belief; plausible**
L credere	to entrust; believe; think; suppose
credulous	**ready to believe; gullible**
Fr crème de la crème	*lit.* = cream of the cream
crème de la crème	**the very best; the highest elite**
L crepitare	to crackle; creak; rustle; rattle
crepitate	**to make a crackling sound**
L crepusculum	twilight; dusk; darkness
crepuscular	**like twilight; glimmering; dim**
Gk krinein	to judge, decide
criterion	**standard on which judgment or decision is made**
Gk chronios	long-lasting
crony	**long-time close friend; chum**

SAMPLE SENTENCES

coup d'état The rebels seized control of the government via a *coup d'état*; they surprised everyone by the *sudden overthrow of the government*

covenant A truce developed between the parties when they signed a *covenant* to balance the budget; it was a *binding agreement*, a *written promise to act.*

covert In certain cases, *covert* operations are necessary. It is important that they be *kept private, hidden,* or *veiled.*

covet In an old book on Latin grammar was the exercise sentence: "I *covet* my uncle's pudding." Can you think of anything better to *desire what belongs to another?*

crass The restaurant manager was nervous about the buffoon's *crass* behavior; it was opening night at the opera, and he was *devoid of refinement* but a big spender.

craven Trying to appease an unreasonable and uncompromising antagonist is a *craven* gesture, one *completely lacking courage* and *contemptibly fainthearted.*

credible The reporters felt that the witness gave a *credible* account of the unusual and complicated incident, a *believable, trustworthy* story.

credulous A simpleton, one deficient in worldly wisdom or informed judgment, is probably *credulous*; he is *ready to believe* almost anything.

crème de la crème Nearly every field or type of activity has its *crème de la crème;* music, sports, literature, etc, - each has its *very best,* its *highest elite.*

crepitate The campers awakened when they heard leaves and twigs *crepitate* outside the tent; something out there *made a crackling sound* on the leaves.

crepuscular At the end of a hot summer day, a *crepuscular* tennis match is the best; the sun has gone down, but there is still plenty of *twilight* time left to play.

criterion Although the SAT score is but one *criterion* for admission to a university, it is in many cases the most important *standard by which to judge* a student.

crony After many years of geographic separation, he was happy that his old *crony* had moved much closer to him. He was his *friend of long standing,* his *chum.*

Etymology	Old Meaning
Word	**New Meaning**
L crux	cross; gallows
crucial	**very important; decisive**
L crux	cross; gallows
crux	**a most important, deciding point; a main or central feature**
Gk kryptos	hidden
cryptic	**secret; serving to conceal; using code**
L culmen	stalk; top, roof, summit; height, acme
culminate	**reach the highest point; bring to a head**
L culpa	blame, fault; guilt; mischief
culpable	**deserving blame or condemnation**
L cumulare	to heap up, pile up; amass; increase
cumulative	**increasing by successive additions**
ME cunnen	to know
cunning	**crafty; wily, tricky; clever; sly**
L cupidus	desirous, eager, fond; greedy
cupidity	**lust; desire for wealth; avarice; greed**
ME currayen favel	to curry (comb) a chestnut horse
curry favor	**seek to gain favor by flattery or attention**
L cursus	running; speed; passage; rapidity
cursory	**rapidly done; hasty; superficial**
L curtus	shortened; broken off; incomplete
curtail	**to make less; shorten; cut off**
Gk kynikos	like a dog
cynic	**a faultfinding, captious critic**

SAMPLE SENTENCES

crucial High grades, test scores, and significant achievements are *crucial* criteria for admission to a university; they are *very important, critical, and decisive* factors.

crux One the last play of regulation time, the *crux* of the problem was whether to go for a tying field goal or a winning touchdown; it was the *most important, deciding point.*

cryptic Classified information is transmitted in *cryptic* messages, so that only the recipient will know the contents; they are *secret* coded data.

culminate Her years of diligent study *culminated* in graduating first in her class; it *brought* her *to the highest point* of her academic career.

culpable Sometimes it takes a jury a long time to decide whether a defendant is *culpable* or not; it is hard to say if someone is *deserving of blame* in some cases.

cumulative Dermatologists warn against the *cumulative* nature of sun radiation; it *increases by successive addition without loss.*

cunning In the airport he eluded the police and other officials by a *cunning* maneuver; he employed a *clever* trick, a *crafty, sly* move.

cupidity The habitual gambler battled his own *cupidity* every time he stepped up to the craps table; his *greed* got the better of him.

curry favor She *curried favor* with her English teacher to allow her one more day in which to complete her essay; her dog ate her work, and she *tried to gain her favor* because her grade and her chance to attend the graduation party depended on it.

cursory One misses many of the subtleties of the language and the beauty of the prose when one does a *cursory* reading of classical literature; fine points are missed with a reading *rapidly done with little attention.*

curtail We had to *curtail* our meeting due to the late hour; we had to *cut it short.*

cynic The *cynics* sneered at the achievers' accomplishments; the *captious critics* and *faultfinders* say people are led by self-interest.

ETYMOLOGY	OLD MEANING
WORD	**NEW MEANING**

| MD dapper | quick; strong |
| **dapper** | **neat, trim; very stylish; alert** |

| L domare | to tame, break in; conquer |
| **daunt** | **subdue through fear; intimidate** |

| ME dere | dear, costly |
| **dearth** | **scarcity; inadequate supply; lack** |

| L debilis | frail; weak; crippled |
| **debilitate** | **impair the strength of; weaken** |

| OFr de bon aire | *lit.*, of good breed or race |
| **debonair** | **easy, carefree; lively; elegant** |

| MFr de- + but | from the starting point |
| **debut** | **first public appearance** |

| LL decadere | to fail, sink; decay |
| **decadence** | **decay; period of decline** |

| Fr décamper | to flee; pack off; move out fast |
| **decamp** | **break camp; depart suddenly** |

| L decimus | tenth |
| **decimate** | **take a tenth from; destroy a lot of** |

| L declivis | sloping down; downhill |
| **declivity** | **downward inclination, slope** |

| L decorus | proper; becoming; beautiful; noble |
| **decorum** | **fitness; good taste; orderliness** |

| Fr décrier | to discredit; bring into disrepute |
| **decry** | **to express strong disapproval of** |

| L deducere | to lead away; escort; subtract |
| **deduce** | **to infer from; trace the course of** |

SAMPLE SENTENCES

dapper Everyone remarked how *dapper* he looked in his new tuxedo. He was *neat, trim,* and *very stylish* at the dinner dance.

daunt A strange new circumstance, like taking a short-cut through a dark alley, will often *daunt* a chary person; it will *intimidate* him, *subdue* him *with fear.*

dearth There was a sudden *dearth* of fresh water on the cruise ship at the half-way point of its journey. The severe *scarcity* meant a careful allotment to everyone.

debilitate An injury such as a stress fracture or hamstring pull will *debilitate* an athlete. It will *impair* his strength, *weaken* him to the extent that he cannot play.

debonair Already dapper in his new tux, his *debonair* style charmed the ladies; his *easy, carefree,* and *elegant* manner impressed them.

debut He made his *debut* at quarterback when the starter was temporarily debilitated by a sprained wrist; it was his *first public appearance* at the position.

decadence A combination of high inflation and massive unemployment can lead to social *decadence*, moral *deterioration*, a *period of decline.*

decamp The players and fans had to *decamp* when the big storm arrived; they decided to *break camp*, to *depart suddenly,* to *get out of there fast.*

decimate The tornado *decimated* the town almost beyond recognition; it *destroyed a lot* of the town.

declivity The beginning skiers were daunted by the steep *declivity* they faced and took the chair lift; they feared the awesome *downward slope.*

decorum The students displayed *decorum* on Parents' Day; some were debonair and almost dapper in showing *good taste* and *orderliness.*

decry The home fans *decried* the failure of the officials to call a foul when the visitors mugged the local hero; they *expressed strong disapproval of* the non-call.

deduce Given enough evidence, one can *deduce* a logical result. One can *infer from* what is known to determine the result.

Etymology **Word**	Old Meaning **New Meaning**
OHG tuomen **deem**	to judge **come to think; have an opinion**
L de- + fallere **default**	to cheat, beguile, deceive; betray **neglect; failure to act, appear, compete, or make good; forfeit**
L defectoris **defection**	deserter; rebel **abandonment of a cause; desertion**
L differre **defer**	to put off, delay; to differ **to delay; postpone; suspend**
L deficere **deficit**	to fail; be lacking; run short **excess of spending over revenue**
L definitivus **definitive**	explanatory **serving to specify, define**
L deflectere **deflect**	to bend down; turn aside **to turn from a straight course**
L defraudare **defraud**	to cheat **to deprive of by deception; cheat**
OFr frai **defray**	expenditure **provide for payment of; pay**
L defunctus **defunct**	discharged; dead **no longer existent; dead; extinct**
L degenerare **degenerate**	to deteriorate; disgrace **to sink to a low state; degrade**
L deus **deify**	god **to make a god of**
L dignus **deign**	worth; worthy; fitting, proper **to condescend to act below one's dignity or to reply; to stoop**

SAMPLE SENTENCES

deem After driving fast through the open countryside, he *deemed* it wise to slow down as he approached the small town; he *judged* it prudent to do so.

default The team bus had a breakdown, and fixing it took several hours, so the players had to *default* the game because they could not arrive on time; they had to *forfeit*.

defection At first the army charged him with *defection*, but instead he was behind enemy lines performing heroic deeds. The charges of *desertion* were dropped.

defer Unable to reach a decision at the late hour, they voted to *defer* further discussion of the issue, to *put* it *off*, to *postpone* it to another time.

deficit If a household or a government spends more money than it takes in, a *deficit* occurs; that is, a *deficiency in amount,* or *an excess of spending over revenue.*

definitive It is better to be *definitive* than vague. An audience prefers a speaker who is *authoritative*, one whose statements are *serving to end something unresolved.*

deflect The defensive back tipped the ball just enough to *deflect* it. The receiver could not catch it because the defender caused it to *turn from a straight course.*

defraud The con artist tried to *defraud* the couple of their savings by having them sign an illegal agreement. He tried to *cheat* them, to *deprive* them *of* their money *by trickery.*

defray It is often customary for the father of the bride to *defray* the young couple's wedding expenses, to *provide for the payment* of them.

defunct He defrauded them by conning them into investing in an enterprise that turned out to be *defunct*, that is, one *no longer in existence*, a *dead, extinct* business.

degenerate Through carelessness and neglect he allowed his life to *degenerate*, that is, to *atrophy, waste away*, or *sink to a low state.*

deify After the second consecutive national championship, the students and alumni alike were eager to *deify* the coach, to *make a god* of him.

deign The dapper politician barely *deigned* to shake hands with a dirt-covered, rough-looking man; he knew it was good press. He *condescended to act below his dignity* for the effect. // She waited for the star to *deign* his reply to her letter, to *condescend to answer.*

ETYMOLOGY	OLD MEANING
WORD	NEW MEANING

Fr déjà vu
déjà vu
already seen
something overly familiar

L delectare
delectable
to charm, delight, amuse
highly pleasing; delicious

Gk deleisthai
deleterious
to hurt
having a harmful effect

L delineare
delineate
to mark out; sketch
portray; depict in words; describe

L delinquere
delinquent
to fail, offend; do wrong
neglectful; overdue in payment

L deludere
delusion
to trick; deceive
something falsely believed

OHG telban
delve
to dig
dig into; explore; seek information

OFr demener
demeaanor
to conduct
behavior; manner; conduct

MFr demettre
demit
to put away; dismiss
to resign; withdraw from

L demorari
demur
to wait; to detain, delay
**to object; take exception to;
hesitate based on doubt**

MFr demourer
demure
to linger, wait
reserved; affectedly modest; coy

L de- + intus
denizen
inside; within, in; from within
inhabitant; one that frequents

L denotare
denote
to point out; specify; observe
**to indicate; announce; mean;
stand for; signify**

SAMPLE SENTENCES

déjà vu Whenever anyone tells you of something that you already know all about, you can say "Been there, done that," but "*déjà vu*" is better.

delectable One of the problems with a big Thanksgiving dinner is that everything is so *delectable* that one overeats. Each item is absolutely *delicious* and *delightful*.

deleterious Second-hand smoke, excessive sun radiation, and high cholesterol levels can have *deleterious* effects; they can lead to *harmful, injurious* results.

delineate To fully appreciate the story, it was necessary that the speaker *delineate* one of the characters, to *describe* him, to *depict* him *in detail*.

delinquent It will be difficult to get a driver's license renewed for anyone *delinquent* on his traffic fines. Those who are *overdue in payment* should pay up.

delusion "If it tastes bad, it must be good for you" is a *delusion* held by some. "If it tastes good, it must be bad for you" is also *something accepted as true that is false*.

delve His project was to find some answers to various uncertainties, so he decided to *delve* into it. He was determined to *explore, seek information,* and *dig into* it.

demeanor Sometimes a player's *demeanor* on the court is very different from that off the court. His or her *behavior to others* or *outward manner* can vary a lot.

demit Because his main plan was not developing the way he had hoped, he decided to *demit.*. He decided to *resign,* or *withdraw from,* the post.

demur He *demurred* at first about going white-water kayaking; he *balked* at the idea; he *delayed through doubt or uncertainty*.

demure Some people are truly *demure*, while others are just playing hard to get. Some are actually *reserved* or *shy*, while others are *affectedly modest* or *coy*.

denizen A deer is a natural *denizen* of the forest, an *inhabitant* thereof. Some people are *denizens* of places, *those who frequent* the places.

denote Red flares *denote* danger; a flag flown upside down *denotes* distress; thickets of aspen and willow *indicate* underlying water. They *mean* these things are there.

ETYMOLOGY **WORD**	OLD MEANING **NEW MEANING**
Fr dénouement **dénouement**	*lit.* = untying **the outcome of a complex sequence of events**
L depingere **depict**	to paint; portray, describe **represent by a picture; describe**
L deplorare **deplore**	weep bitterly; bewail; mourn **be sorry; regret; disapprove of**
L displicare **deploy**	to scatter; display **extend in width; spread out**
L deponere **deposition**	lay down; set aside; put away **testimony under oath or in court**
L depravare **deprave**	to distort; pervert, corrupt **to make bad; corrupt; debase**
L deprecari **deprecate**	to avert by prayer; intercede for **show mild disapproval**
L derelinquere **derelict**	to abandon; forsake **abandoned; run-down; negligent; lacking sense of duty;** *also,* **a bum**
Fr de rigueur **de rigueur**	required by fashion; proper **required by etiquette or custom**
L deridere **derision**	to laugh at **contemptuous laughter; ridicule**
L derivare **derive**	to lead off, draw off **take from; deduce; have origin**
L dis- + cantus **descant**	singing; playing; music; magic spell **to talk at considerable length**
OFr descrier **descry**	to proclaim, decry **catch sight of; find out; discover**

SAMPLE SENTENCES

dénouement A book, movie, or sometimes a newspaper article can have a *dénouement* that is unusual. Everything builds up to the *outcome of a complex series of events.*

depict The speaker was able to *depict* clearly his climb up Mount Everest. The audience was thrilled to hear him *describe*, to *picture in words*, his ordeal.

deplore He *deplored* the death of his close friend; he *was sorry about* it. She *deplored* her boyfriend's rude behavior; she *viewed* it as *unfortunate* and *disapproved* of it.

deploy The police lieutenant *deployed* his squad on both sides of the bank; he *spread* the squad *out* so as to cut off an escape route for the robber inside.

deposition The witness' story on the stand differed from his *deposition*; what he said was not the same as his *sworn testimony under oath.*

deprave Some think that certain types of entertainment will *deprave* the morals of society. They fear that some kinds will *corrupt* or *debase* the accepted standards.

deprecate The man *deprecated* his son's pranks at the parents night open house at the school. He expressed *mild* but *regretful disapproval* of them.

derelict He was fired because he was *derelict* in his responsibilities; he was *negligent, lacking in sense of duty*. The books lie *derelict* on the top shelf, *abandoned*.

de rigueur He had been invited to a an exclusive, formal party, but he had no tuxedo, which was *de rigueur* at such an affair. A tux was *required by etiquette or custom.*

derision The mention of his name was greeted by *derision* by the opposing forces; they reacted with *contemptuous laughter* and *ridicule*.

derive A street *derives* its name from someone in the history books, whereas a building on campus *takes* its name *from* a living big donor.

descant Some people will *descant* at the dinner table about their chief activities whether others are interested or not; they will *talk at considerable length* about them.

descry At their 30th class reunion two old room-mates *descried* each other from across the crowded ball-room; they *caught sight of, discovered* each other.

QUIZ

Match the following words with their meanings:

(1) caterwaul   [ ] to persuade with flattery
(2) cavalier   [ ] lacking adult sophistication
(3) cabal   [ ] informal conversation; chat
(4) cajole   [ ] to punish; criticize severely
(5) cacophony   [ ] sudden change of mind; whim
(6) captious   [ ] able to contain much; spacious
(7) callous   [ ] casual in dismissal of urgent matters
(8) castigate   [ ] to cry harshly; quarrel noisily
(9) cachet   [ ] group joined in a secret plot
(10) causerie   [ ] harsh or discordant sound
(11) caprice   [ ] approved great prestige, status
(12) capacious   [ ] feeling no emotion or sympathy
(13) callow   [ ] quick to find fault; critical

(1) circumlocution   [ ] magnetic charm or appeal
(2) chary   [ ] held in or conducted in secrecy
(3) charlatan   [ ] conclusion of a musical; finale
(4) cavil   [ ] to inflict punishment; scold
(5) choleric   [ ] unusually perceptive; clear-sighted
(6) chimerical   [ ] cautious; vigilant about risks
(7) charisma   [ ] wordiness; evasion in speech
(8) clandestine   [ ] careful; on the lookout
(9) coda   [ ] a pretender to expertise; a fake
(10) chastise   [ ] to blame; find fault with; criticize
(11) clairvoyant   [ ] easily angered; hot-tempered
(12) censure   [ ] to raise trivial objections to
(13) circumspect   [ ] unreal, improbable; imaginary

 (1) comatose   [ ] powerful; convincing; valid
 (2) coerce, compel   [ ] to compare; put in proper order
 (3) collusion   [ ] friendly quality; social harmony
 (4) cognizant   [ ] related; generally alike
 (5) commensurate [ ] conveniently spacious; roomy
 (6) cogent   [ ] lethargic; drowsy; dull, inactive
 (7) cogitate   [ ] force; cause to do by pressure
 (8) colloquial   [ ] aware; having special knowledge
 (9) comity   [ ] secret agreement for an illegal plot
(10) cognate   [ ] equal in extent; proportionate
(11) collate   [ ] to ponder; to plan; think deeply
(12) commodious   [ ] used in informal conversation

 (1) complacent   [ ] driven by force or necessity
 (2) concierge   [ ] official who audits accounts
 (3) compunction   [ ] component that completes
 (4) comprehensive [ ] demanded by authority; required
 (5) concomitant   [ ] deserved; appropriate; merited
 (6) condescending [ ] self-satisfied; smug; unconcerned
 (7) conation   [ ] anxiety from guilt; qualm; misgiving
 (8) comptroller   [ ] an all-purpose hotel desk manager
 (9) condign   [ ] covering broadly; inclusive
(10) compulsory   [ ] having an air of superiority
(11) compulsive   [ ] occurring along with; at the same time
(12) complement   [ ] instinct; a wish or craving

 (1) conciliate   [ ] to create as if by magic; invent
 (2) conjecture   [ ] a coming together; meeting
 (3) consensus   [ ] sympathy with one in sorrow
 (4) congenital   [ ] agreeable; pleasant; attractive
 (5) connote   [ ] to overwhelm in argument; disprove
 (6) confrere   [ ] an expert; critical judge
 (7) connive   [ ] to gain favor by pleasing acts; pacify; appease
 (8) condolence   [ ] an uncertain inference; a guess
 (9) congenial   [ ] in agreement; coinciding
(10) confute   [ ] to imply or suggest more than the exact meaning
(11) connoisseur   [ ] a colleague; fellow worker
(12) conjure   [ ] pretend ignorance of wrongdoing; conspire
(13) congruent   [ ] existing at birth; inherent; innate
(14) confluence   [ ] opinion held by all or most; general agreement

(1) consign   [   ] to call together for a meeting
(2) consternation   [   ] something reversed in relation
(3) consummate   [   ] fond of feasting and good company
(4) contrite   [   ] likely to argue; quarrelsome
(5) contemn   [   ] devise; fabricate; invent; concoct
(6) convoke   [   ] to transfer to the care of someone else
(7) contingent   [   ] in actual contact; adjacent
(8) convivial   [   ] complete in every detail; perfect
(9) contrive   [   ] to treat or view with contempt; to scorn
(10) converse   [   ] confused and distressing excitement
(11) contentious   [   ] possible; dependent on something else
(12) contiguous   [   ] grieving for sin; remorseful

(1) copious   [   ] having worldwide sophistication
(2) coup de grace   [   ] an inexhaustible store; abundance
(3) corroborate   [   ] to show a relationship between
(4) convoluted   [   ] can be set straight; correctable
(5) corollary   [   ] a brilliant, sudden stroke or act
(6) cosmopolitan   [   ] in large quantity; profuse in words
(7) countenance   [   ] a decisive finishing blow, act, or event
(8) correlate   [   ] to support with evidence; confirm
(9) corpulent   [   ] twisted; coiled; involved; intricate
(10) cornucopia   [   ] something that naturally follows
(11) coup   [   ] calm expression; composure; look, expression; face
(12) corrigible   [   ] having a large, bulky body; fat

(1) criterion   [   ] the very best; the highest elite
(2) covet   [   ] to make a crackling sound
(3) credulous   [   ] kept private; hidden; veiled
(4) crass   [   ] lacking courage; fainthearted
(5) coup d'état   [   ] a formal, binding agreement
(6) covert   [   ] worthy of belief; plausible
(7) crème de la crème   [   ] standard on which judgment or decision is made
(8) credible   [   ] lacking delicacy or refinement; stupid
(9) craven   [   ] ready to believe, *esp.* on uncertain evidence; gullible
(10) covenant   [   ] a sudden overthrow of government
(11) crepitate   [   ] to desire what belongs to another

(1) crux   [   ] lust; desire for wealth; avarice; greed
(2) cryptic   [   ] rapidly and often superficially done; hasty
(3) culminate   [   ] to make less; shorten; cut off
(4) culpable   [   ] very important; decisive
(5) cunning   [   ] increasing by successive additions
(6) cupidity   [   ] a most important, deciding point
(7) curtail   [   ] to seek to gain favor by flattery
(8) cursory   [   ] secret; serving to conceal; using code
(9) crucial   [   ] deserving blame or condemnation
(10) cumulative   [   ] crafty; wily; tricky; sly
(11) curry favor   [   ] to reach the highest point; bring to a head

(1) deduce   [   ] to subdue through fear; intimidate
(2) decadence   [   ] downward inclination; slope
(3) dapper   [   ] easy, carefree; lively; elegant
(4) debilitate   [   ] to express strong disapproval of
(5) decamp   [   ] to take a tenth from; destroy a lot of
(6) debut   [   ] fitness; good taste; orderliness
(7) declivity   [   ] scarcity; inadequate supply; lack
(8) daunt   [   ] to break camp; depart suddenly
(9) decry   [   ] to infer from; trace the course of
(10) debonair   [   ] neat, trim; very stylish; alert
(11) decimate   [   ] to impair the strength of; weaken
(12) decorum   [   ] first public appearance
(13) dearth   [   ] decay; period of decline

(1) deem   [   ] to make a god of
(2) deficit   [   ] abandonment of a cause; desertion
(3) definitive   [   ] no longer existent; dead; extinct
(4) deflect   [   ] to deprive of by deception; cheat
(5) deign   [   ] to delay; postpone; suspend
(6) defray   [   ] come to think; have an opinion
(7) deify   [   ] to sink to a low state; degrade
(8) defunct   [   ] serving to specify, define
(9) defer   [   ] to turn from a straight course; bend; deviate
(10) defraud   [   ] to condescend to act below one's dignity
(11) defection   [   ] excess of spending over revenue
(12) degenerate   [   ] to provide for payment of; pay

(1) default   [   ] behavior; manner; conduct
(2) demit   [   ] to portray; depict in words; describe
(3) deleterious   [   ] reserved; affectedly modest; coy
(4) delve   [   ] to indicate; signify; stand for
(5) delinquent   [   ] highly pleasing; delicious
(6) déjà vu   [   ] something falsely believed
(7) demeanor   [   ] neglect; failure to act; a forfeit
(8) demur   [   ] to resign; withdraw from
(9) demure   [   ] neglectful; overdue in payment
(10) delusion   [   ] something overly familiar
(11) delectable   [   ] having a harmful effect
(12) delineate   [   ] to dig into; explore; seek information
(13) denote   [   ] to object; hesitate based on doubt

(1) deplore   [   ] to take from; deduce; have origin
(2) derelict   [   ] required by etiquette or custom
(3) descant   [   ] to extend in width; spread out
(4) dénouement   [   ] testimony under oath or in court
(5) depict   [   ] to show mild disapproval
(6) deprave   [   ] to be sorry; regret; disapprove of
(7) deposition   [   ] contemptuous laughter; ridicule; scorn
(8) derive   [   ] to catch sight of; find out; discover
(9) deploy   [   ] to talk at considerable length
(10) derision   [   ] the outcome of a series of events
(11) deprecate   [   ] to represent by a picture; describe
(12) de rigueur   [   ] negligent; lacking a sense of duty
(13) descry   [   ] to make bad; corrupt; debase

QUIZ

1. The term "crepuscular" refers to:
   (a) a heavy storm   (b) a skin condition
   (c) twilight time   (d) a hot day

2. Members of a coterie want it to be:
   (a) choleric   (b) the crème de la crème
   (c) contentious   (d) defunct

3. A person prefers his crony to be:
   (a) captious   (b) comatose
   (c) cynical   (d) convivial

4. A woman wants her consort to
   (a) cavil   (b) confute
   (c) be congenial   (d) be condescending

5. A young lady making her debut into society prefers an escort who is:
   (a) debonair   (b) crass
   (c) craven   (d) callow

6. In making an important purchase in art or wine, it is best to consult the consummate:
   (a) comptroller   (b) confrere
   (c) concierge   (d) connoisseur

7. In going over school assignments, the good student tends to be:
   (a) desultory   (b) cursory
   (c) cognizant   (d) complacent

8. At the ball the debutante's escort's decorum is:
   (a) contingent   (b) de rigueur
   (c) déjà vu   (d) derisive

9. One usually prefers a dinner guest noted for his/her:
   (a) circumlocution   (b) charisma
   (c) cupidity   (d) diatribes

10. An employer seeks to hire someone who is
    (a) cavalier   (b) derelict
    (c) congenial   (d) cunning

SEGMENT THREE

ETYMOLOGY WORD	OLD MEANING NEW MEANING
L desiderare **desideratum**	feel the want of; miss; long for **something needed and wanted**
L desolare **desolate**	to leave, abandon **deserted; barren; lifeless; gloomy**
L despoliare **despoil**	to rob, plunder **to strip of possessions; pillage**
L desuetus **desuetude**	unaccustomed; unused **discontinuance from exercise; disuse**
L desultura **desultory**	jumping down **lacking in plan; erratic, shifting**
L de- + via **deviate**	away from the road, street, way **to turn aside from a norm; to stray from; change course**
L dexter **dexterity**	right; right hand; skillful; favorable **skill in using hands; mental skill**
L diabolus **diabolical**	devil **relating to the devil; fiendish**
Gk diakritikos **diacritical**	separative **distinctive; capable of distinguishing**
Gk diagignoskein **diagnose**	to distinguish **recognize, identify a disease by signs; investigate, analyze problems**
Gk diatribe **diatribe**	study, pastime, discourse **a bitter, abusive denunciation**
Gk dichotomein **dichotomous**	to cut in half **dividing into two opposing parts**
Gk didaskein **didactic**	to teach **meant to teach, instruct**

SAMPLE SENTENCES

desideratum A tall glass of cool, clear water under a shade tree is a *desideratum* after a long, hot hike across the desert; it is truly *something needed and wanted.*

desolate Nearly out of gas, they approached the settlement; but it turned out to be a *desolate* ghost town. It was *deserted, barren* and *lifeless*—only tumbleweeds.

despoil He arose early one morning only to find that a flock of birds had *despoiled* his bing cherry tree. The birds had *pillaged* it, *stripped it of all its cherries.*

desuetude Couch potatoes are classic examples of muscular *desuetude*; they suffer from *discontinuance of exercise*, and thus from the *disuse* of muscles.

desultory It was hard to follow the logic of her *desultory* shopping spree. It was *lacking in plan,* very *erratic* and *shifting* in its course.

deviate Thinking he was being followed, he decided to suddenly *deviate* from the main road; he decided to *change course*, to *turn aside from the expected* route.

dexterity She not only played the piano with great *dexterity* but also showed it in debate; she thus demonstrated *skill in using hands* as well as *mental skill.*

diabolical Unhappy with the new office boss, a cabal cooked up a *diabolical* plot to undermine her. It was a *fiendish* scheme.

diacritical Not knowing what wines to buy for the special dinner, he sought the advice of a connoisseur, who had *diacritical* powers, *capable of distinguishing* good from average.

diagnose It is part of a doctor's job to *diagnose* diseases, but this one is a good camper. He can *recognize, identify, investigate,* and *analyze* mechanical and engine problems.

diatribe She regretted the *diatribe* against her husband, a *bitter, abusive denunciation* of him, for being seen with another woman. As it turned out, the other woman was helping her husband select her birthday present, since he was such a klutz about women's gifts.

dichotomous This man led what might be called a reverse *dichotomous* life; he was a lion at the office and a lamb at home—a *dividing into two contradictory parts* kind of life.

didactic The class nicknamed the teacher "Socrates" because of his *didactic* manner. He had a certain *teacher-like* way; he was *fitted to teach, concerned with teaching.*

ETYMOLOGY	OLD MEANING
WORD	**NEW MEANING**
L diffidere	to distrust, despair
diffident	**hesitant; lacking self-confidence**
L digredi	to separate; part; deviate
digress	**depart temporarily from subject**
Gr di- + lemma	two + proposition, assumption
dilemma	**choice between unpleasant options**
It dilettare	to delight
dilettante	**one whose interests are superficial;**
	an art lover; a dabbler; amateur
L dirus	ominous; fearful; bad luck
dire	**warning of disaster; desperately urgent**
Fr dés = dis- + abuser	dis- + to abuse
disabuse	**to free from error or fallacy**
L discernere	to divide, separate; distinguish between
discern	**recognize as separate and distinct**
OFr des- = dis- + clamer	dis- + to cry out, complain
disclaimer	**a denial, disavowal; repudiation**
L dis- + concerer	not + to join together
disconcert	**upset the composure of; confuse**
L dis- + consolari	not + to console
disconsolate	**dejected; downcast; cheerless**
L discordare	to disagree; quarrel; to be unlike
discordant	**disagreeing; harsh; quarrelsome**
L discursus	running hither and thither
discourse	**exchange of ideas; expression of thought**
L discernere	to divide, separate; distinguish between
discreet	**showing good judgment; tactful**

SAMPLE SENTENCES

diffident He was *diffident* when asked to speak about something he knew little about. He was *hesitant, lacking in self-confidence* because of his shaky knowledge about it.

digress A professor will sometimes *digress* during his lecture to tell a story which supports his point; that is, he will *depart temporarily from the subject* to do it.

dilemma The escapee faced a *dilemma*—to call the cops or face the mob, to which he owed money he was unable to pay. He had a *choice between unpleasant alternatives*.

dilettante He is a *dilettante* when it comes to cultural matters. For example, he is a *dabbler* in the arts, *one whose interests are superficial, not deep*.

dire She was in *dire* circumstances as the thug was breaking into her house and she had no gun or other means of protection. She was in a *desperately urgent* situation.

disabuse It is often difficult to *disabuse* certain people from errors in thinking; it is hard to *free* them *from false ideas*.

discern Most people can't *discern* the difference between a good and mediocre piano recital, play, or wine; but a connoisseur can *recognize* them *as separate and distinct*

disclaimer His line of defense was a *disclaimer* of having been seen at the scene of the crime; his *denial* of having been there was backed up by proving he was on a plane.

disconcert The district attorney tried to *disconcert* the defense attorney by his constant objections to everything she said; he tried to *upset* her *composure*, to *confuse* her.

disconsolate After the game the happy winning coach walked off the field with the *disconsolate* losing coach. The latter was *dejected, downcast, cheerless*.

discordant The city council held a very *discordant* meeting over the leaf-blower issue. The opposing forces were *disagreeing, harsh,* and *quarrelsome*.

discourse Various elements of society met for a *discourse* on the needs of the school district; to have an *exchange of ideas*, to hear *expression of thought on the matter*, was a good idea.

discreet He was very *discreet* in not correcting the speaker's grammatical error in front of the others; he was *tactful, showing good judgment*, to avoid embarrassment.

ETYMOLOGY **WORD**	OLD MEANING NEW MEANING
L discrepare **discrepancy**	to be out of tune; disagree, differ **difference; disagreement; inconsistency**
L discrimen **discriminate**	interval; dividing line; difference **carefully distinguishing**
L discursus **discursive**	running hither and thither **passing from one topic to another; digressive; rambling; desultory**
L dedignari **disdain**	to scorn, reject **look with scorn on; treat with contempt**
OFr descheveler **disheveled**	to disarrange the hair **being in loose disorder; ruffled, untidy**
dis- + L ingenuus **disingenuous**	dis- + native; free-born; noble; frank **giving false look of frankness; calculating**
OFr desparagier **disparage**	to marry one of inferior rank **to discredit; speak slightingly of; belittle**
L disparare **disparate**	to separate; segregate **distinct in character; unequal; dissimilar**
L dispar **disparity**	unlike, unequal (par = equal) **inequality; difference; incongruity**
L dissimulare **dissemble**	to conceal; pretend that; give false look **hide under false pretense; hide feelings**
L disseminare **disseminate**	to sow; broadcast **to spread widely; scatter; publicize**
L dissentire **dissent**	to disagree, differ; be unlike, inconsistent **withhold assent; not to approve; object; differ; disagree**
L dissidere **dissident**	to be distant; disagree; quarrel; differ **not agreeing; dissenting; quarrelsome**

SAMPLE SENTENCES

discrepancy The auditor found a *discrepancy* in the account between the income statement and the amount listed—a huge *difference* and *inconsistency*.

discriminate Neither the charlatan nor the dilettante is truly *discriminate* in tastes, but the connoisseur is *carefully distinguishing* when it comes to matters of taste.

discursive She dominated the dinner table discussion by giving a *discursive* speech about her year's activities. Her talk was *rambling, desultory, passing from one topic to another.*

disdain Many motorists *disdain* those who mess up normal traffic patterns by talking on their cell phones; they *look on* them *with scorn, regard* them *with contempt.*

disheveled Despite his use of hair spray, the "Dapper Dan" arrived *disheveled* at the party. He rode in the back seat of the convertible and his hair got *ruffled, untidy.*

disingenuous The charlatan was *disingenuous* with people. He was *lacking in candor, giving a false look of frankness,* and *calculating,* in an effort to fool them.

disparage A jealous person or a self-promoter will often *disparage* the success or great accomplishment of a rival; he will *discredit, belittle,* or *speak slightingly of* it.

disparate He is interested in such *disparate* attractions as grand opera and duck-hunting. These activities are *distinct in character, unequal,* and *dissimilar.*

disparity There is a *disparity* in the wealth of nations that have economic and political freedoms and those that do not. There is usually a huge *inequality* or *difference.*

dissemble Being a good sport, she *dissembled* her disappointment in losing the match with a smile. She *concealed* her true *feelings.*

disseminate It was supposed to be secret information, but some jerk *disseminated* it to everyone. He *spread* it *widely, publicized* it.

dissent In the game preserve the antelopes advocated universal vegetarianism, but the lions *dissented.* The big cats *did not approve* of the idea; they strongly *objected.*

dissident Whenever a controversial bill is introduced in congress, the *dissident* groups will be heard; they are *dissenting, quarrelsome,* and *contentious* over each other's ideas.

ETYMOLOGY WORD	OLD MEANING NEW MEANING
L dissipare **dissipate**	to scatter, disperse; destroy **waste, squander; expend foolishly**
L dissolvere **dissolute**	to unloose; dissolve; destroy **lacking restraint; loose in morals**
L dissuadere **dissuade**	to advise against; oppose **advise a person against something**
L distorquere **distort**	to twist **to twist out of proportion or shape**
L distrahere **distrait**	to tear apart; distract **absentminded; inattentive; upset**
L diurnus **diurnal**	daily; for a day; by day; day **recurring every day; daily**
L divulgare **divulge**	to publish, make public **to make known; disclose; reveal**
L docere **docile**	to teach; inform; tell **easily taught, led, or managed**
L doctrina **doctrinaire**	instruction, education, learning; science **dogmatic; dictatorial**
Gk dogma < dokein **dogmatic**	to seem good; think **asserting an opinion as if it were fact; dictatorial**
OE dol **doldrums**	foolish, silly; dull **a spell of listlessness; blues; slump**
L dolor **dolorous**	pain **expressive of misery or grief**
OE dol **dolt**	foolish, silly; dull **a stupid fellow; blockhead; numskull**

SAMPLE SENTENCES

dissipate The gambler and spendthrift *dissipated* his inheritance to the point of poverty. He *wasted* it, *squandered* it; he *expended aimlessly and foolishly.*

dissolute Whenever he got drunk at a restaurant, ball game, or town meeting, he was escorted out because of *dissolute* behavior; i.e., *being unrestrained in conduct.*

dissuade Although the sales pitch sounded good (they always do), he had to *dissuade* her from putting money into the deal. He *advised her against* it.

distort The reporters badly *distorted* the facts and what was said at the meeting; they *twisted* the true story *out of proportion, twisted* it *out of shape*, to suit their needs.

distrait She was *distrait* during the inquiry after the accident. She could not talk clearly because she was *distraught*, very *upset*, and momentarily *absentminded.*

diurnal Most people expect to eat on a *diurnal* basis, while only some keep up with their exercise programs on a *daily* basis; in both cases, it means *recurring every day.*

divulge It is natural to not wish to *divulge* certain bits of personal information at a public gathering. Why should one willingly *disclose, reveal*, or *make* them *known?*

docile A *docile* person is like a tame animal—he is *obedient* and *easily directed, led*, or *managed.*

doctrinaire The professor was *doctrinaire* in his opinions. He was *dogmatic* and *dictatorial* in his statements.

dogmatic When asked who will win an election, or which team will win a game, many people are *dogmatic* in their statements; they are *asserting an opinion as if it were fact.*

doldrums If a top team goes into a losing streak, it is in the *doldrums*, that is, a feeling of *listlessness* or *despondency*. It can also mean a *stagnation* or *slump.*

dolorous The plight of people in poor countries, especially beggars, is a *dolorous* sight. It is a condition *expressive of misery or grief.*

dolt Here was this *dolt* driving 35 miles per hour on the freeway, causing traffic to pile up behind him. This *blockhead*, or *numskull*, was chatting away aimlessly on his cell-phone.

ETYMOLOGY WORD	OLD MEANING NEW MEANING
OHG toug **doughty**	is useful; have worth **fearless; able; strong; valiant**
L durus **dour**	hard; rough; tough; cruel **stern; harsh; forbidding; gloomy; obstinate; unyielding; sullen**
L ducere **ductile**	to lead, guide; bring **capable of being molded; pliant; easily led or influenced**
L dulcis **dulcet**	sweet; pleasant; delightful; lovely **luscious; melodious; agreeable; soothing**
Fr duper **dupe**	to trick, fool, deceive **to trick; fool, deceive; a person easily fooled or tricked**
L duplicis **duplicity**	double; twofold; both; false **belying one's true intentions; bad faith; double-dealing**
L durus **duress**	hard; rough; painful; cruel **restraint by force; compulsion by threat; coercion**
Gk dyspeptos **dyspeptic**	hard to digest < dys- = bad **showing a sour disposition; ill-tempered**
NL dys- + Gk topos **dystopia**	bad + place **an imaginary depressingly wretched place, one of dreadful existence**
L ebullire **ebullience**	to bubble up; to brag about **enthusiastic feelings; exuberance**
Gk ekklesiastes **ecclesiastical**	member of an assembly **of or relating to a church**

SAMPLE SENTENCES

doughty The strongly opinionated, dogmatic odds makers declared them as heavy under dogs, but with a spirited, *doughty* struggle they won; it took a *strong, valiant* effort.

dour A bollixed up play at the end of the game cost the team the championship. The locker room was *dour* in mood, *gloomy, sullen,* and silent.

ductile Citizens of statist regimes are far more *ductile* than those in free societies; they are *easily led or influenced.*

dulcet After a hectic week of final exams the *dulcet* sounds of the forest eased his tensions. The *melodious, soothing* experience was good for the mind.

dupe He was a *dupe* of their false promises; he was *someone easily fooled or tricked* by them. They *duped* him with their promises; they *tricked* or *fooled* him.

duplicity Some politicians are guilty of *duplicity* when they tell people they are for something yet vote against it. Their *double-dealing, belying true intentions,* is bad.

duress He signed the papers under *duress.* He signed them unwillingly by *coercion,* under *compulsion by threat.*

dyspeptic A broken shoestring, then a flat tire, followed by bumper-to-bumper traffic, and finally a speeding ticket, left him *dyspeptic* for the rest of the day. This series of events caused him to miss an important meeting, and he was *ill-tempered* and *of sour disposition.*

dystopia The country had no freedoms, was poverty-stricken, and was run by drunken soldiers—in short, it was a virtual *dystopia.* It was like *an imaginary depressingly wretched place, one of dreadful existence.*

ebullience He danced into the room with *ebullience* over his exciting, good news. He showed a *feeling of enthusiasm,* an *exuberance.*

ecclesiastical He wanted to know if his friend had any *ecclesiastical* duties to perform at the ceremony, if he had to do something *relating to the church.*

ETYMOLOGY	OLD MEANING
WORD	**NEW MEANING**

Fr éclat	splinter; burst
éclat	**dazzling effect; brilliance; brilliant, conspicuous success**
Gk eklegein	to select, pick out
eclectic	**selecting from various sources**
L edacis	gluttonous; devouring
edacious	**relating to eating; voracious**
L edicere	to declare
edict	**an order; a command**
L aedificare	to build, construct
edify	**to instruct; to enlighten**
L effetus	exhausted
effete	**worn out; spent; weak; outmoded**
L efficere	to make; accomplish; bring about
efficacy	**the power to produce an effect**
L effingere	to form; portray; represent
effigy	**a crude image of a hated person**
LL effrons	shameless
effrontery	**crass, offensive boldness, discourtesy**
L aequalitas	evenness; equality; similarity
egalitarianism	**a belief in human equality**
L ego	I
egotism	**excessive talk and use of "I"**
L egregius	outstanding, distinguished; illustrious
egregious	**conspicuously bad; outrageous**
L egressus	departure; way out; digression
egress	**a coming out; way out; exit**

SAMPLE SENTENCES

éclat Her piano recital was done with *éclat*. It was a *showy display*, done with *brilliance* and *dazzling effect*—a truly *conspicuous success*.

eclectic He has an *eclectic* art collection. It is *composed of elements from various sources* or *consisted of styles drawn from various sources*.

edacious It was a splendid array of hors d'oeuvres until an *edacious* buffoon devoured all the little crab cakes, the favorite choice. He was a *voracious* dolt.

edict After several complaints the librarian posted a stern *edict* about talking in the library; it was an *order* not to talk.

edify People who have experienced foreign tyranny try to *edify* indifferent Americans about how bad it is. They try to *instruct* them, to *enlighten* them about it.

effete Perhaps the best example of an *effete* person is one who just completed a marathon run; at this point he or she is *worn out, spent,* and *weak*.

efficacy The best player on the team showed great *efficacy* in making difficult shots and getting fouled in the process. She demonstrated enormous *power to produce*.

effigy The expatriates hanged and burned the *effigy* of the ruthless dictator of their native land. They destroyed the *crude image of the hated tyrant* in a symbolic gesture.

effrontery Seeing a long line, the late arrival had the *effrontery* to cut in near the front, to everyone's shock. He showed *offensive boldness* and *crass discourtesy*.

egalitarianism There are those who advocate *egalitarianism* over individualism and freedom; they put *a belief in human equality* above liberty.

egotism He would be a more interesting speaker were it not for his *egotism*, which turns people off. His *excessive talk and use of "I"* reduce his audience.

egregious The crowd reacted to the referee's *egregious* call; it was *outrageous, conspicuously bad*.

egress Lost in the woods, nobody wanted to be the first to ask about an *egress*. Everyone wanted to find a *way out*, an *exit*.

ETYMOLOGY **WORD**	OLD MEANING **NEW MEANING**
MFr eslan **élan**	rush, dash **vigor; spirit; enthusiasm; zest; liveliness of imagination**
LL eleemosyna **eleemosynary**	alms **relating to charity; charitable**
Gk elegos **elegy**	song of mourning **a song, poem, or speech of sorrow**
L elicere **elicit**	to lure out; to draw out **call forth, bring out (a response)**
L elidere **elide**	squeeze out; drive out; crush; destroy **to strike out (a word); leave out**
L eloqui **eloquent**	to speak out **forcefully and fluently expressive**
L luidus **elucidate**	bright; clear **to give a clear explanation**
L eludere **elude**	to foil; outplay; outmaneuver **escape the notice of; avoid adroitly**
L emanare **emanate**	to flow out; spring from **come out from a source; give out**
L emancipare **emancipate**	to declare independent; give up; sell **release from, free from restraint**
L emendare **emend**	to correct, improve **correct by textual change**
L emeritus **emeritus**	superannuated, worn out; veteran **retired from a position**
L eminere **eminent**	to stand out, project; be prominent **conspicuous; evident; noteworthy**

SAMPLE SENTENCES

élan He demonstrated great *élan* in producing and directing the school play. Everyone admired his *spirit, enthusiasm,* and *liveliness of imagination.*

eleemosynary Despite a busy schedule involving studies and athletics, they found time for *eleemosynary* causes, those *relating to charity*, or *charitable* ones.

elegy He delivered the *elegy* at the funeral ceremony of his close friend; it was a touching *speech of sorrow* over the loss of one who meant much to him.

elicit While the girls looked askance or confused, his jokes never failed to *elicit* bent-over laughter among the guys. The jokes would always *bring out* knee-slapping laughs.

elide When people asked questions about his career, he emphasized the favorable aspects but would *elide* references to embarrassing parts; he would *omit* or *pass over* them.

eloquent Ask him a question about anything and he will give a lengthy, *eloquent* reply. His response will be *forcefully and fluently expressive.*

elucidate If a professor happens to elide part of an abstruse concept, it is a good idea to ask him/her to *elucidate*, to *give a clear explanation* of the matter in detail.

elude He tried to *elude* the agents looking for him in the airport. It would be difficult to *escape the notice of* them, *adroitly avoid* them, with the suitcase full of money.

emanate He saw smoke *emanate* from the cabin. When he saw the smoke *come out from* the building, he deduced from the adage, "Where there's smoke there's fire."

emancipate To take a vacation is to *emancipate* oneself from the rigors of the hectic life. It is good to *release* oneself *from* them, to *free* oneself *from restraint.*

emend If someone discovers an error in a text, it becomes necessary to *emend* it; if, for example, wrong statements are found, the editor must *correct* certain parts.

emeritus When a professor finally leaves the teaching profession, he/she is thereafter known as Professor *Emeritus*, indicating he is *retired from his professorship.*

eminent Ben Franklin, Thomas Jefferson, James Madison, and Alexander Hamilton were among the *eminent* contributors to the Constitution; they were *noteworthy* individuals.

ETYMOLOGY	OLD MEANING
WORD	NEW MEANING

Gk empiria	experience
empirical	**based on observation or experience**
aemulari	to rival, copy; to be jealous
emulate	**strive to equal or excel; imitate**
MFr encombrer	to obstruct, burden
encumber	**to weigh down; burden; impede**
L dot, dos	gift; dowry
endow	**provide an income; give freely to**
L inducere	to bring in; lead on; introduce
endue	**to provide, endow; transfuse**
L aenigma	riddle
enigma	**something hard to explain; mystery**
L injungere	to join, attach; to impose, inflict
enjoin	**to direct by order; forbid, prohibit**
OFr enui	annoyance
ennui	**boredom; feeling of dissatisfaction**
Fr entreprendre	to undertake; enter upon; attempt
entrepreneur	**one who organizes, manages, and assumes the risks of a business**
Gk ephemeros	for the day, short-lived
ephemeral	**lasting a very short time**
Gk epos	word, speech; poem
epic	**beyond the ordinary; heroic; big**
Gk epikoinos	common
epicene	**common to both sexes or neither**
Gk epigonos	born after
epigone	**imitative follower; inferior imitator of a great achiever, thinker, or artist**

SAMPLE SENTENCES

empirical His statements were strictly *empirical* data, not opinion, abstract theory, transcendentalism, or imagination; they were *based on observation* and *experience*.

emulate Although he joined a club which had many wealthy members, he knew it would be futile to *emulate* them in lifestyle. It would be useless to *strive to equal or excel* them, or to try to *imitate* them.

encumber If fewer than the full complement of nurses are on duty, a sudden emergency can severely *encumber* them; it can *overburden* them, *impede* them in their work.

endow He *endowed* the university; he *provided* it *with an income*. Nature *endows* some people with rare talents; it *provides* or *equips* them freely with such gifts.

endue After a string of losses to start the season, their first win *endued* the team with confidence. It *transfused* confidence into the team, *provided* it with confidence.

enigma The case was a real *enigma* to solve, having many conflicting bits of evidence. It was *something hard to explain*, a *puzzle*, a *mystery* for the problem solvers.

enjoin The captain *enjoined* the squad not to shoot; he *directed* them *by order* not to do so. The restaurant owner *enjoined* smoking; he *forbade* it, *prohibited* it.

ennui The secret to being dull is to tell everything, which she did. The result was *ennui* for everyone at the table. The listeners suffered *boredom* as she droned on.

entrepreneur He was the *entrepreneur* of the business, i.e., the one who *organized, managed, and assumed the risks of a business.*

ephemeral A substitute's playing time is often *ephemeral*, that is, it is *of short duration*, or *lasting a very short time.*

epic Johann Gutenberg's invention of the printing press in 1453 and the moon-landing in 1969 were *epic* events; they were *beyond the ordinary, heroic, big* happenings.

epicene Volleyball and tennis are *epicene* sports, that is, *common to both sexes*. Football is not, nor are public rest rooms.

epigone To the untrained eye, the works of an *epigone*, or an *imitative follower*, may seem indistinguishable from those of the noted artist.

John Eshleman / 119

ETYMOLOGY	OLD MEANING
WORD	**NEW MEANING**

Gk epigraphein — to write on, inscribe
epigram — **a terse or witty saying**

L epistula — letter
epistle — **a formal or elegant letter**

Gk epithetos — added
epithet — **disparaging, abusive word or phrase**

Gk epitemnein — to cut short
epitome — **a summary; brief description; typical or ideal example**

Gk epi- + onyma — name
eponym — **a person for whom something is named**

L aequanimitas — goodwill, calmness
equanimity — **evenness of mind, esp. under stress**

LL aequivalere — to have equal power
equivalent — **equal or like; corresponding to**

LL aequivocus — equal voice
equivocate — **deceive; speak evasively; lie; use double meanings; mislead**

L eradicare — to root out; destroy
eradicate — **uproot; get rid of; wipe out**

L erraticus — roving, shifting
erratic — **lacking consistency; eccentric**

OHG sciuhen — to frighten off
eschew — **to avoid habitually; to shun**

L esculentus — edible, tasty
esculent — **edible**

Gk esoteros <eso- — within
esoteric — **of knowledge restricted to a small group; abstruse**

Sample Sentences

epigram He likes to tell one-liners, jokes, and *epigrams* at gatherings, parties, and dinners; He comes up with funny *terse or witty sayings*.

epistle He prefers to say that he penned an *epistle* to his girl friend, rather than he wrote an *elegant letter* to her.

epithet It seems natural to write a favorable or praiseworthy epitaph for the deceased but an *epithet* for the living, a *disparaging, abusive word or phrase*.

epitome He bought the *epitome* of the great book, the *summary,* the *brief description* of it. She is the *epitome* of the gracious hostess, the *ideal representation* of one.

eponym If one is the *eponym* of a building, street, field, or holiday, it means that he/she is *the person for whom it is named*. Example: Hoover Institution, Sproul Hall, Martin Luther King Day, Chavez Plaza, Woody Hayes Drive, Eiffel Tower, etc.

equanimity Although beleaguered by a rush of late customers at closing time, he finished the job with *equanimity*, with *composure*, with *evenness of mind under stress*.

equivalent The academic credit for two semesters at Cal is *equivalent* to three quarters at Stanford, that is, the credits are *equal*. Other examples are six francs to the dollar and 2.2 pounds to the kilo.

equivocate When asked by the committee about his role in the affair he seemed to *equivocate* in his answers; he would *speak evasively* and *use double meanings*.

eradicate A program to *eradicate* illiteracy is necessary for a healthy society; plans to *get rid of,* to *wipe out* the problem, will help a lot.

erratic It is scary to see someone drive a car on the freeway in an *erratic* manner. Such *shifting, inconsistent* behavior keeps people guessing and is dangerous.

eschew It is wise to *eschew* harmful substances such as drugs, alcohol, and tobacco. For a better life, *avoid* them *habitually, shun* them.

esculent At some fund-raisers or long rides on a chartered bus, expect an *esculent* box lunch. It is *edible*, but that's about all one can say for it.

esoteric At one table the lawyers discussed *esoteric* legal doctrine; at the next one the scientists were into *abstruse* research, *understood only by a small group*.

ETYMOLOGY	OLD MEANING
WORD	**NEW MEANING**

L aestimare
esteem

to value; estimate the value of
high regard; to regard highly; to consider

Gk etymon + logia

etymology

literal meaning of a word from its origin
+ science of
history and analysis of a word from its origin

Gk euphemos
euphemism

auspicious, sounding good
**use of agreeable expression for an unpleasant
one**

L evanescere
evanescent

to vanish, die away, lose effect
of short duration; like vapor

L evertere
evert

to eject; overturn; ruin, destroy
overthrow, upset; turn inside-out

L evincere
evince

overcome, conquer, prevail over
to prove; show clearly; reveal

L evocare
evoke

to call out, call forth; summon
conjure; bring to mind or memory

L evolvere
evolve

to roll out; roll along, unroll; unfold
**give off, emit; derive; develop;
undergo upward gradual change**

L ex- + acerbus
exacerbate

bitter, harsh; violent; troublesome
to make matters worse

L exaggerare
exaggerate

to pile up; heighten, enhance
overstate the truth; enlarge upon

L exasperare
exasperate

to roughen; to provoke
cause the anger of; enrage; irritate

L ex- + culpa
exculpate

out of + blame, fault, mischief
to clear from alleged fault or guilt

L exemplum
exemplary

copy; example, sample
deserving imitation, commendable

SAMPLE SENTENCES

esteem He *esteemed* the suggestion foolish; he *deemed, considered* it foolish. He has *esteem* for his friend; he has *high regard* for him.

etymology In this book we use a "quick" *etymology*, that is, a one-word meaning of an old Latin or Greek word to best illustrate why a modern word means what it does. It is a quick *history and analysis of a word from its origin* or later.

euphemism "pass away" instead of "die," "took a position" for "got a job," work "with IBM" rather than "for IBM," are *euphemisms*; they are *substitutions of agreeable expressions for less pleasant ones.*

evanescent After a long, hard week at work, the weekend outing seemed *evanescent*. It seemed to be *of short duration, like vapor.*

evert The speaker became nervous when he realized that new evidence might *evert* his theory. He feared it would *upset, overthrow* his belief.

evince Unable to dissemble his true feelings, he *evinced* his disappointment and disgust; his expression *clearly showed* how he felt. It *revealed* it.

evoke A rare California snowfall *evoked* childhood memories of the Mid-west in winter; it *brought to mind* those experiences.

evolve Who would have thought that the huge corporation, employer of thousands of wealthy people, *evolved* from a one-car garage? It *developed, derived* from it.

exacerbate She was playing in the third set, fighting the flu and the heat, when a blister formed on her foot to *exacerbate* the situation; it served to *make matters worse.*

exaggerate Over time, people often *exaggerate* the length of a putt or the size of a fish that got away; they tend to *overstate the truth* or *enlarge upon* the incident.

exasperate A driver at the head of the line who "falls asleep" when the light turns green can *exasperate* those behind him; he can *enrage* them, *cause* their *anger.*

exculpate A jury will usually *exculpate* a defendant if there is a lack of evidence against him; the members will *clear* him *from alleged fault or guilt.*

exemplary Everyone praised his *exemplary* action in saving the two little kids from certain death; his effort was highly *commendable, deserving imitation*

ETYMOLOGY	OLD MEANING
WORD	NEW MEANING

L exempli gratia   **for example** (*expressed as*, **e.g.**)

L eximere   to take out, remove, release, to free
exempt   **not liable or subject to; free from liability to which others are subject**

L exserer   to put out, stretch out
exert   **put forth strength or tiring effort**

L exhortari   to encourage
exhort   **to incite; urge strongly; to warn**

L exogere   to enforce; demand; claim
exigent   **requiring immediate aid or action**

L exonerare   to unload; discharge; unburden
exonerate   **to relieve; to clear from blame**

L ex- + orbita   out of + rut, track, path
exorbitant   **beyond the customary limits; excessive; too much**

L exoticus   foreign
exotic   **strikingly or excitingly different or unusual**

L expatiari   to wander; digress
expatiate   **speak at length or in detail**

L expatriare   to leave one's own country
expatriate   **one who lives in a foreign country**

L expedire   be advantageous; prepare; put right
expedient   **fit, proper, or advantageous under the circumstances**

L expedire   be advantageous; prepare; put right
expedite   **act promptly; speed up progress**

L explicare   to unfold, spread out; to open
explicit   **clearly visible; specific; definite; unambiguous; not vague at all**

SAMPLE SENTENCES

exempli gratia We hardly ever use the full expression, *exempli gratia*; we usually say *for example*, or use the abbreviation, *e.g.*

exempt People with handicap or disabled certificates are *exempt* from paying to park; they are *free from* this obligation, *not liable or subject to it.*

exert Everyone in the group had to *exert* himself to reach the top of the mountain; they all had to *put forth a tiring effort* to do so.

exhort The coach *exhorted* the swimmers to exert themselves if they wanted to win; she *strongly urged* them to "give everything you've got."

exigent A fire starting in the barn created an *exigent* circumstance; it was one *requiring immediate action*, especially in order to save the horses.

exonerate Enough evidence convinced the court to *exonerate* him from the charges; it served to *clear* him *from any blame.*

exorbitant Prices for simple items like hot dogs and lemonade at ball games seem *exorbitant*; they are *excessive, too much,* for what you get.

exotic The divers saw all kinds of *exotic* fish and other marine life. What they saw was *strikingly or excitingly different or unusual..*

expatiate The trapped guests at the dinner table listened as she *expatiated* on the exploits of her nephew. She *spoke at length* and *in detail* about simple accomplishments.

expatriate An American who lives permanently in Paris, France, is an *expatriate*, that is, a *native of one country who lives in a foreign country.*

expedient Since he had to be on the other side of campus in five minutes, he found it *expedient* to appropriate a loose bike. It was an act *advantageous under the circumstances* but wrong.

expedite If a project is going too slowly, and time is getting short, it is time to *expedite* matters; it is necessary to *act promptly*, to *speed up the progress.*

explicit The rules of the club are very *explicit* on many points; they are *clearly visible, specific, definite,* and *unambiguous.*

ETYMOLOGY	OLD MEANING
WORD	NEW MEANING

L explicitus
exploit

easy
deed, act; to use; use unjustly

L exponere
exponent

set out; expose, display; explain
interpreter; one who advocates

L expostulare
expostulate

to demand urgently; complain of
to reason earnestly; to dissuade

L expungere
expunge

to cancel
to erase or remove; delete

L expurgatus
expurgate

to purify, to justify; cleanse
expunge material from; delete

L extraneous
extraneous

stranger; external, foreign
from the outside; irrelevant

L extricare
extricate

to disentangle; clear up
**to free from entanglement or
difficulty; disencumber**

L ex- + sudare
exude

to sweat; to work hard
to ooze; display abundantly

L exsultare
exult

to jump up; prance; boast
be extremely joyful; rejoice

SAMPLE SENTENCES

exploit Catching a purse-snatcher is a notable *exploit*; it is a good *deed*. A person should *exploit* his talent at what he does best, should *make use of* it. Don't *exploit* a friend.

exponent She is a leading *exponent* of a strong defense combined with economic and political freedom; she is *one who advocates* such a plan.

expostulate It is hard to *expostulate* with a stubborn person, to *reason earnestly* with or to *dissuade* such a person from his false ideas.

expunge If a frantic director wishes to *expunge* certain parts of "Hamlet," it is no longer "Hamlet." To *remove* or *delete* parts of a play makes it something different from what was originally intended, in most cases.

expurgate Many parents wish to *expurgate* certain materials from the internet; they seek to *expunge* or *remove passages considered objectionable* from the internet.

extraneous A good director will expunge *extraneous* parts of a play for the benefit of the audience; he will take out *irrelevant* parts, those *not forming a vital part*.

extricate He climbed the tree to escape the savage lunges of the cross dog. He awaited the return of the dog's owner to *extricate* him from the awkward predicament, to *free* him *from the difficulty*.

exude Wherever she went, she seemed to *exude* radiance and happiness, cheering those about her in the process. She would *abundantly display* the joyful life.

exult Events worthy of huge celebrations will cause people to *exult*; for example, teachers and students *rejoice* and *are extremely joyful* on the last day of school in the Spring while parents usually *exult* when classes resume in the Fall.

QUIZ

Match the following words with their meanings:

(1) desideratum   [ ] a bitter, abusive denunciation
(2) desolate   [ ] meant to teach, instruct
(3) despoil   [ ] to recognize, identify a disease; investigate, analyze problems
(4) desuetude   [ ] skill in using hands; mental skill
(5) desultory   [ ] dividing into two opposing or contradictory parts
(6) deviate   [ ] to strip of possessions, belongings, or value; pillage
(7) diatribe   [ ] something needed and wanted
(8) diacritical   [ ] relating to the devil; fiendish
(9) diagnose   [ ] to turn aside from a norm; to stray from; change course
(10) dexterity   [ ] discontinuance from use or exercise; disuse
(11) didactic   [ ] deserted; barren; lifeless; gloomy
(12) diabolical   [ ] distinctive; capable of distinguishing
(13) dichotomous   [ ] lacking in plan, regularity, or purpose; erratic; shifting

(1) diffident   [ ] disagreeing; harsh; quarrelsome
(2) dilemma   [ ] a denial, disavowal; repudiation
(3) digress   [ ] to upset the composure of; confuse
(4) discreet   [ ] warning of disaster; desperately urgent
(5) discourse   [ ] a choice between unpleasant options
(6) discern   [ ] to free from error or fallacy
(7) disconsolate   [ ] hesitant; lacking self-confidence
(8) dilettante   [ ] an exchange of ideas; expression of thought
(9) disconcert   [ ] to depart temporarily from the subject
(10) dire   [ ] showing good judgment; tactful
(11) disclaimer   [ ] one whose interests are superficial; a dabbler
(12) disabuse   [ ] to recognize as separate and distinct
(13) discordant   [ ] dejected; downcast; cheerless

(1) dissident   [ ] distinct in character; unequal; dissimilar

(2) disparity   [ ] difference; disagreement; inconsistency

(3) disdain   [ ] withhold assent; not to approve; object; differ; disagree

(4) discursive   [ ] not agreeing; dissenting; quarrelsome

(5) discrepancy   [ ] inequality; difference; incongruity

(6) disingenuous   [ ] carefully distinguishing

(7) disparage   [ ] to hide under false pretense; to hide one's feelings

(8) disheveled   [ ] passing from one topic to another; digressive; rambling

(9) disseminate   [ ] to look with scorn on; to treat with contempt

(10) discriminate   [ ] giving a false look of frankness; calculating; lacking candor

(11) dissemble   [ ] to discredit; speak slightingly of; belittle

(12) dissent   [ ] to spread widely; scatter; publicize

(13) disparate   [ ] being in loose disorder; ruffled; untidy

(1) doctrinaire   [ ] expressive of misery or grief

(2) dissolute   [ ] easily taught, led, or managed

(3) distort   [ ] to waste, squander; expend foolishly

(4) dolt   [ ] a spell of listlessness; blues; a slump

(5) dissuade   [ ] to make known; disclose; reveal

(6) dolorous   [ ] dogmatic; dictatorial

(7) dissipate   [ ] to twist out of the true meaning or proportion

(8) doldrums   [ ] a stupid fellow; blockhead; numskull

(9) diurnal   [ ] lacking restraint; loose in morals

(10) docile   [ ] absent-minded; inattentive or distracted by anxiety

(11) divulge   ['] to advise a person against something

(12) distrait   [ ] recurring every day; daily

(1) dystopia   [ ] enthusiastic feelings; exuberance
(2) ductile   [ ] showing a sour disposition; ill-tempered
(3) dour   [ ] luscious; melodious; agreeable; soothing
(4) duress   [ ] an imaginary depressingly wretched
                          place; a dreadful place
(5) dogmatic   [ ] capable of being molded; easily led or
                          influenced; pliant
(6) duplicity   [ ] a person easily fooled or tricked
(7) dyspeptic   [ ] fearless; able; strong; valiant
(8) dulcet   [ ] stern, harsh; forbidding; gloomy; obsti
                          nate; unyielding; sullen
(9) dupe   [ ] restraint by force; compulsion by
                          threat; coercion
(10) doughty   [ ] asserting an opinion as if it were fact;
                          dictatorial
(11) ebullience   [ ] belying one's true intentions; bad faith;
                          double dealing

(1) élan   [ ] the power to produce an effect
(2) effete   [ ] of or relating to a church
(3) egalitarianism   [ ] a crude image of a hated person
(4) effrontery   [ ] a dazzling effect; brilliance; a brilliant,
                          conspicuous success
(5) edacious   [ ] composed of elements selected from
                          various sources
(6) edict   [ ] vigor, spirit; enthusiasm; zeal; liveliness of
                          imagination
(7) ecclesiastical   [ ] worn out; spent; weak; outmoded
(8) efficacy   [ ] a coming out; a way out, an exit
(9) enigma   [ ] a belief in human equality
(10) eclectic   [ ] relating to eating; voracious
(11) effigy   [ ] an order; a command
(12) éclat   [ ] something hard to explain; mystery
(13) egress   [ ] crass, offensive boldness; discourtesy

(1) edify   [ ] to release from; to free from restraint
(2) elicit   [ ] to escape the notice of; avoid adroitly, cleverly
(3) elegy   [ ] excessive talk and use of "I"
(4) elide   [ ] to come out from a source; give out
(5) eleemosynary   [ ] conspicuously bad; outrageous
(6) emancipate   [ ] to call forth, bring out (a response)
(7) elucidate   [ ] to instruct; to enlighten
(8) elude   [ ] to strike out (a word); leave out
(9) eloquent   [ ] relating to charity; charitable
(10) egotism   [ ] a song, poem, or speech of sorrow, esp. for one who is dead
(11) emanate   [ ] to give a clear explanation
(12) egregious   [ ] forcefully and fluently expressive

(1) emeritus   [ ] lasting a very short time
(2) epicene   [ ] conspicuous; evident; noteworthy
(3) entrepreneur   [ ] an imitative follower; inferior imitator of a great achiever
(4) emend   [ ] to direct by order; to forbid, prohibit
(5) epic   [ ] based on observation or experience
(6) ephemeral   [ ] retired from a position (like a professor)
(7) endow   [ ] to weigh down; burden; impede
(8) eminent   [ ] common to both sexes or neither
(9) epigone   [ ] one who starts and takes the risks of running a business
(10) enjoin   [ ] to provide, endow; transfuse
(11) encumber   [ ] to correct by textual change
(12) empirical   [ ] beyond the ordinary; heroic; big
(13) endue   [ ] to provide an income; give freely to

(1) epigram   [ ] history and analysis of a word from its origin
(2) esculent   [ ] equal or like; corresponding to
(3) epithet   [ ] high regard for
(4) equivocate   [ ] to uproot; get rid of; wipe out
(5) erratic   [ ] edible
(6) eponym   [ ] a summary; brief description; a typical
                      example
(7) equivalent   [ ] lacking consistency; eccentric
(8) eschew   [ ] to deceive; speak evasively; lie; mislead; use
                      double meanings
(9) esteem   [ ] a disparaging, abusive word or phrase
(10) epistle   [ ] boredom; feeling of dissatisfaction
(11) epitome   [ ] a terse or witty saying
(12) eradicate   [ ] to avoid habitually; to shun
(13) etymology   [ ] a formal or elegant letter
(14) ennui   [ ] a person for whom something is named

(1) evert   [ ] to prove; show clearly; reveal
(2) evoke   [ ] to cause the anger of; enrage; irritate
(3) esoteric   [ ] for example
(4) evolve   [ ] to clear from alleged fault or guilt
(5) exasperate   [ ] to make matters worse
(6) evanescent   [ ] free from liability to which others are
                        subject; not liable to
(7) exaggerate   [ ] to conjure; to bring to mind or memory
(8) evince   [ ] to overthrow, upset; turn inside-out
(9) exempli gratia [ ] deserving imitation; commendable
(10) exacerbate   [ ] give off, emit; derive, develop; undergo
                        gradual upward change
(11) exempt   [ ] of short duration; like vapor
(12) exculpate   [ ] to overstate the truth; enlarge upon
(13) exemplary   [ ] of knowledge restricted to a small group;
                        abstruse

(1) exert   [   ] to incite; to urge strongly; to warn

(2) explicit   [   ] strikingly or excitingly different or unusual

(3) exigent   [   ] fit, proper, or advantageous under the circumstances

(4) euphemism   [   ] a deed or act

(5) exhort   [   ] to relieve; to clear from blame

(6) exorbitant   [   ] clearly visible; specific; definite; unambiguous; not vague at all

(7) expatriate   [   ] one who interprets; one who advocates something

(8) exotic   [   ] beyond the customary limits; excessive; too much

(9) expedient   [   ] from the outside; irrelevant

(10) exonerate   [   ] to put forth strength or tiring effort

(11) exponent   [   ] one who lives in a foreign country

(12) exploit   [   ] the use of an agreeable expression for a less pleasant one

(13) extraneous   [   ] requiring immediate attention, aid, or action

(1) expunge   [   ] to act promptly; speed up progress

(2) extricate   [   ] to speak at length or in great detail

(3) exult   [   ] to reason earnestly with someone to dissuade him or her

(4) exude   [   ] to free from entanglement or difficulty; disencumber

(5) expostulate   [   ] to erase or remove; delete; expurgate

(6) expatiate   [   ] to be extremely joyful; to rejoice

(7) expedite   [   ] to ooze; display abundantly

QUIZ

1. A good diplomat is:
(a) diffident   (b) disconsolate   (c) discreet   (d) discordant

2. An edifice on a campus usually bears the name of:
(a) a dolt   (b) an eponym   (c) an epigone   (d) an expatriate

3. A person most likely to succeed in business is:
(a) a dilettante   (b) an expatriate   (c) a dupe   (d) an entrepreneur

4. A girl on her way to a party prefers that her escort be:
(a) doughty   (b) disheveled   (c) erratic   (d) effete

5. Someone who is concerned about the disparity of wealth is noted for his:
(a) egotism   (b) effrontery   (c) egalitarianism   (d) éclat

6. In order to edify the class on an abstruse topic, the students want the professor to:
(a) disconcert   (b) elucidate   (c) elide   (d) eradicate

7. If a wheel of your car gets stuck in a deep, narrow ditch, you want to be:
(a) exasperated   (b) dolorous   (c) extricated   (d) distrait

8. A person who extricates someone from an exigent circumstance is considered:
(a) dogmatic   (b) exemplary   (c) docile   (d) dour

9. A person known for his use of duplicity is probably:
(a) eminent   (b) discordant   (c) disingenuous   (d) discriminate

10. Knowledge gained by observation or experience is:
(a) eclectic   (b) ephemeral   (c) esoteric   (d) empirical

REVIEW QUIZ

Match these important words with their meanings:

(1) abeyance   [   ] contrast, opposition; direct opposite
(2) duplicity   [   ] pretentious inflated style of speech; self-importance
(3) crux   [   ] something that naturally follows, accompanies, or parallels
(4) aura   [   ] a bitter, abusive, and usu. lengthy speech or writing
(5) bombast   [   ] a choice between equally unsatisfactory alternatives
(6) criterion   [   ] a temporary suspension of activity
(7) antithesis   [   ] doubtless of thought; deception by pretense; bad faith
(8) corollary   [   ] a most important, deciding point; a main or central feature
(9) dilemma   [   ] a distinctive surrounding atmosphere or impression
(10) diatribe   [   ] a standard to judge by; a standard of reference; a "yardstick"

(1) abstract   [   ] asserting an opinion as if it were fact; dictatorial
(2) exempt   [   ] not willing; opposed to; disinclined
(3) arbitrary   [   ] giving a false look of frankness; lacking in candor
(4) empirical   [   ] showing a likeness; comparable; similar
(5) dogmatic   [   ] likely but not certain; dependent on something else
(6) contingent   [   ] having special knowledge; aware; conscious
(7) analogous   [   ] detached from specifics; not real; abstruse; theoretical
(8) averse   [   ] based on direct experience, not theoretical
(9) cognizant   [   ] left to one's whim; selected at random and without reason
(10) disingenuous   [   ] not subject to; not liable to; excepted from some law

(1) ad lib   [   ] to show relationship of or correspondence to
(2) expedite   [   ] to assert positively but without proof
(3) ascribe   [   ] emit; derive; develop; undergo upward gradual change
(4) equivocate   [   ] be sorry; regret; disapprove of
(5) edify   [   ] withhold assent; not to approve; to differ in opinion
(6) allege   [   ] to improvise; speak offhand; speak without prior preparation
(7) correlate   [   ] to refer to a cause; give a reason for; to attribute; to credit
(8) deplore   [   ] to act promptly; speed up the progress of
(9) evolve   [   ] to deceive; speak evasively; lie; use double meanings; mislead
(10) dissent   [   ] to instruct; to enlighten; to elevate, uplift

SEGMENT FOUR

ETYMOLOGY	OLD MEANING
WORD	**NEW MEANING**

L facetus	witty, humorous; fine; elegant
facetious	**given to joking; light, pleasant; witty**

L factio	making; doing; group, party
faction	**party or group; clique**

L facere	to make, create; compose
factitious	**man-made; artificial; not natural**

L fac totum!	do everything!
factotum	**a person of many diverse activities**

L fallere	to deceive, cheat; to beguile; be mistaken
fallacy	**a false idea; unsound argument**

L fallere	to deceive, cheat; to beguile; be mistaken
fallible	**liable to be wrong or make a mistake**

OE fealg	piece of plowed land
fallow	**left untilled; dormant; inactive; having large unused potential**

L farcire	to stuff, fill full
farce	**satirical comedy; empty show; mockery**

L fastus + taedium	arrogance + irksomeness, disgust
fastidious	**hard to please or satisfy; demanding excessive delicacy or care; fussy**

L fatuus	foolish, silly; unwieldy
fatuous	**complacently ignoring reality; stupid**

Fr faux pas	*lit.,* false step
faux pas	**a blunder, esp. a social blunder**

L fidelis	faithful, loyal; trustworthy, sure
fealty	**intense, compelling loyalty; allegiance**

MFr fais, faire	to make, to do
feasible	**suitable; reasonable, likely; possible**

SAMPLE SENTENCES

facetious At almost any social gathering there is usually someone who likes to tell *facetious* stories, those that are *characterized by joking* and *wit*.

faction Within a large group there is often a smaller group known as a *faction*, which hangs out together. It is also called a *clique* or *set*, an *exclusive circle or group*.

factitious When we read or hear conflicting reports, we try to determine which is real or genuine and which is *factitious* or *artificial*. The latter is *sham* or *false*.

factotum It is advantageous to have a *factotum* in an organization along with the specialists; that is, a *person of many diverse activities and functions*.

fallacy To disabuse a stubborn person from a *fallacy* is difficult but worth a try; to free him from a *phony idea* or *unsound argument* is hard.

fallible All people are *fallible*, that is, *capable of making a mistake*. We often hear a *fallible* generalization, one *liable to be erroneous*.

fallow At any given moment there are probably important inventions lying *fallow*; that is, they are *dormant, inactive,* and *have large unused potential*.

farce The show was a *farce*, a *light drama of satirical comedy and improbable plot*. Loud rude interruptions make a *farce* of debate; it is a *mockery*.

fastidious The *fastidious* hostess wanted everything to be perfect for her grand ball; she is *fussy* and *hard to please*.

fatuous It is *fatuous* to persist in presenting a fallacy to the listeners; to be *complacently foolish, silly,* or *stupid* is not a way to convince rational persons.

faux pas He committed a *faux pas* at the reception by calling the guest of honor by the wrong name, a *social blunder*.

fealty Elected officials and some appointees take an oath of *fealty* to the Constitution, an oath of *allegiance*, or *compelling loyalty*, to it.

feasible She came up with a *feasible* solution to the problem. It seemed a *reasonable, possible,* even a *suitable* and *likely* way out of the enigma.

ETYMOLOGY	OLD MEANING
WORD	**NEW MEANING**

ME fek
feckless
effect
ineffectual, weak; worthless; irresponsible helpless; incompetent

L fingere
feign
to form; imagine; suppose; invent
give a false appearance of; pretend

L felicitas
felicity
happiness; good luck
happiness; great happiness

L fera
feral
wild beast, animal
savage; escaped and become wild

L fidere
fiduciary
to trust, rely on
held in trust; depending on public confidence for its value

Fr fief
fief
preserve; stronghold; private kingdom
something over which one has rights or exercises control

L fingere
figment
to form; imagine; suppose; invent
something made up or contrived

L figurare
figurative
to form, shape
not in the literal or exact sense; metaphoric

OFr fin
finesse
fine
skillful handling of a situation

L fiscus
fiscal
purse; moneybox; basket; treasury
of the treasury; financial

L findere
fission
to split, divide; to burst
a splitting or breaking up of parts

L flaccidus
flaccid
flabby; feeble
lacking firmness; lacking force; limp

L flagitium
flagitious
offence; disgrace, shame; scoundrel
shamefully wicked; vile; villainous

SAMPLE SENTENCES

feckless After one day the boss had to fire his *feckless* nephew; on the job he was *weak, ineffectual, incompetent, worthless, irresponsible,* and had the mind of a turnip.

feign With time running out and his team behind, he decided to *feign* being hurt to stop the clock; he decided to *give a false appearance of* an injury, to *pretend* he was hurt.

felicity His dour expression changed to one of *felicity* upon finding his golf ball in a surprisingly good lie for his next shot; he had the look of *great happiness.*

feral The hikers in the forest were chary and circumspect because of *feral* dogs and pigs. They are known to be *savage*; many *having escaped and become wild.*

fiduciary He had *fiduciary* duties, those *of a trustee.* Paper money is *fiduciary,* that is, *valuable because of public confidence* in it, rather than of any intrinsic value.

fief In governments there are many *fiefs*, or fiefdoms, e.g., bureaus, agencies, and offices, each run by a honcho. Like little kingdoms, each is *something over which one has charge.*

figment The dénouement of a novel thriller is usually a *figment* of the author's imagination, *something made up, fabricated, or contrived.*

figurative "That receiver can fly" (He is fast) and "I could eat a horse" (I am hungry) are *figurative* or *metaphoric* expressions. They are *not in the literal or exact sense.*

finesse The team accomplished by *finesse* what could not be done by force; the team used *adroit maneuvering* and *skillful handling of the situation.*

fiscal We expect our representatives to use sound *fiscal* policy with our money; we want a practice of good *financial* judgment in matters *of taxation, revenues, and debt.*

fission Children are the victims when there is a *fission* of the family, a *splitting up* of the parents. Great energy is released with atomic *fission,* or the *splitting* of the atom.

flaccid A person can become *flaccid* from lack of proper exercise (muscular desuetude); no one wants to be *lacking firmness or force,* or to be *limp.*

flagitious Totalitarian governments have been guilty of *flagitious* acts such as mass murders of "enemies of the state;" these acts are *shamefully wicked, vile,* and *villainous.*

ETYMOLOGY	OLD MEANING
WORD	**NEW MEANING**

L flagrans	hot; blazing; brilliant
flagrant	**extremely conspicuous because of uncommon evil; very bad; egregious**

Fr flamboyer	to blaze; flame up; to flash
flamboyant	**given to dashing display; showy**

L fluctus	a wave; a flowing
fluctuate	**to shift back and forth uncertainly**

L fluxus	flowing; loose; lax
flux	**continuous change; state of uncertainty; lack of clear direction**

OFr feble	feeble
foible	**a minor flaw in character or behavior**

OFr fol	fool
folly	**foolish act or idea; very costly undertaking**

L forensis	public; of the marketplace
forensic	**belonging to public discussion and debate; argumentative**

L formidabilis	terrifying
formidable	**causing fear; discouraging approach; awe-inspiring**

L fortuitus	casual; accidental
fortuitous	**occurring by chance; fortunate, lucky**

L frivolus	empty; of little worth
frivolous	**of little weight or importance**

L fructus	enjoyment; revenue; fruit; reward
fruition	**the bearing of fruit; accomplishment conclusion; realization**

L fugere	to flee, escape; vanish
fugacious	**fleeting, ephemeral; lasting a short time**

L fungi	to perform, discharge; do, be acted upon
fungible	**interchangeable; capable of substitution**

SAMPLE SENTENCES

flagrant The *flagrant* poverty in some societies is usually due to neglect and lack of education; it is *egregious* and *extremely conspicuous because of uncommon evil.*

flamboyant Arriving late as usual, she made a *flamboyant* grand entrance to the ball. Her arrival was *showy, given to dashing display.*

fluctuate Diurnal temperatures *fluctuate*, as do stock prices; they *shift back and forth with uncertainty.*

flux Take the weather or the stock market; each is in a state of *flux*; each undergoes *continuous change*, is in a *state of uncertainty*, and has a *lack of clear direction.*

foible It is hard to imagine anyone without a *foible*, someone who has no *minor flaw in character or behavior, weakness,* or *fault.*

folly To sue somebody for $25,000 at a cost of $40,000 in attorney's fees is sheer *folly*. It is a *foolish idea* and a *very costly undertaking.*

forensic Suggested legislation, court cases, and ballot propositions are *forensic* matters; they are *argumentative* and *belonging to public discussion and debate.*

formidable The steep, craggy mountains presented a *formidable* barrier to the hikers; the mountains were *awe-inspiring* yet *discouraging approach* and *causing fear.*

fortuitous The *fortuitous* meeting between a former prisoner of war and his former camp guard in a Los Angeles department store really set things off. The meeting, of course, was *accidental, happening by chance.*

frivolous Thinkers and achievers waste little time indulging in *frivolous* conversation; they tend to avoid discussions *of little weight or importance.*

fruition The building of a large, useful vocabulary can lead to successful *fruition* in the university and later on to great *realization, accomplishment* or *conclusion.*

fugacious Close-up visits by a hummingbird or a lizard are *fugacious*, here one moment, gone the next. They are *fleeting, ephemeral,* and *lasting a short time.*

fungible The simpler the tasks one performs, the more *fungible* he becomes; the easier the job, the more *capable of substitution, replaceable*, and *readily interchangeable* he is.

ETYMOLOGY	OLD MEANING
WORD	**NEW MEANING**

L furtum | theft, robbery; trick
furtive | **done secretly, done by stealth; sneaky**

L futilis | that pours out easily; useless
futile | **serving no useful purpose; ineffective**

Fr gaffe | blunder, booboo
gaffe | **social blunder; clumsy mistake; faux pas**

ME gain- + sayen | against + to say
gainsay | **to deny, dispute; contradict; oppose**

MFr gambade | spring of a horse
gambol | **to skip or leap about in play**

L granum | seed, grain
garner | **acquire by effort; earn; pick up**

L garrulus | talkative, babbling
garrulous | **tediously, pointlessly, or annoyingly talkative**

Fr gasconner | to boast
gasconade | **bravado, boasting**

Gk gastro- + -nomia | belly + knowledge
gastronomy | **the art of good eating; epicurism**

Fr gauche | left, on the left
gauche | **lacking social grace; crude; awkward**

MFr gant | glove
gauntlet | **a challenge to combat; cross fire; ordeal**

L gelidus | cold, frosty; stiff, numb; chilling
gelid | **extremely cold; icy**

Fr genre | kind, type, sort
genre | **kind; sort; category (of art) by style, form, or content**

Sample Sentences

furtive The stranger at the party had a *furtive* aura, which aroused a little suspicion. He had a *sneaky* look, one *trying not to be seen, done in a secret manner.*

futile His efforts to disabuse the dolt from his fallacy proved *futile*; try as he might, his reasoning was *ineffective, serving no useful purpose.*

gaffe The program chairman made a *gaffe* while introducing the 360 pound guest speaker as "huge in stature in her field." It was a *clumsy mistake*, a genuine *faux pas.*

gainsay A debater must be careful to make points which nobody can *gainsay*, to assert claims that are hard to *deny, dispute, contradict,* or *oppose.*

gambol After the last day of school in the spring, children *gambol* happily; after a touchdown in the fall, students and alumni *leap about in play* with glee.

garner The volunteer group managed to *garner* considerable support for the symphony. The members were able to *acquire by effort*, to *earn, pick up* the needed support.

garrulous The sensitive poet felt uncomfortable while seated among the *garrulous* types. He wanted to get away from the *tediously* and *pointlessly talkative* simpletons.

gasconade He resorted to excessive *gasconade* to call attention to his recent minor accomplishments. He showed too much *bravado* or *boasting.*

gastronomy One of the interests of many cosmopolitan individuals is *gastronomy*, which is *the art of good eating*, or *epicurism.*

gauche Buffoons and dolts are usually *gauche;* that is, they are *crude, awkward*, and *lacking in social grace.*

gauntlet To qualify for the position, each candidate or applicant must run a demanding *gauntlet* of critical judges. Each must face a *cross fire* of questions, which is a severe *test*, or *ordeal.*

gelid The hikers looked up at the *gelid* rocky slopes; the *extremely cold, icy* slopes were formidable, indeed.

genre What is your favorite *genre* in music? Jazz? Classical? How about art? Cubism? Romanticism? Impressionism? What *kind, sort, category* or *class* do you like?

ETYMOLOGY	OLD MEANING
WORD	**NEW MEANING**

ME germain
germane
having the same parents
relevant and appropriate; fitting

L gestus
gesticulate
posture; gesture
to make gestures esp. when speaking

LG glibberig
glib
slippery
spoken in a smooth, offhand manner; nonchalant; lacking depth; slick

Gk gignoskein
gnome
to know
maxim, aphorism

King Gordius
Gordian knot
tied an intricate knot that can't be undone
seemingly insoluble, perplexing problem; extreme difficulty

MFr grand
grandeur
large; grand
state of being grand; magnificence

L grandiloquus
grandiloquent
grandis = grand + loqui = to speak
using lofty, colorful, or bombastic speech

L grandis
grandiose
large, great; grand
characterized by affectation of grandeur, splendor, or absurd exaggeration

L gratuitus
gratuity
costing nothing; free
something given voluntarily; a tip

Gk agora
gregarious
assembly; marketplace
liking companionship; sociable; social

OHG grisenlich
grisly
terrible
inspiring intense fear; ghastly; horrible

ME gilen
guile
to deceive
crafty or deceitful cunning; duplicity

ME gulle
gullible
silly fellow; *lit.*, an unfledged bird
easily deceived, cheated, or duped

SAMPLE SENTENCES

germane A moderator expects questions from the audience to be *germane* to the topic or discussion. They should be *relevant and appropriate* and *fitting*.

gesticulate To see a barber *gesticulate* wildly with razor in hand can make one nervous. Must he *make* sweeping *gestures while talking*, especially with that razor?

glib In an effort to "play it cool," the witness was *glib* with his answers to the District Attorney's questions; he was *smooth, offhand,* and *nonchalant*.

gnome "What goes up must come down" and "What goes around comes around" are *gnomes*, also known as *aphorisms, general truths,* or *sayings*.

Gordian knot He fully intended to replace the money he took, but he lost the key to get back in and found out the bank examiner was coming in Sunday to go over the books. He faced a *Gordian knot*, an *extreme difficulty,* a real *stickler of a problem*.

grandeur They looked in awe and wonder at the scenic *grandeur* of the mountains and valleys and later saw the *magnificence* of the ocean bashing the rocks.

grandiloquent He delivered a *grandiloquent* address at the graduation ceremony; it was one *using lofty, colorful,* and sometimes *bombastic* speech.

grandiose Madame Bovary had *grandiose* ideas and dreams, those *characterized by affectation of grandeur, splendor, or absurd exaggeration,* compared to her simple life.

gratuity It is customary to leave a *gratuity* to someone for services given; a generous *tip, something given voluntarily* in anticipation of some services, is appreciated.

gregarious People elected to various offices are usually *gregarious*. They are *social, tending to associate with others, liking companionship,* and *sociable*. They are not loners.

grisly The jury heard the district attorney describe the *grisly* details of the murder, the *ghastly, horrible* descriptions.

guile It is one thing to use *guile* at the card table to throw the opponents off yet quite another to be guilty of *crafty or deceitful cunning,* or *duplicity,* in human relationships.

gullible It would take a very *gullible* Eskimo to buy a refrigerator from a slick salesman, or for an Arab who is *easily deceived, cheated, or tricked* to buy a bucket of sand from him.

ETYMOLOGY	OLD MEANING
WORD	**NEW MEANING**

Fr habituer
habitué
to frequent
one who frequents a type of place

Gk hagio + graphein
hagiography
holy + to write
biography of saints; idealizing biography

Gk alkyon
halcyon
fabled kingfisher which calmed the waves
peaceful; happy; golden; prosperous

OFr herberge
harbinger
army encampment; hostelry
something that tells what is to come; a sign; an omen

?Fr haridelle
harridan
old horse; tall, lean, gaunt ugly woman
an ill-tempered, scolding woman

MFr haut
haughty
lit., high
brazenly and disdainfully proud

OHG horechen
hearken
to listen, hark
to give respectful attention

L hebetis
hebetude
blunt; dull; obtuse; stupid
absence of mental alertness; dullness

Gk Hektor
hector
Trojan champion slain by Achilles
to bully; swagger; harass; intimidate

Gk hedone
hedonism
pleasure
doctrine that pleasure or happiness is the sole or chief good in life

Gk hegemonia
hegemony
leadership
influence or dominance, esp. of one nation over others

Gk hetero- + doxa
heterodox
different + opinion
not following tradition; unconventional

L hiatus
hiatus
an opening; open mouth
a break or gap; lapse in continuity

SAMPLE SENTENCES

habitué He is an *habitué* of golf courses and ski slopes. He is *one who frequents* such places. Ex. *habitué* of Paris, the theater, Las Vegas, the racetrack, etc.

hagiography Admissions deans receive thousands of *hagiographies* each year. They get many *idealizing biographies* from friends, relatives, and loved ones of each applicant.

halcyon Far from home and beleaguered by life in the complaint department, he reflected on the *halcyon* days of summer, those *calm, happy, golden* days of yore.

harbinger A robin in late winter is a *harbinger* of spring, just as a yellow leaf in late autumn is a *sign*, or *omen*, of winter.

harridan The boys were careful not to let their ball go over the fence into the yard of the *harridan*. Getting it back from the *nasty, mean old woman* poses a real problem.

haughty The *haughty* young beauty never deigned to notice the crew members on the yacht. She was *disdainfully proud*, condescending, and *overbearing*.

hearken It is advisable for incoming freshmen to *hearken* to the words of the dean. It is wise to *give respectful attention* to him.

hebetude A person driving down the highway while talking on a cellphone shows the *hebetude* of a dolt, the *absence of mental alertness* in traffic.

hector The two tough guys tried to *hector* the poor imbecile playing the pinball machine. Their intention was to *bully, harass*, and *intimidate* him.

hedonism He felt that adopting *hedonism* was the ultimate escape from life's problems. The *doctrine that pleasure is the chief good in life* suited him just fine.

hegemony Prior to the euro, German economic *hegemony* was the case in Europe. The German economic *dominance over the rest of* Europe prevailed.

heterodox It is good to challenge conventional wisdom with occasional *heterodox* ideas; To hearken to *unconventional* ideas, those *not following tradition*, is healthy.

hiatus The personnel manager noticed a two-year *hiatus* in the applicant's employment history. He wanted the details of this *gap*, or *lapse in continuity*, explained.

ETYMOLOGY	OLD MEANING
WORD	**NEW MEANING**

L histrio	actor
histrionics	**display of emotion for effect; theatrics**

Hobson, 1631 Eng.	one must take the horse nearest the door
Hobson's choice	**an apparently free choice when there is no real alternative**

Gk homilia	conversation, discourse
homily	**sermon; lecture on moral conduct**

Fr hors d'oeuvre	*lit.,* outside of work
hors d'oeuvre	**any of savory foods served as appetizers; tidbit**

L hortatus	encouragement
hortatory	**exhorting; serving to urge; advisory**

?D heiden	country lout; heathen
hoyden	**boisterous, carefree girl or woman; tomboy**

Gk hybris	out
hubris	**exaggerated pride often resulting in punishment**

MD hoeken	to peddle, bear on the back; squat
huckster	**hawker, peddler; adman**

Gk hyperballein	to exceed (hyper- + ballein = to throw)
hyperbole	**extravagant exaggeration**

Gk hypotithenai	to put under; suppose (hypo- + tithenai = to put)
hypothesis	**a tentative assumption; concession made for the sake of argument**

SAMPLE SENTENCES

histrionics The plaintiff's *histrionics* was designed to win the jury's sympathy; he hoped his *display of emotion for effect,* his *theatrics,* would work in his favor.

Hobson's choice The group faced a *Hobson's choice*: vanilla only was available at the store; i.e., they had a *seemingly free choice where there is no real alternative.*

homily "Silent Cal", back at the White House after the Sunday *homily,* was asked by his wife, Grace, "How was the *sermon?*" "Fine." "What was it about?" "Sin," "Well, what did he have to say about it?" "He was against it."

hors d'oeuvre It was time to put out the *hors d'oeuvres,* the *tasty tidbits served as appetizers,* just before the guests were due to arrive.

hortatory In the closing moments of the close game the *hortatory* home fans yelled, "Defense! Defense!" The crowd was *exhortative, serving to urge* the team to win.

hoyden The girls heading for camp were glad the *hoyden* came along, for she was the only one capable of changing the wheel after the tire blew out. She was a *carefree* and *boisterous girl,* a real *tomboy,* who learned things in her dad's garage.

hubris "A haughty spirit goeth before a fall," aptly illustrates *hubris,* which, simply put, means *exaggerated pride often resulting in retribution* (punishment).

huckster A ticket scalper, or *huckster,* must sell for less after the kick-off; whereas a hot-dog *peddler,* or *hawker,* does very well during the game.

hyperbole The "Mile High" Stadium in Denver is a reality; but "mile-high ice cream cones" is an example of *hyperbole,* that is, *extravagant exaggeration.*

hypothesis To make a point in a discussion it is helpful to offer a *hypothesis,* that is, a *tentative assumption,* or a *concession made for the sake of argument.*

ETYMOLOGY	OLD MEANING
WORD	**NEW MEANING**

Gk iatros
iatric

healer, physician
relating to a physician; medical

L ibidem
ibid

in the same place
abbr., used in footnotes

MGk eokonoklastes
iconoclast

lit., image destroyer
**one who attacks established
beliefs or institutions**

Gk idio-
+ synkarannynai
idiosyncrasy

one's own + to mingle, mix
peculiarity of habit, character

Gk eidos
idyll

form, image
short description of rural serenity

L ignominia
ignominious

dishonor, disgrace
disgraceful, shameful; humiliating

L illudere
illusory

to play; to mock; to jeer at
based on illusion; deceptive

L imbibere
imbibe

to drink in; conceive
to assimilate; take in; to drink

It imbrogliare
imbroglio

to entangle; confuse; embroil
**a complicated situation; an
embarrassing misunderstanding**

L imbuere
imbue

to wet, dip; fill; inspire
to fill with; permeate; infuse; inspire

L imminere
imminent

to overhang, project; be near; threaten
ready to take place; menacingly near

L immoderatus
immoderate

limitless; excessive; unbridled
exceeding suitable bounds; unreasonable

L immutabilis
immutable

not subject to change; unalterable
unchangeable; unchanging

SAMPLE SENTENCES

iatric The student applicant has shown potentially outstanding *iatric* ability. The dean was impressed by his probable *medical* talent, i.e., talent *relating to a physician*.

ibid The expression *ibid* is used, as in a footnote, to avoid repetition of source data, e.g., references, authors, etc. It is an abbreviation of *ibidem*, meaning *in the same place*.

iconoclast An *iconoclast* preaches on the steps of a public building, in a park, or on a university campus; he is the *one who attacks established beliefs or institutions*.

idiosyncrasy Captain Queeg's *idiosyncrasy* was clicking steel balls in his hand when he got nervous, a *peculiarity of habit*, a *quirk*.

idyll A beleaguered clerk would like to be the subject of an *idyll* now and then, to be part of a *light-hearted, carefree episode,* or a *romantic interlude.*

ignominious He made an *ignominious* exit after pushing the official, creating a technical foul, and costing his team the game; it was a *disgraceful, shameful,* and *humiliating* exit.

illusory His optimism about winning was *illusory*; he was filled with *unreal, deceptive* hopes.

imbibe She *imbibes* a lot of strong coffee each morning. She *drinks* much coffee.

imbroglio He faced a real *imbroglio* when he found out that the two girls he had been dating turned out to be roommates; it was a very *complicated situation.*

imbue Although trailing, scoring on the final play of the half served to *imbue* the team with confidence; it *inspired, infused, filled* the team *with* great promise.

imminent The unusual noise downstairs at 2 A.M. made her feel she was in *imminent* danger, one *ready to take place, menacingly near at hand.*

immoderate He seemed to show an *immoderate* appetite at the dinner table, asking for third helpings of everything. It was *excessive, unreasonable* food consumption.

immutable His opinion on the matter is *immutable*; all attempts to reason with him will find him *unchangeable, unchanging.*

Etymology	Old Meaning
Word	**New Meaning**

Etymology / Word	Old / New Meaning
L in- + peccare **impeccable**	not + to make a mistake, to sin **free from blame or fault; flawless**
L in- + pecunia **impecunious**	not + property, money **habitually without money; penniless**
L impedimentum **impediment**	hindrance, obstacle; baggage **something that holds up or blocks**
L impendere **impending**	to overhang; to threaten **that is about to occur; imminent**
L imperiosus **imperious**	powerful, imperial; tyrannical **dominant; arrogant; domineering; very urgent; compelling**
L in- + perturbare **imperturbable**	not + to throw into disorder; to upset **extremely calm; steady; serene**
L impetus **impetuous**	attack; charge; rapid motion; rush **furious; hastily or rashly energetic; impulsively passionate**
L impingere **impinge**	to dash; force against; force upon **to come into sharp contact; encroach**
L in- + placabilis **implacable**	not + easily appeased **incapable of being appeased or changed**
L implere **implement**	to fill; satisfy; make up, complete; fulfill **to carry out; accomplish; fulfill**
L implicare **implicate**	to entwine, enfold; entangle; connect closely **to involve as a consequence; to involve deeply or unfavorably**
L implicare **implicit**	to entwine, enfold; entangle; connect closely **understood quietly; potential; absolute**
L implorare **implore**	to invoke, entreat, appeal to **to beseech; call or pray for earnestly; to beg**

SAMPLE SENTENCES

impeccable If someone under investigation has an *impeccable* record, the police detective says "he's clean;" his credentials are *flawless, free from fault or blame.*

impecunious Regardless of economic times, there are *impecunious* people, mainly in big cities; they are *habitually broke, with little or no money,* or *penniless.*

impediment Indecision can be an *impediment* to one's progress; like a fallen tree across the road, it is *something that holds up or blocks* your pathway.

impending Approaching a steep cataract in the canoe seemed like *impending* disaster. A catastrophe *that was about to occur,* an *imminent* tragedy, seemed likely.

imperious Many of the ladies in the club did not like her *imperious* attitude in planning for the event; they objected to her *arrogant, domineering* ways.

imperturbable Despite impending delays and inconveniences, she was *imperturbable* the whole trip; she remained *extremely calm, steady,* and *serene* throughout.

impetuous The coach became *impetuous* when no foul was called, losing his temper and berating the referee; he was *rashly energetic* and *passionate.*

impinge The landowner felt that the new regulation might *impinge* on his property rights; it could *encroach* or *infringe* upon them.

implacable No matter how urgently they expostulated, he remained *implacable* in his belief. He was *adamant, incapable of being appeased, changed, or modified.*

implement It is one thing to come up with a plan or idea and another to *implement* it; but someone has to *carry out* the project, *accomplish* it, *fulfill* it.

implicate The district attorney sought to *implicate* the suspect in the crime. Based on the evidence, he wished to *involve* him *as a consequence* of it, to *involve* him *deeply.*

implicit He didn't offer his opinion, but it was *implicit*; that is, *capable of being inferred or understood.* The oak is *implicit* in the acorn; it is *potential.* An *implicit* trust, i.e., one *lacking in doubt or reserve,* is a *wholehearted* trust.

implore The boys *implored* the harridan to throw the ball back to them; they *begged* her, *beseeched* her, *called earnestly for* her to return the ball.

ETYMOLOGY	OLD MEANING
WORD	**NEW MEANING**

L implicare	to entwine, enfold; entangle; connect
imply	**to indicate, suggest; to contain potentially; express indirectly**
L importunus	unsuitable; troublesome; bullying
importune	**to beg or solicit persistently; annoy**
L in- + prehendere	not + take hold of; to catch; seize
impregnable	**unconquerable; unassailable; beyond question or criticism**
L in promptu	at hand; in readiness; easy
impromptu	**on the spur of the moment; improvised**
L improvisus	*lit.,* unforeseen; unexpected
improvise	**to make, invent, or arrange offhand**
L impugnare	to attack; oppose
impugn	**assail by words; oppose as false; deny**
L impunitus	unpunished
impunity	**exemption from punishment or loss**
L imputare	to put to one's account; to ascribe, credit
impute	**to blame, charge; to credit to a person**
L in- + advertere	not + to turn, direct towards; call attention
inadvertent	**inattentive; unintentional**
L inanis	empty, void; unsubstantial; useless, idle
inane	**lacking meaning or point; silly**
L carcer	prison; jailbird; barrier
incarcerate	**to put in prison; subject to confinement**
L incipere	to begin
inception	**process of beginning; commencement**
L in- + cessare	not + to stop, delay; rest; do nothing
incessant	**continuing without interruption; continuous**

SAMPLE SENTENCES

imply His facial expression seems to *imply* disappointment with the report. His look *indicates, suggests* displeasure with the news; it *expresses* it *indirectly.*

importune In certain cities the local bums *importune* tourists for handouts; they *beg* or *persistently solicit* the visitors; in fact they *annoy* travelers.

impregnable His business is good because of *impregnable* honesty and candor. His reputation is *unassailable, beyond question or criticism.*

impromptu She can ad lib, is able to speak *impromptu* on many topics, *on the spur of the moment.* Her *impromptu* speech went smoothly. Her *improvised* speech was better than the prepared one.

improvise He *improvised* a way to secure the loose muffler by the use of a coat hanger; he *invented, arranged offhand,* a way to solve the problem.

impugn Two fierce debaters will *impugn* each other's arguments in a hearing; they will *assail verbally, oppose as false,* and *deny* each other's points or claims.

impunity Some people commit egregious acts with *impunity,* or so it seems. They seem to have *exemption from punishment* for their actions.

impute Few things can screw up a situation like a communications breakdown, but whom does one *impute* for it? Whom does one *lay the blame* for bollixing it up?

inadvertent Shipping all her luggage to Philadelphia instead of Paris was *inadvertent*; it was *unintentional,* the result of *inattentive, negligent* baggage handling.

inane One way to turn people off is to make frequent *inane* remarks in conversation. Don't make *empty, pointless,* or *silly* statements, those *lacking in meaning.*

incarcerate The police had reason to *incarcerate* him, based on strong evidence of too many shenanigans; they had to *put* him *in prison* for a while.

inception The *inception* of the large corporation took place in a one-car garage; its *process of beginning,* its *commencement,* actually happened there.

incessant After two weeks of *incessant* rainfall, one guy started building an ark; the downpour was *continuing without interruption;* it was *continuous.*

ETYMOLOGY	OLD MEANING
WORD	**NEW MEANING**

L incohatus	unfinished
inchoate	**only partly in existence; imperfectly formulated**
L incipere	to begin
incipient	**beginning to come into being**
L incitare	to urge on; rouse; encourage
incite	**to move to action; stir up; spur on**
L inclemens	severe
inclement	**physically severe; stormy**
L incognitus	unknown, unrecognized; untried
incognito	**with one's identity concealed**
L in- + congruere	not + to coincide, correspond, agree
incongruous	**incompatible; not conforming**
L in- + consequens	not + coherent, reasonable, logical
inconsequential	**illogical; irrelevant; unimportant**
L incrementum	growth, increase, addition
increment	**one of a series of additions; an increase**
L inculcare	to tread on; force upon; impress on
inculcate	**to teach and impress by frequent repetitions or admonitions**
L incumbere	to lean on; fall upon; lie heavily upon
incumbent	**imposed as a duty or obligation**
L incurrere	to run into; meet with; get involved in
incur	**bring down upon oneself; become liable to**
L in- + defatigare	to tire out; exhaust
indefatigable	**incapable of being fatigued; untiring**
OF enditer	to write down
indict	**to charge with some offense; accuse**

SAMPLE SENTENCES

inchoate They were not yet ready for the "Grand Opening" sign; their business was still *inchoate, in the beginning stages, only partly in existence, just barely begun.*

incipient One can tell the *incipient* stages of a cold by the first sign of a sore throat and congestion, by the *initial, commencing,* or *inchoate* stages of such discomfort.

incite Campus activists usually wait until spring to *incite* a crowd, rarely in fall or winter. They *stir up, spur on, move* a crowd *to action* over some cause.

inclement It is wise not to go sailing during *inclement* weather; it is advisable not to try most outdoor activities in *physically severe, stormy* conditions.

incognito He was successful in going *incognito* to the costume ball; no one could recognize him. He came *with his identity concealed.*

incongruous His tan shoes were *incongruous* with his black suit; they were *incompatible* or *not conforming* with it.

inconsequential The prosecuting attorney objected that the defense attorney's question was *inconsequential,* that is, *irrelevant, illogical,* and *unimportant.*

increment He built his stock portfolio one *increment* at a time. Each month he invested an *increase,* an *addition* of a fixed amount, to the growth of his shares.

inculcate Different societies *inculcate* different ideas in their children; they *fix in the mind, teach by repetition,* the ideas of the prevailing culture.

incumbent It is *incumbent* upon the CEO and the board of directors to maximize the long term gains of the shareholders; it is *imposed as a duty or obligation* to do so.

incur The driver yakking on his cell phone *incurred* the anger of others for his dangerous and reckless driving; he *brought down upon himself* their bitter disapproval.

indefatigable The factotum seemed to be *indefatigable* in shifting from one task to the next; she was *untiring, incapable of being fatigued,* in her many duties.

indict It is one thing to *indict* someone and another to convict him; to *accuse* someone, to *charge* him *with some offense,* is very different from finding him guilty.

ETYMOLOGY **WORD**	OLD MEANING **NEW MEANING**
L indigena **indigenous**	native **original in a particular region; inborn; innate; native**
L indigere **indigent**	to need, want; require; crave **poor; impoverished; needy**
L indolentia **indolent**	freedom from pain **averse to activity or effort; habitually lazy**
L inducere **induce**	to bring in, lead on; persuade **to persuade, influence; bring about**
L ineluctabilis **ineluctable**	inescapable **not to be avoided; inevitable**
L inaestimabilis **inestimable**	incalculable; invaluable **too valuable to measure**
L inevitabilis **inevitable**	inescapable **incapable of being avoided**
L inexorablili **inexorable**	not sympathetic; severe **not to be persuaded or moved; unyielding; relentless; inflexible**
L inexplicabilis **inexplicable**	not feasible; not usable; unending **incapable of being explained**
L inexpugnabilis **inexpugnable**	impregnable, safe **incapable of being subdued; steady**
L inextricabilis **inextricable**	not able to untangle **impossible to get free from; unable to disentangle or untie; unsolvable**
L infatuare **infatuate**	to make a fool of **inspire with a foolish or extravagant love or admiration**
L inferre **infer**	to carry in; bring to **to conclude from facts or assumption**

SAMPLE SENTENCES

indigenous Aborigines, koalas, and eucalyptus trees are *indigenous* to Australia; they are *original* or *native* to it.

indigent Typical citizens of a statist country would be considered *indigent* by U.S. standards; they would be seen as *poor, impoverished,* and *needy,* by comparison.

indolent The *indolent* nephew of the CEO had to be let go because of his disruptive attitude. He was *averse to activity or effort* and *habitually lazy.*

induce The indigence of his family was enough to *induce* him to study well, in order to seek a better life. It *persuaded* him, *influenced* him to do so.

ineluctable Fatuous people ignore or deny *ineluctable* conclusions of logical deduction; they disregard *unavoidable* facts, those that *cannot be changed or resisted.*

inestimable She performed an *inestimable* service for the project; without her efforts it would have failed. Her input was *too valuable to be measured or appreciated.*

inevitable When the two star players were sidelined with severe injuries, the loss of the playoff game was *inevitable*; it was *incapable of being avoided.*

inexorable She had to maintain her doughty spirit while playing against an *inexorable* opponent, one whose game was *unyielding* and *relentless.*

inexplicable His sudden, *inexplicable* departure confused his coaches and team mates. His action was *incapable of being explained or accounted for.*

inexpugnable In animal societies the position of the alpha-male is *inexpugnable*, that is, he is *incapable of being subdued.*

inextricable The spider weaves an *inextricable* web which traps insects. It is a tangle *from which it is impossible to get free.* Also, one is *unable to disentangle or untie it.*

infatuate Quite often, if a girl is *infatuated* with a boy, her father objects; if a boy is *inspired with a foolish or extravagant love for* a girl, his mother is opposed.

infer We see smoke and *infer* that there is fire (we *conclude from facts*). We see the professor's car parked on campus, we *infer* (*conclude from assumption*) he is in his office.

QUIZ

Match the following words with their meanings:

(1) facetious   [ ] liable to be wrong, or make a mistake

(2) faux pas   [ ] a false idea; unsound argument

(3) fallow   [ ] ineffectual; weak; worthless; irresponsible; incompetent

(4) fatuous   [ ] man-made; artificial; not natural

(5) faction   [ ] intense, compelling loyalty; allegiance

(6) fastidious   [ ] given to joking; light, pleasant; witty

(7) farce   [ ] a blunder, esp. a social blunder

(8) feckless   [ ] left untilled; dormant; inactive; having large, unused potential

(9) fallacy   [ ] a party or group; a clique

(10) factitious   [ ] complacently ignoring reality; stupid

(11) fealty   [ ] a satirical comedy; empty show; a mockery

(12) fallible   [ ] hard to please or satisfy; demanding excessive delicacy or care

(1) felicity   [ ] skillful handling of a situation

(2) feral   [ ] lacking firmness; lacking force; limp

(3) fief   [ ] a splitting or breaking up of parts

(4) figurative   [ ] held in trust; depending on public confidence for its value

(5) figment   [ ] happiness; great happiness

(6) fiscal   [ ] shamefully wicked; vile; villainous

(7) finesse   [ ] something over which one has rights or exercises control

(8) flagrant   [ ] suitable; reasonable, likely; possible

(9) flaccid   [ ] not in the literal or exact sense; metaphoric

(10) fission   [ ] something made up or contrived

(11) flagitious   [ ] of the treasury; financial

(12) fiduciary   [ ] extremely conspicuous because of uncommon evil

(13) feasible   [ ] savage; escaped or lost and become wild

(1) flamboyant   [   ] fleeting; ephemeral; lasting a short time
(2) futile   [   ] done secretly, done by stealth; sneaky
(3) flux   [   ] the bearing of fruit; accomplishment;
                        conclusion; realization
(4) feign   [   ] to shift back and forth uncertainly
(5) frivolous   [   ] occurring by chance; fortunate; lucky
(6) forensic   [   ] interchangeable; capable of substitution
(7) foible   [   ] continuous change; state of uncertainty;
                        lack of clear direction
(8) formidable   [   ] given to dashing display; showy
(9) furtive   [   ] serving no useful purpose; ineffective
(10) fugacious   [   ] belonging to public discussion and debate;
                        argumentative
(11) fluctuate   [   ] to give a false appearance of; pretend
(12) fruition   [   ] a minor flaw in character or behavior
(13) fungible   [   ] causing fear; discouraging approach; awe-
                        inspiring
(14) fortuitous   [   ] of little weight or importance

(1) folly   [   ] the art of good eating
(2) gaffe   [   ] a challenge to combat; cross-fire; ordeal
(3) gainsay   [   ] to make gestures, esp. when speaking
(4) garrulous   [   ] relevant and appropriate; fitting
(5) gasconade   [   ] kind; sort; category (of art, e.g.) by style,
                        form, or content
(6) gauche   [   ] extremely cold; icy
(7) gauntlet   [   ] foolish act or idea; very costly undertaking
(8) gambol   [   ] to acquire by effort; earn; pick up
(9) germane   [   ] tediously, pointlessly, or annoyingly
                        talkative
(10) genre   [   ] a social blunder; clumsy mistake; faux pas
(11) gesticulate   [   ] to deny, dispute; contradict; oppose
(12) gelid   [   ] lacking social grace; crude; awkward
(13) gastronomy   [   ] bravado, boasting
(14) garner   [   ] to skip or leap about in play

(1) glib   [ ] tending to associate with others; social; liking companionship
(2) gnome   [ ] something given voluntarily; a tip
(3) grandiloquent   [ ] easily deceived, cheated, or duped
(4) Gordian knot   [ ] crafty or deceitful cunning; duplicity
(5) gregarious   [ ] inspiring intense fear; ghastly; horrible
(6) gratuity   [ ] state of being grand; magnificent
(7) grandiose   [ ] spoken in a smooth, offhand, carefree manner; nonchalant; slick
(8) grandeur   [ ] a seemingly insoluble, perplexing problem; extreme difficulty
(9) gullible   [ ] using lofty, colorful, or bombastic speech
(10) guile   [ ] maxim, aphorism
(11) grisly   [ ] characterized by affectation of grandeur or absurd exaggeration

(1) hagiography   [ ] doctrine that pleasure or happiness is the chief good in life
(2) halcyon   [ ] not following tradition; unconventional
(3) hearken   [ ] to bully; swagger; harass; intimidate
(4) habitué   [ ] an ill-tempered, scolding woman
(5) harbinger   [ ] a break or gap; lapse in continuity
(6) hebetude   [ ] influence or dominance, esp. of one nation over others
(7) haughty   [ ] peaceful; happy; golden; prosperous
(8) hedonism   [ ] something that tells what is to come; a sign; an omen
(9) hector   [ ] to give respectful attention
(10) hiatus   [ ] a biography of saints; an idealizing biography
(11) harridan   [ ] one who frequents a type of place
(12) heterodox   [ ] brazenly and disdainfully proud
(13) hegemony   [ ] absence of mental alertness; dullness; lethargy

(1) factotum [ ] a boisterous, carefree girl or woman; a tomboy

(2) histrionics [ ] extravagant exaggeration

(3) hortatory [ ] disgraceful, shameful; humiliating

(4) Hobson's choice [ ] any of tasty foods served as appetizers; tidbit

(5) hypothesis [ ] exaggerated pride often resulting in retribution (punishment)

(6) hoyden [ ] a person of many diverse activities or responsibilities

(7) hyperbole [ ] display of emotion for effect; theatrics

(8) ignominious [ ] exhorting; serving to urge; advisory

(9) homily [ ] tentative assumption; concession for the sake of argument

(10) hubris [ ] an apparently free choice when there is no real alternative

(11) hors d'oeuvre [ ] a sermon; a lecture on moral conduct

(1) iatric [ ] ready to happen; menacingly near

(2) idiosyncrasy [ ] a complicated situation; an embarrassing misunderstanding

(3) huckster [ ] one who attacks established beliefs or institutions

(4) imbibe [ ] to fill with; permeate; infuse; inspire

(5) immoderate [ ] based on illusion; deceptive

(6) ibid [ ] unchangeable; unchanging

(7) imminent [ ] relating to a physician; medical

(8) iconoclast [ ] a hawker; peddler; ad man

(9) idyll [ ] a peculiarity of habit or character

(10) imbue [ ] to assimilate; take in; to drink

(11) illusory [ ] exceeding suitable bounds; unreasonable

(12) imbroglio [ ] a short description of rural serenity

(13) immutable [ ] in the same place (abbreviation used in footnotes)

(1) impecunious   [ ] incapable of being appeased or changed
(2) impinge   [ ] to beseech; to call or pray for earnestly
(3) impediment   [ ] process of beginning; commencement
(4) impending   [ ] understood quietly; potential; absolute
(5) impetuous   [ ] free from blame or fault; flawless
(6) implement   [ ] to involve deeply or unfavorably
(7) implacable   [ ] furious; hastily or rashly energetic;
                              impulsively passionate
(8) imperious   [ ] that is about to occur; imminent
(9) inception   [ ] something that holds up or blocks
(10) imperturbable   [ ] dominant; arrogant; domineering; urgent;
                              compelling
(11) implore   [ ] to carry out; accomplish; fulfill
(12) implicit   [ ] habitually without money; penniless
(13) implicate   [ ] to come into sharp contact; encroach
(14) impeccable   [ ] extremely calm; steady; serene

(1) inadvertent   [ ] on the spur of the moment; improvised
(2) importune   [ ] to put in prison; subject to confinement
(3) impregnable   [ ] continuing without interruption; continuous
(4) imply   [ ] to blame, charge; to credit to a person
(5) improvise   [ ] to assail by words; oppose as false; deny
(6) inane   [ ] unconquerable; unassailable; beyond
                              question or criticism
(7) impute   [ ] to beg or solicit persistently; to annoy
(8) incessant   [ ] beginning to come into being; commencing
(9) incarcerate   [ ] to indicate, suggest; to contain potentially;
                              express indirectly
(10) impromptu   [ ] lacking meaning or point; silly
(11) impugn   [ ] to make, invent, or arrange offhand
(12) incipient   [ ] inattentive; unintentional

(1) inchoate   [   ] illogical; irrelevant; unimportant

(2) incite   [   ] to teach and impress by frequent repetitions or admonitions

(3) incongruous   [   ] with one's identity concealed

(4) inclement   [   ] incapable of being fatigued; untiring

(5) incur   [   ] to charge with some offense; accuse

(6) incumbent   [   ] only partly in existence; imperfectly formulated

(7) impunity   [   ] one of a series of additions; an increase

(8) inculcate   [   ] to bring down upon oneself; become liable to

(9) inconsequential   [   ] physically severe; stormy

(10) indict   [   ] to move to action; stir up; spur on

(11) incognito   [   ] imposed as a duty or obligation

(12) increment   [   ] exemption from penalty or loss

(13) indefatigable   [   ] incompatible; not conforming

(1) indigenous   [   ] incapable of being avoided

(2) indolent   [   ] poor; impoverished; needy

(3) infer   [   ] to persuade, influence; bring about

(4) inextricable   [   ] too valuable or excellent to be measured; cannot be estimated

(5) ineluctable   [   ] not to be persuaded or moved; unyielding; relentless; inflexible

(6) induce   [   ] to inspire with a foolish or extravagant love or admiration

(7) inexplicable   [   ] incapable of being subdued or overthrown; s   teady

(8) indigent   [   ] original in a particular region; inborn; native; innate

(9) inevitable   [   ] impossible to get free from; unable to disentangle; unsolvable

(10) infatuate   [   ] to conclude from facts or assumption

(11) inexpugnable   [   ] not to be avoided; inevitable

(12) inexorable   [   ] incapable of being explained

(13) inestimable   [   ] averse to activity or effort; habitually lazy

QUIZ

1. Children just out of school in spring are most likely to:
(a) hearken   (b) gambol   (c) implore   (d) gesticulate

2. College students just after mid-terms are most likely to:
(a) hearken   (b) hector   (c) imbibe   (d) incite

3. Most people would prefer a neighbor known for his:
(a) hubris   (b) gasconade   (c) hyperbole   (d) felicity

4. On a long plane ride you wish to relax; you prefer the one seated next to you to be:
(a) impetuous   (b) garrulous   (c) haughty   (d) imperturbable

5. The group encounters a Gordian knot. To solve it, we prefer someone noted for his:
(a) finesse   (b) hedonism   (c) histrionics   (d) hebetude

6. An employer seeks to hire someone whose records, credentials, and résumés are:
(a) illusory   (b) impeccable   (c) frivolous   (d) inexplicable

7. To "brainwash" someone, it is necessary to:
(a) impugn   (b) implicate   (c) inculcate   (d) indict, that person

8. Ideas involving public debate or discussion are:
(a) facetious   (b) forensic   (c) gauche   (d) inconsequential

9. An iconoclast is known for being:
(a) heterodox   (b) gullible   (c) glib   (d) gregarious

10. Coaches want their players to be:
(a) feckless   (b) flaccid   (c) fatuous   (d) formidable

BONUS QUIZ

The etymology and old meaning are given. Enter a word derived from each set.

Example: L ab- + origine **ETYMOLOGY**	from the beginning **OLD MEANING**	aborigine **WORD**
L abscondere	to hide from	
L abstinere	to hold back	
L absurdus	not to be heard of	
L adulari	to wag the tail	
L affluere	to flow abundantly	
L ambigere	wander about; be in doubt	
L amicus	friend	
Gk amnestia	forgetfulness	
Gk ana- + chronos	against time	
Gk analogos	proportionate; in due ratio	
L ancilla	servant	
L ad- + nihil	to nothing	
Gk anomalos	uneven	
L arbiter	a witness; judge; umpire	
L astus	craft, cunning	
L augere	to increase; enrich	
L auxilium	help	
L avarus	greedy	

SEGMENT FIVE

ETYMOLOGY	OLD MEANING
WORD	**NEW MEANING**

L infinitus	infinite, boundless, endless; indefinite
infinitesimal	**immeasurably small; close to zero**
L inflatus	blown up, swollen
inflation	**more money and fewer goods leading to higher prices**
L infligere	to dash against; to strike
inflict	**to give by striking; to impose**
L infringere	to break; to bruise
infringe	**to encroach upon; to trespass**
L infundere	to pour in or on
infuse	**to introduce; inspire, animate**
L ingenuus	native, innate; free-born
ingenue	**a naïve or inexperienced person**
L ingenuus	native, innate; free-born
ingenuous	**innocent; childlike; simple; candid**
L ingratus	disagreeable; unwelcome; thankless
ingrate	**an ungrateful person**
L in- + gratia	in + charm, grace; favor, influence
ingratiating	**capable of, or intended to, gaining favor**
L inhaerere	cling to, adhere; to be always in
inherent	**involved in the nature of; belonging by nature or habit**
L inimicus	unfriendly, hostile; enemy
inimical	**hostile, unfriendly; harmful, adverse**
L in- + imitabilis	not + imitable
inimitable	**not capable of being imitated; matchless**
L iniquus	unequal, uneven; adverse; unfair
iniquity	**gross injustice; wickedness; sin**
L injungere	to join, attach; to impose, inflict
injunction	**court order to require an act to be done, or to refrain from doing it**

SAMPLE SENTENCES

infinitesimal The differences in their political ideologies are *infinitesimal*. They are *immeasurably small*, practically *next to zero*.

inflation Higher prices result when there is *inflation*. When there is an *increase in the money supply with no increase in available goods*, it is called *inflation*.

inflict Many thought the scandal would *inflict* a damaging blow to his career. As it turned out, it did not *give a striking blow* to his career at all.

infringe Totalitarian governments *infringe* upon the rights of their citizens routinely. They *encroach upon, trespass upon*, the lives of their people.

infuse The return of the star player *infused* the team with renewed confidence; it *inspired* the players, *animated* them.

ingénue It is unwise to appoint an *ingénue* to a position of great responsibility and importance. A *naïve* or *inexperienced person* belongs elsewhere.

ingenuous If you want the truth, go to an *ingenuous* individual; try to find an *innocent, childlike, simple, naïve, and candid* person.

ingrate He chased the man for several blocks to give him the wallet he had dropped on the sidewalk The *ingrate* didn't even thank him. What an *ungrateful person*!

ingratiating The little girl's *ingratiating* smile won her dad over to her wishes nearly every time. Her expression was *capable of*, and *intended for, gaining* his *favor*.

inherent Some talents are *inherent*, not learned or acquired; they are abilities *belonging by nature* to some individuals.

inimical Sneezing in crowded, public areas can cause *inimical* effects in other people; it can cause *unfavorable, adverse* results.

inimitable Certain comedians and actors possess *inimitable* gestures and ways of portrayal. These inherent talents are *matchless, not capable of being imitated*.

iniquity Some think that inequality among humans is an *iniquity*. In reality, it is a law of nature and a benefit to mankind, not a *gross injustice* or *sin*.

injunction One example of an *injunction* is a restraining order, which is a *court order to refrain from doing something*.

ETYMOLOGY	OLD MEANING
WORD	**NEW MEANING**

L innasci	to be born in
innate	**belonging to the nature of something; native; inherent**
L in- + nocere	not + to harm, hurt
innocuous	**producing no injury; harmless**
L innuere	to give a nod
innuendo	**oblique allusion; a hint; insinuation**
L inordinatus	disordered, irregular
inordinate	**exceeding reasonable limits; immoderate**
L in- + satiare	not + to satisfy, appease, fill, saturate
insatiable	**incapable of being satisfied**
L in-+ scrutari	not + to search, probe into, find out
inscrutable	**hard to grasp; mysterious**
L insidiari	to lie in ambush; lie in wait for; plot against
insidious	**harmful but enticing; developing undetected gradually**
L insinuare	bring in stealthily; creep in
insinuate	**convey in indirect wording; hint; imply**
L in- + sapidus	not + savory
insipid	**lacking qualities that interest; dull; flat**
L insolens	unusual; excessive; extravagant
insolent	**insultingly contemptuous; overbearing**
Fr in- + soucier	not + to trouble, disturb
insouciant	**lighthearted; unconcerned; nonchalant**
L instigare	to goad, incite
instigate	**to goad or urge forward; provoke**
L interdicere	to forbid
interdict	**to prohibit, forbid**
L internecinus	murderous; of extermination
internecine	**mutually destructive; involving conflict within a group**

SAMPLE SENTENCES

innate Some characteristics of an individual are acquired, while others are *innate*; that is, they are *existing from birth, belonging to the nature of* (*something*), or *inherent*.

innocuous The man tells his friends that his dog is *innocuous*, that he's "all bark and no bite;" he is *harmless, unlikely to cause hostility*, and *producing no injury*.

innuendo He attacked his opponent's position by *innuendo*; that is, he did not come out directly against it, but by *devious, indirect allusion*, by a *hint*.

inordinate Many tools and machines make an *inordinate* amount of noise, e.g., buzz saws, jack hammers, leaf blowers, etc. They make *immoderate* amounts of racket, the kind *exceeding reasonable limits*.

insatiable Learning leads to an *insatiable* desire for more knowledge, a desire that is *incapable of being satisfied*.

inscrutable Trying to figure out the *inscrutable* tax code is a challenge for millions of citizens each year; it is *hard to grasp, mysterious*, and *not readily interpreted*.

insidious There are *insidious* diseases, eating habits, and commitments; they are *harmful but enticing, treacherous*, and *developing undetected gradually*.

insinuate To say that any fool can understand this, even a certain person we know, is to *insinuate* that the person is a fool; it *conveys in indirect wording, hints*, and *implies* such a message.

insipid A garrulous speaker who descants is *insipid*; he is *dull, flat*, and *uninteresting*.

insolent The *insolent* nephew of the CEO had to be let go because of his *insultingly contemptuous* attitude.

insouciant He was trying to impress her with his knowledge, but she was *insouciant* about the details of the grain market. She was *unconcerned, nonchalant*.

instigate Who in his right mind would *instigate* a plan to build housing on the fairway of a famous golf course? Who would *provoke, incite*, or *urge forward* such an idea?

interdict Current laws *interdict* the presence of weapons in airports and in courtrooms. The laws *prohibit*, or *forbid*, weapons in these places.

internecine Any organization, e.g., a team, military unit, or political party, that engages in *internecine* warfare, is doomed to disaster. A *mutually destructive* battle, one *involving conflict within a group*, will severely damage its cause.

ETYMOLOGY	OLD MEANING
WORD	**NEW MEANING**

L in toto
in toto

on the whole
totally, entirely; altogether

L in- + transigere
intransigent

not + to carry through; finish; settle
uncompromising

L intrepidus
intrepid

calm; brave; undisturbed
fearless, brave, and able to withstand hardship, adversity, or stress

L intrinsecus
intrinsic

on the inside
belonging to the essential nature of

L intuitus
intuition

look at, watch; contemplate, consider
knowledge of conviction; quick insight

L inundare
inundate

to overflow, flood
to cover with a flood; to overwhelm

ME en- + ure
inure

en- + the use, custom
accustom to accept something undesirable; to habituate

L invehere
invective

to bring in, carry in; attack
insult, abuse; violent verbal attack

MFr aveugler
inveigle

to blind, hoodwink
to win over by trickery; to entice

L inveteratus
inveterate

of long standing
firmly established; habitual

L invidia
invidious

envy, jealousy, ill-will; unpopularity
causing discontent, envy, or resentment

L in- + violare
inviolable

not + to violate or break or do violence to
secure from violation or assault

L invocare
invoke

to call, call upon; appeal to
call forth, put into effect; implement

SAMPLE SENTENCES

in toto The committee agreed to the plan *in toto*. The members were in accord with the idea *totally* and *entirely*.

intransigent He was *intransigent* about any ideas of appeasement of those with different viewpoints; he was *uncompromising* in his attitude.

intrepid The two men managed their kayak through the fiercely raging white waters in an *intrepid* manner; they were *fearless* and *brave* throughout the ordeal.

intrinsic Certain traits, e.g., head shape, eye color, and foot size, are *intrinsic*; that is, they are *belonging to* or *situated within* the body.

intuition Despite very little study, she wrote the right answers by *intuition*. She was able to do this by virtue of *knowledge of conviction* and *quick and ready insight*.

inundate The beleaguered secretary was *inundated* by a flood of paperwork and phone calls. She was *overwhelmed* by it all, but faced it in an intrepid manner.

inure Their dilemma was whether to *inure* themselves to the bad neighbors or move at great cost. Should they *accustom* themselves *to accept something undesirable*, to *habituate?* In short, to *get used to something* they *don't particularly like*.

invective He abided the *invective* of the hostile disrupters with equanimity. He handled their *violent verbal attacks*, *abusive speech*, and *insults* with aplomb.

inveigle Using clever means, the coach *inveigled* the highly prized recruit into coming to the university; he *won him over by sly means;* he *enticed* him into coming.

inveterate He is the *inveterate* baseball fan, attending not only all the home games, but the away games as well. He is a *long time, firmly established,* and *habitual* fan.

invidious In a partisan speech, he made an *invidious* distinction between the candidates; it was a distinction *causing resentment*.

inviolable An armed citizen feels far more *inviolable* in his home than an unarmed one, in the event of facing an assailant.The former is more *secure from violation or assault*.

invoke The witness *invoked* the Fifth Amendment in order to avoid answering the question. He *put it into effect,* or *implemented* it.

| ETYMOLOGY | OLD MEANING |
WORD	NEW MEANING
Gk eiron **irony**	dissembler in speech **incongruity between result and expectation; reversal between them**
L in- + refragari **irrefragable**	not + to oppose, thwart **impossible to deny or refute**
L irresolutus **irresolute**	not slackened **uncertain how to act; vacillating**
L iterum **iterate**	again, a second time **to say or do again; repeat**
L itineris **itinerary**	journey, way; route, road **the route of a planned journey**
Fr *tour d'ivoire* **ivory tower**	*lit.,* tower of ivory **a dreamy attitude divorced from reality or practical matters**
L jejunus **jejune**	lacking food; hungry **devoid of interest; dull; immature**
OFr jeu parti **jeopardy**	divided game **danger, hazard**
Ar jihad **jihad**	a contest, war **a holy war; a crusade for a belief**
Fr joie de vivre **joie de vivre**	*lit.,* joy of living **keen enjoyment of life**
L jocosus **jocose**	humorous; playful **given to joking; humorous, witty**
L jungere **junta**	to join together, unite **a group controlling a government after a revolutionary takeover**
L juxta + E position **juxtapose**	near; next door to **to place side by side**

SAMPLE SENTENCES

irony That a conference on global warming had to be postponed because of heavy snows and sub-freezing temperatures is a touch of *irony*; it is a *reversal between the result and the expectation.*

irrefragable That an extensive vocabulary is a great asset in school and beyond is *irrefragable*, that is, *impossible to deny or refute.*

irresolute Tourists in a strange city sometimes appear *irresolute*; that is, they seem *uncertain how to act, vacillating* about what to do or where to go.

iterate Sometimes it is necessary for a professor to *iterate* an abstruse point. In order that the students don't miss the idea, he should *say it again, repeat* it.

itinerary Before going on a vacation trip, it can be advantageous to make an *itinerary*. It helps to determine the *route of a planned journey* before leaving.

ivory tower To say that someone should come down from his *ivory tower* means he has a *dreamy attitude divorced from reality or practical matters* and should "get real."

jejune People lacking knowledge of a subject will make *jejune* statements in attempts to analyze or discuss it. They will make *dull, insipid,* or *immature* comments.

jeopardy His bad grade on the final examination put his chances of getting into graduate school in *jeopardy*. He was in *danger* of not being accepted.

jihad In certain foreign countries a soccer match takes on the character of a *jihad*; it becomes a seeming *holy war* among the fans..

joie de vivre A hedonist hopes to have *joie de vivre* all the time. His main goal is to have *keen enjoyment of life* as much as possible.

jocose After listening to jejune commentary from the discursive dullard, it is refreshing to hear *jocose* remarks by a comedian. His epigrams are *humorous* and *witty.*

junta An unstable country will sometimes be run by a *junta*; that is, a *group controlling the government after a revolutionary takeover.*

juxtapose The club committee was trying to decide whether to put the two tennis courts in separate places, or to *juxtapose* them, that is, *place* them *side by side.*

ETYMOLOGY **WORD**	OLD MEANING **NEW MEANING**
Gk kinetos **kinetic**	moving **relating to motion; active, lively; dynamic, energizing**
Gk kleptein + menos **kleptomania**	to steal + spirit **impulse to steal without economic motive**
L labis **labile**	sinking, fall; ruin, destruction **open to change or breakdown; unstable**
L lacrimosus **lachrymose**	tearful; lamentable **tending to cause tears; mournful**
Gk lakonikos **laconic**	*from* Spartan terseness of speech **using a minimum of words; concise**
L lambere **lambent**	to lick, lap; touch **flickering; softly radiant; brilliant playing lightly over a surface**
L lamentarius **lament**	sorrowful **express sorrow; regret strongly; deplore**
Fr lampons! **lampoon**	let us guzzle! (gulp or swig down!) **to mock or ridicule**
L languere **languish**	to be weary, weak; droop; be idle, dull **be depressed; have less vitality; become dispirited; suffer neglect**
OFr large **largesse**	generous **liberal giving; excessive gratuities; big tips**
L lassitudinis **lassitude**	fatigue; heaviness **weariness; debility; fatigue; listlessness**
L latere **latent**	to lie hidden; be unknown, escape notice **present but not now visible or active**
L levis **levity**	light; slight, trivial; fickle, unreliable **excessive frivolity; lack of seriousness; fickleness**

SAMPLE SENTENCES

kinetic A class will listen to, and be inspired by, a *kinetic* professor who teaches even a somewhat dull subject. Students like a *lively, dynamic,* and *energizing* professor.

kleptomania Some unfortunate kids are afflicted with *kleptomania.* It is the *impulse to steal without economic motive.*

labile Some people are emotionally *labile;* many substances are heat-*labile* or acid-*labile;* that is, they are *subject to change or breakdown,* or *unstable,* in these cases.

lachrymose Some *lachrymose* circumstances are *mournful,* but equally *lachrymose* is the peeling of raw onions, a process *tending to cause tears.*

laconic It is often funny to hear someone give a *laconic* answer to a lengthy, highly detailed and garrulous question, one *using a minimum of words,* a *concise* answer.

lambent It is delightful to see the *lambent* rays of the sunset on a lake. They are the *softly radiant, flickering* rays that signal the end of the day.

lament The management, the waiter, and the dinner guests *lamented* the spilling of a bottle of a rare Château Petris '89 all over the table. They *mourned aloud, wailed,* and *strongly regretted* the horrible tragedy.

lampoon During election years it is common for cartoonists to *lampoon* the politicians. They find it fun to *mock or ridicule* them in their cartoons.

languish The reasons why some people *languish* should be investigated. Why should people *be depressed, have less vitality, become dispirited,* or *suffer neglect?*

largesse The big spender displayed his *largesse* in the restaurant, ordering expensive wines for his guests. He was noted for *liberal giving, excessive gratuities,* and *leaving big tips.*

lassitude He was in a state of *lassitude* just after finishing the marathon. A friend asked him to play tennis, unaware of his *weariness, debility, fatigue,* and *listlessness.*

latent The management thought the new salesman had a *latent* talent; they believed it was *present but not now visible or active,* that it would show up later.

levity Many attendees looked askance at the *levity* on the part of two boys at the funeral; *excessive frivolity* and *lack of proper seriousness* are very inappropriate at such occasions.

ETYMOLOGY	OLD MEANING
WORD	**NEW MEANING**

| MFr lier + -aison | to bind, tie + action |
| **liaison** | **a close connection; interrelationship** |

| L locus | place, site, locality, region |
| **lieu** | **place, stead; (in lieu = instead)** |

| L limbus | fringe, hem; edge, border |
| **limbo** | **a place of neglect or oblivion; intermediate or transitional state** |

| L illuminare | to light up; enlighten; embellish |
| **limn** | **draw; to outline in sharp detail; describe** |

| L limpidus | clear |
| **limpid** | **clear; simple in style; serene, untroubled** |

| Gk litanos | entreating |
| **litany** | **a repetitive recital or chant** |

| L littera | letter |
| **literal** | **actual, obvious; exact, word for word** |

| L litteratus | with letters on it; educated, learned |
| **literati** | **the educated class; men of letters** |

| L litigare | to quarrel; to go to law |
| **litigation** | **the practice of taking legal action** |

| Gk logistike | art of calculating |
| **logistics** | **the handling of the details of an operation; strategy** |

| L loqui | to speak, talk, say; talk about |
| **loquacious** | **given to excessive talking; garrulous** |

| L lucere | to shine, be light, clear |
| **lucid** | **sane; intelligible; clear to the understanding; clear** |

| L lucrari | to gain, win, acquire |
| **lucrative** | **producing wealth; profitable** |

SAMPLE SENTENCES

liaison It is important that a university maintain a strong *liaison* with its alumni. A *close connection*, or *interrelationship*, is an advantage to both.

lieu This word literally means *place* or *stead* but is usually used with the preposition *in*. The expression *in lieu* means *instead*. One often hears *in lieu of*, meaning *instead of*.

limbo The plan is in *limbo* since the committee didn't know what to do about it. It is in *an intermediate or transitional state* for an indefinite period.

limn The star witness was called upon to *limn* the situation as best she could. She was able to verbally *draw* a picture, to *outline in sharp detail* the circumstances.

limpid a *limpid* stream, *clear, transparent;* a *limpid* essay, *simple in style;* a *limpid* forest, *serene and untroubled.* (phrases only for a change).

litany One is likely to hear at least one *litany* at a football game or a political convention. A *repetitive recital* or *chant* from the partisans is not uncommon.

literal We have already seen many examples of *literal* "Old Meanings" of etymological words. They are the *actual, exact, word for word* meanings.

literati They are members of the *literati, the educated class.* He is a *literati*, a *man of letters.*

litigation Such things as lawsuits, estate settlements, divorces, and restraining orders are settled by *litigation*, which is *the practice of taking legal action.*

logistics Those in charge of a group tour, for example, are responsible for the *logistics*. They take care of the *handling of the details of the operation*, the *strategy.*

loquacious It has been demonstrated that a few adult beverages can make even a laconic person *loquacious*, that is, *given to excessive talking*, or *garrulous.*

lucid Students are happy if the professor's lectures are *lucid*, that is, *intelligible* or *clear to the understanding*, especially when covering abstruse material.

lucrative The more *lucrative* enterprises in a country, the healthier its economy. Those *profitable* businesses, the ones *producing wealth*, benefit the society.

Etymology	Old Meaning
Word	**New Meaning**
L lugubris	mourning; disastrous
lugubrious	**sad; disposed to gloom; dismal**
L lumen	light; lamp, torch
luminary	**a brilliantly outstanding person**
L luridus	pale yellow; ghastly pallid
lurid	**causing horror; gruesome**
after Niccolo Machiavelli	1469 – 1527 Italian philosopher
machiavellian	**characterized by political cunning, duplicity, or bad faith**
L machinari	to devise, contrive; plot, scheme
machinate	**to plan or plot, esp. to do harm**
L magnanimus	great, brave
magnanimous	**generous of mind; forgiving**
Fr maître d'	maître d'hôtel, *lit.*, master of house
maître d'	**a head steward; headwaiter**
Fr maladroit	clumsy, awkward
maladroit	**lacking adroitness; inept; awkward**
Fr mal- + aise	bad + comfort
malaise	**a vague, indefinite feeling of ill-being**
from Mrs. Malaprop	character in *the Rivals*, 1775 comedy
malapropism	**humorous use of a word sounding like another but ludicrously wrong in context**
L malignus	unkind, ill-natured, spiteful
malign	**to injure by speaking ill of; defame**
Fr malingre	sickly
malinger	**to feign incapacity (e.g., sickness) in order to avoid work or duty**
L mandatus	command
mandatory	**constituting a command; obligatory**

SAMPLE SENTENCES

lugubrious After the tough loss, there was a *lugubrious* aura in the locker room. It was a *mournful, dismal,* and *gloomy* atmosphere.

luminary He was both a *luminary* in his field as well as an inspiration to beginning students; they were grateful to this *brilliantly outstanding person.*

lurid The witness was averse to describing the *lurid* details of the case. It was a most *gruesome* scene.

machiavellian Some societies had to endure *machiavellian* governments. They were *characterized by political cunning, duplicity, or bad faith.*

machinate A cabal intended to *machinate* against the new office manager; those involved met to *plan or plot to do harm* to her by undermining her efforts on the job.

magnanimous In victory he was *magnanimous* toward his former enemy; he was very *forgiving* and *showing generosity of mind.*

maître d' Habitués of a famous restaurant find it advantageous to know the *maître d'* quite well; he is the *headwaiter,* who makes certain that everything is excellent.

maladroit A beginning waiter who is *maladroit* has a long way to go before becoming a maître d'. He must get over being *inept* or *awkward.*

malaise Unfortunate is he who suffers from *malaise* on an important day, one involving a big interview or final examination. Who needs a *vague, indefinite feeling of ill-being?*

malapropism She likes to use a *malapropism* now and then. The *humorous misuse of a word,* such as "polo bear" and "an allegory on the banks of the Nile," are good examples.

malign Part of the machination was to *malign* him, to *say damaging things about* him, to *speak ill of* him, to *defame* him.

malinger He decided to *malinger* that Saturday in order to attend a football game in which his brother was the visiting team's quarterback. He *pretended sickness in order to avoid work* that day. He *faked his illness.*

mandatory It is *mandatory* to have a driver's license in order to operate an automobile. It is *required* by law; it is *obligatory.*

ETYMOLOGY **WORD**	OLD MEANING **NEW MEANING**
L manifestare **manifest**	to disclose **make evident by showing; reveal**
L manipulus **manipulate**	a bundle (esp. of hay) **to manage, control, change, or doctor by artful means to one's advantage**
Skt. *akin to* mantar **mantra**	thinker **a mystical formula; verbal spell; incantation**
after Gen Jean Martinet **martinet**	17th Cent. French drillmaster **strict disciplinarian; stickler for rigid rules**
of Mary Magdalene **maudlin**	a weeping, regretful sinner **weakly, gushingly sentimental**
ME mawke **mawkish**	maggot **sickly, childishly sentimental**
L maximus **maxim**	greatest, largest **a general truth; proverbial saying**
L mea culpa **mea culpa**	through my fault **acknowledgement of personal fault**
Gk meandros **meander**	Meandros (Menderes) river in Asia Minor **follow a winding course; ramble; wander aimlessly or casually**
L medius **mediate**	middle, middle of; neutral **interpose between parties; reconcile differences**
L meditari **meditate**	think over, contemplate; reflect **focus one's thoughts on; ponder over**
Gk melan + chole **melancholy**	black + bile **depression of spirits; dejection**
Fr mêler **mélange**	to mix; blend; mingle **a mixture often of incongruous elements**

SAMPLE SENTENCES

manifest Given a chance to play, she was able to *manifest* her athletic skills and talents. She could *show plainly* her abilities.

manipulate He was able to *manipulate* the numbers in such a way so as to make his rival look bad. He *changed them by artful means to his advantage.*

mantra It is common to hear a *mantra* repeated by a partisan group. It is a *verbal spell* or *incantation, a formula of words designed to produce a particular effect.*

martinet The new office manager was a *martinet*, which upset the easy-going routine. A cabal was formed to "get" the *strict disciplinarian* and *stickler for rigid rules.*

maudlin People were turned off by his overly *maudlin* pleas; the *weakly, gushingly sentimental* lamentations did not go over well.

mawkish Rather than malinger, he made up this *mawkish* story about a sick aunt. It was a *sickly, childishly sentimental* tale of woe.

maxim "There's no such thing as a free lunch," and "You can't score if you don't have the ball," are common maxims. Each is a *general truth*, or a *proverbial saying.*

mea culpa If a person finds out later that he screwed up, he says or writes *mea culpa* to those involved. In brief, it means *my fault*, an *acknowledgement of personal fault.*

meander After being on a structured and rigid guided tour, it is relaxing to *meander*. It is sometimes exciting to *wander aimlessly or casually* about.

mediate To prevent internecine warfare, he decided to *mediate* between the two board members. He sought to *interpose between* them and *reconcile* their *differences.*

meditate She wanted to *meditate* on the proposition before making a final decision. She decided to *focus* her *thoughts on* the offer, to *ponder over* it.

melancholy It is important to avoid *melancholy* after a loss or setback. Eschew any *depression of spirits* or *dejection.*

mélange Send for the maître d'! This new waiter is making a strange-looking *mélange*, a *mixture of incongruous elements.*

ETYMOLOGY	OLD MEANING
WORD	NEW MEANING

L mel + fluere	honey + to flow
mellifluous	**having a smooth rich flow**
L mendax	lying; deceptive, unreal
mendacious	**deceptive; false; dishonest**
ME meynie	household
menial	**of servants; lowly; servile; lacking dignity**
after F. A. Mesmer	Austrian mystic of "animal magnetism"
mesmerize	**to hypnotize; to spellbind, fascinate**
L metus	fear, alarm, anxiety
meticulous	**excessively careful about details; fussy**
L minationis	threat
minatory	**having a menacing quality; threatening**
Fr mignon	darling; dainty
minion	**a servile dependent; subordinate official**
L minutus	small; paltry
minutia	**a minute or minor detail** (usu. used in pl.-**ae**)
Gk misanthropos	hating mankind
misanthrope	**one who hates or distrusts mankind**
L miscere	to mix, mingle, blend; combine
miscible	**capable of being mixed or mixing in**
MFr mescroire	to disbelieve
miscreant	**one who behaves criminally**
MFr mesnommer	to misname
misnomer	**use of a wrong name; a wrong name**
L mitigare	to ripen, soften; to calm, pacify
mitigate	**make or become milder, less harsh; alleviate**

SAMPLE SENTENCES

mellifluous His sales pitch was nearly irresistible because of his *mellifluous* voice, one *having a smooth, rich flow.*

mendacious He went from hyperbole to *mendacious* tales about his latest fishing trips and golf scores. The details were *deceptive* and *false.*

menial He resented being relegated from decision-making functions to *menial* chores. He did not like doing *lowly, servile* work, or tasks *lacking dignity.*

mesmerize He was able to *mesmerize* quite a few people with his mendacious accounts. He seemed to *spellbind* them, *fascinate* them with his stories.

meticulous In preparing for the big party, the hostess was *meticulous* about everything; indeed, she is noted for being *excessively careful about details,* or *fussy.*

minatory The dinner conversation stopped as one of the guests started making *minatory* remarks to one across the table. He used *threatening* words, those *having a menacing quality.*

minion He acted like a big shot at social functions, but in the main office he was but a *minion,* a *minor, subordinate official.*

minutia The martinet was meticulous even with a *minutia,* with each and every *minute or minor detail.*

misanthrope The *misanthrope* is overly cynical. He is *one who hates or distrusts mankind.*

miscible Oil and water don't mix, but alcohol and water are *miscible;* that is, they are *capable of being mixed or mixing in.* So are oil and kerosene.

miscreant It is important to keep a wide variety of weapons, e.g., knives, nooses, ice picks, guns, or explosives, out the hands of any *miscreant,* or *one who acts criminally.*

misnomer To refer to a spider as an insect is a *misnomer.* It is an arachnid, so the term, insect, is the *use of a wrong term or wrong terminology.*

mitigate New medicines can *mitigate* severe pains and illnesses. They can *alleviate* them, *make* them *less severe or painful, make* them *milder.*

ETYMOLOGY	OLD MEANING
WORD	**NEW MEANING**

Gk mimneskesthai	to remember
mnemonic	**assisting or intended to assist memory; of or relating to memory**

L modicus	moderate; middling; small
modicum	**a small portion; a limited quantity**

L medius	middle, the middle of; intermediate
moiety	**one of two approximately equal parts**

L mollis	soft, supple; tender, gentle
mollify	**to soothe in temper; appease; assuage**

Gk mon- +lithos	one + stone
monolithic	**showing rigidly fixed uniformity**

OE mot, *akin to* metan	to meet
moot	**open to question or discussion; made abstract or academic; debatable**

L mordere	to bite, bite into; to sting, hurt
mordacious	**biting in style or manner; caustic**

L mos	nature, manner; mood; custom
mores	**moral attitudes; habits, manners**

L mors, mortis	death; corpse
mortify	**to subject to severe embarrassment; to shame**

ME *perhaps* mot	mote, speck
motley	**aried in color; composed of diverse and often incongruous elements**

L mundus	toilet gear; universe, world; mankind
mundane	**practical, temporary; ordinary; earthly**

MFr muser	to gape; to idle
muse	**be absorbed in thought; meditate; ponder**

Gk myrioi	countless, ten thousand
myriad	**ten thousand; an immense number**

SAMPLE SENTENCES

mnemonic He had trouble remembering names, especially at fairly large gatherings, so he took a *mnemonic* course, one *relating to memory*.

modicum He gave a speech with barely a *modicum* of sincerity in it. His talk contained a *small, limited amount* of sincerity.

moiety It was agreed that whoever cut the remainder of the pie into two slices, the other boy would get to choose his *moiety* first. After a careful cut by the first boy, the second, after some hesitation, chose his *approximately equal part*.

mollify Thinking she had not been invited to the party, the fact that her invitation showed up at a neighbor's house served to *mollify* her; it served to *appease* or *assuage* her.

monolithic A great diversity of ideas is much better than a *monolithic* dogma. Free and open inquiry is preferable to an opinion *showing rigidly fixed uniformity*.

moot Whether he caught the ball inbounds or out of bounds was a *moot* point, *open to question or discussion, debatable*. However, a penalty nullified the play, so the issue was *moot*, or *made abstract or academic*.

mordacious She writes *mordacious* articles; they are *biting, caustic* columns.

mores Before visiting a foreign country for the first time, it is wise to learn the *mores* of the populace. It is advisable to know the *moral attitudes, habits,* and *manners*.

mortify Some of her husband's actions in public and at social gatherings *mortify* her. They *shame* her; they *subject her to severe embarrassment*.

motley While most college bands are precisely, neatly, and uniformly attired, there is a certain *motley* group of musicians, one *varied in color* and *composed of diverse elements*.

mundane He mortified the more sensitive guests at the table by asking something so *mundane* as the price of the house special, something so *practical* and *ordinary*.

muse She *mused* whether to hold or sell her stocks; she *meditated* and *pondered* over it.

myriad A dean of admissions is faced with a *myriad* of applications, dinner invitations, and letters of recommendation each year – an *immense number* of them.

ETYMOLOGY	OLD MEANING
WORD	**NEW MEANING**

Ar nab
nabob
governor
an important or rich man

Ar nazir
nadir
opposite
the lowest point

L nativus
naïve
inborn, native, natural
simple, artless, ingenuous; credulous

L nasci
nascent
to be born, originate; be produced
coming into existence; beginning to develop

L nebulosus
nebulous
misty, cloudy
indistinct, vague

L nefas
nefarious
wickedness, sin, wrong; horror!
flagrantly wicked; evil; vicious

Gk nemesis
nemesis
punishment; righteous anger
a formidable and usu. victorious opponent or rival; bane

Gk neophytos
neophyte
newly planted, newly converted
a new convert; novice; beginner

L nepos
nepotism
grandson; nephew
favoritism shown a relative in hiring

L nectere
nexus
to tie, fasten, bind; weave
connection, link

L nihil
nihilism
nothing
belief that existence is senseless, that destruction of society is desirable

L nimius
nimiety
too great, too much, excessive
an excess, a redundancy

Skt nirvana
nirvana
lit. act of extinguishing
place of oblivion to care or pain; hoped for but unattainable goal; dream

SAMPLE SENTENCES

nabob There are many *nabobs* in the club, *men of great wealth or prominence.*

nadir The temperature in the area reaches its *nadir* in January, that is, its *lowest point*

naïve The disingenuous salesman sold the *naïve* young man far more bags of salt than he needed. The *simple, ingenuous,* and *credulous* man bought an excess of salt.

nascent The project is in the *nascent* stage. It is not yet underway, but it is *coming into existence, beginning to develop.*

nebulous Many students were totally lost by the professor's *nebulous* explanation of the abstruse principle. They felt that his presentation was *indistinct,* or *vague.*

nefarious Looters come up with *nefarious* schemes during disasters such as earthquakes. Their ideas are *flagrantly wicked, evil,* and *vicious.*

nemesis She was scheduled to play her *nemesis* in the quarter-final later in the day. She was going up against her *formidable and usually victorious opponent,* her *bane.*

neophyte The big boss was hesitant about putting a *neophyte* in charge of such a great responsibility; he was a *beginner,* a *novice,* a true *greenhorn.*

nepotism Although his nephew was a neophyte, the nabob hired him for an important position. It was a clear case of *nepotism,* that is, a *favoritism for a relative on the basis of the relationship.*

nexus There is a fairly strong *nexus* between education and success and happiness in life. A close *connection,* or *link,* exists between them.

nihilism It is probable that an advocate of *nihilism* would not get many votes on election day. One pushing the *belief that existence is senseless and useless,* that the *destruction of society is desirable,* is certain to get very few votes.

nimiety Some restaurants serve a *nimiety* of food, that is, an *excess* of it. Advertisers often iterate a *nimiety* of statements about the product, a *redundancy.*

nirvana To get away from mundane matters, some folks muse about a *nirvana,* a *place of oblivion to care or pain,* or *a hoped for but unreachable goal.*

ETYMOLOGY	OLD MEANING
WORD	**NEW MEANING**

L nisus **nisus**	pressure, effort; striving **perfective urge to reach a goal**
L nodus **nodus**	knot; knob; girdle **complication; difficulty**
Gk noetikos **noetic**	intellectual **relating to or based on the intellect**
L nomenclator **nomenclature**	a slave who told his master the names of people **process of naming; system of terms**
ME to then anes **nonce**	for the one purpose **used only once or for a special occasion**
non- + L describere **nondescript**	not + to copy out; draw, sketch **of no particular kind or class; not easily described**
L non sequitur **non sequitur**	it does not follow **a remark that does not follow logically from what has just been said**
MFr nuance **nuance**	shade of color **shade of difference; tiny variation**
L nubere **nubile**	to be married **of marriageable condition or age; attractive**
L nugatorius **nugatory**	futile **of little or no consequence; trifling; having no force; inoperative**
L nullus **nullify**	no, none; not, not at all; non-existent **to make of no value or consequence; to reduce to nothing; negate**

SAMPLE SENTENCES

nisus In going against her nemesis that day, she felt a *nisus* toward winning, a *striving, strong urge to reach that goal.*

nodus He explained to his meticulous boss, a martinet, that a *nodus* foiled his getting to work on time; it was a *complication*, a *difficulty,* involving a highway patrol cop.

noetic Instead of saying, "It doesn't take a rocket scientist..etc," why not say," It is hardly a *noetic* challenge to figure out such and such."? It's not very *intellectual* in scope.

nomenclature A student will encounter a *nomenclature* in a biology or organic chemistry course, a *system of naming* various classes, families, or other categories.

nonce The group had been scanning the trees for more than an hour, when Bob finally spotted a koala. Thus, "Koala Bob" was his *nonce* nickname, one *used only once.*

nondescript When pressed for details, the witness said the suspect was *nondescript* in his deposition; he was *of no particular type, not easily described.*

non sequitur His attorney said, "You are being charged with murder!" He replied, "I've got to get rid of the crabgrass in my lawn." That is a *non sequitur*, a *remark that has nothing to do with what was just said.*

nuance Dilettantes, while in art museums, like to point out *nuances* in color, lines, and forms, of the various paintings. They spot the *shades of difference,* the *slight variations.*

nubile A year or two after graduation, the proud, young heiress would consider herself *nubile*. She felt she would be *of marriageable condition* as well as *attractive.*

nugatory The neophyte's ideas for solving the Gordian knot proved to be *nugatory*; they were *trifling, of little or no consequence,* and *inoperative.*

nullify She wanted to *nullify* the contract after reading the fine print. She sought to *negate* it, *make* it *of no value, annul* it.

QUIZ

Match the following words with their meanings:

(1) ingenuous   [   ] hostile, unfriendly; harmful, adverse
(2) iniquity   [   ] increase in money supply relative to goods;
higher prices
(3) inflict   [   ] to encroach upon; to trespass
(4) ingénue   [   ] an ungrateful person
(5) inherent   [   ] not capable of being imitated; matchless
(6) inflation   [   ] court order to require an act or refrain
from one
(7) ingratiating   [   ] immeasurably small; next to or almost zero
(8) infuse   [   ] to give by striking; to impose
(9) inimical   [   ] involved in the nature of; belonging by
nature or habit
(10) injunction   [   ] gross injustice; wickedness; sin
(11) infinitesimal   [   ] innocent; childlike; simple; candid
(12) ingrate   [   ] a naïve or inexperienced person
(13) infringe   [   ] to introduce; inspire; animate
(14) inimitable   [   ] capable of, or intended to, gaining favor

(1) innate   [   ] insultingly contemptuous; overbearing
(2) insatiable   [   ] hard to grasp; mysterious
(3) internecine   [   ] exceeding reasonable limits; immoderate
(4) insinuate   [   ] to goad or urge forward; provoke
(5) innocuous   [   ] lighthearted; unconcerned; nonchalant
(6) insipid   [   ] treacherous; harmful but enticing;
developing undetected
(7) inscrutable   [   ] belonging to the nature of; native; inherent
(8) interdict   [   ] to convey in indirect wording; hint; imply
(9) inordinate   [   ] incapable of being satisfied
(10) insidious   [   ] producing no injury; harmless
(11) insouciant   [   ] deadly; mutually destructive; involving
conflict within a group
(12) instigate   [   ] to prohibit, forbid
(13) insolent   [   ] lacking qualities that interest; dull; flat

(1) in toto   [ ] firmly established; habitual
(2) inviolable   [ ] uncompromising
(3) inundate   [ ] accustom to something undesirable; to habituate, get used to
(4) innuendo   [ ] insult, abuse; violent verbal attack
(5) intransigent   [ ] fearless, brave, able to withstand hardship, adversity, or stress
(6) inure   [ ] to win over by trickery; to entice
(7) inveterate   [ ] secure from violation or assault
(8) invective   [ ] knowledge of conviction; quick insight
(9) intrinsic   [ ] totally, entirely; altogether
(10) intuition   [ ] oblique allusion; a hint; insinuation
(11) intrepid   [ ] belonging to the essential nature of
(12) inveigle   [ ] to cover with a flood; to overwhelm

(1) invidious   [ ] given to joking; humorous, witty
(2) invoke   [ ] to say or do again; to repeat
(3) irony   [ ] a dreamy attitude divorced from reality or practical matters
(4) irrefragable   [ ] uncertain how to act; vacillating
(5) jihad   [ ] danger, hazard
(6) iterate   [ ] to place side by side
(7) irresolute   [ ] causing discontent, envy, or resentment
(8) ivory tower   [ ] keen enjoyment of life
(9) itinerary   [ ] incongruity between result and expectation; reversal of them
(10) jejune   [ ] impossible to deny or refute
(11) juxtapose   [ ] to call forth, put into effect; implement
(12) jeopardy   [ ] the route of a planned journey
(13) jocose   [ ] devoid of interest; dull; immature
(14) joie de vivre   [ ] a holy war; crusade for a belief

(1) junta   [ ] the educated class; men of letters
(2) kinetic   [ ] tending to cause tears; mournful
(3) kleptomania   [ ] excessive frivolity; lack of seriousness;
                             fickleness
(4) lampoon   [ ] to express sorrow; regret strongly; deplore
(5) lachrymose   [ ] using a minimum of words; concise
(6) levity   [ ] impulse to steal without economic motive
(7) lament   [ ] to draw; to outline in sharp detail; to
                             describe
(8) lambent   [ ] open to change or breakdown; unstable
(9) literati   [ ] a group controlling a government after a
                             revolutionary coup
(10) labile   [ ] relating to motion; active, lively; dynamic,
energizing
(11) languish   [ ] to mock or ridicule
(12) laconic   [ ] flickering; softly radiant; brilliant; playing
                             lightly over a surface
(13) limn   [ ] to be depressed; have less vitality; be
                             dispirited; suffer neglect

(1) largesse   [ ] a close connection; interrelationship
(2) liaison   [ ] weariness; debility; fatigue; listlessness
(3) limpid   [ ] present but not now visible or active
(4) lieu   [ ] the practice of taking legal action
(5) lassitude   [ ] the handling of the details of an operation;
                             strategy
(6) limbo   [ ] a place, a stead
(7) litany   [ ] liberal giving; excessive gratuities; big tips
(8) loquacious   [ ] clear; simple in style; serene, untroubled
(9) latent   [ ] bright, lit up; sane; intelligible; clear to the
                             understanding; clear
(10) litigation   [ ] a place of neglect or oblivion; intermediate
                             or transitional state
(11) logistics   [ ] a repetitive recital or chant
(12) lucid   [ ] given to excessive talking; garrulous

(1) lugubrious　　　　[　] lacking adroitness; inept; awkward
(2) machiavellian　　　[　] actual, obvious; exact, word for word
(3) malaise　　　　　　[　] humorous misuse of a word sounding like another but wrong
(4) malign　　　　　　[　] to plan or plot, especially to do harm
(5) luminary　　　　　[　] a head steward; head waiter
(6) magnanimous　　　[　] causing horror; gruesome
(7) maladroit　　　　　[　] characterized by political cunning, duplicity, or bad faith
(8) lucrative　　　　　[　] constituting a command; obligatory
(9) malapropism　　　[　] a vague, indefinite feeling of ill-being
(10) literal　　　　　　[　] sad; disposed to gloom; dismal
(11) malinger　　　　　[　] to injure by speaking ill of; defame
(12) mandatory　　　　[　] generous of mind; forgiving
(13) maître d'　　　　　[　] a brilliantly outstanding person
(14) lurid　　　　　　　[　] producing wealth; profitable
(15) machinate　　　　[　] to feign injury or illness to avoid work or duty

(1) manifest　　　　　[　] to control or doctor by artful means to one's advantage
(2) maxim　　　　　　[　] a mystical formula; verbal spell; incantation
(3) maudlin　　　　　[　] sickly, childishly sentimental
(4) minion　　　　　　[　] a strict disciplinarian; stickler for rigid rules or details
(5) meander　　　　　[　] to interpose between parties; to reconcile (their) differences
(6) mélange　　　　　[　] a depression of spirits; dejection
(7) mantra　　　　　　[　] an acknowledgement of personal fault
(8) mediate　　　　　[　] to make evident by showing; reveal
(9) martinet　　　　　[　] a servile dependent; subordinate official
(10) mawkish　　　　　[　] weakly, gushingly sentimental
(11) melancholy　　　[　] a mixture often of incongruous elements
(12) mea culpa　　　　[　] a general truth; proverbial saying
(13) manipulate　　　[　] follow a winding course; wander aimlessly or casually

(1) meditate   [ ] to hypnotize; to spellbind, fascinate
(2) mellifluous   [ ] capable of being mixed or mixing in
(3) mendacious   [ ] of servants; lowly; servile; lacking dignity
(4) minutia   [ ] a wrong name; use of a wrong name
(5) mesmerize   [ ] make or become milder, less harsh or
                           severe; alleviate
(6) menial   [ ] deceptive; false; dishonest
(7) misanthrope   [ ] one who behaves criminally or viciously
(8) miscible   [ ] having a smooth rich flow
(9) misnomer   [ ] a tiny or minor detail
(10) mitigate   [ ] to focus one's thoughts on; ponder over
(11) miscreant   [ ] one who hates or distrusts mankind

(1) meticulous   [ ] varied in color; composed of diverse,
                           incongruous elements
(2) minatory   [ ] open to question or discussion; made aca
                           demic; debatable
(3) monolithic   [ ] practical, temporary; ordinary; earthly
(4) modicum   [ ] ten thousand; an immense number
(5) mollify   [ ] to make of no value or consequence;
                           reduce to nothing; negate
(6) motley   [ ] intended to assist memory; of or relating to
                           memory
(7) moiety   [ ] moral attitudes, habits, manners
(8) moot   [ ] showing rigidly fixed uniformity
(9) mortify   [ ] be absorbed in thought; meditate; ponder
(10) mordacious   [ ] excessively careful about details; fussy
(11) myriad   [ ] a small portion; a limited quantity
(12) mundane   [ ] having a menacing quality; threatening
(13) mores   [ ] one of two approximately equal parts;
                           approximate halves
(14) mnemonic   [ ] biting in style or manner; caustic
(15) muse   [ ] to soothe in temper; appease; assuage
(16) nullify   [ ] to subject to severe embarrassment; to shame

(1) nadir   [   ] a perfective urge to reach a goal

(2) nimiety   [   ] "existence is senseless, destruction of society is desirable"

(3) nabob   [   ] a new convert; novice; beginner

(4) nascent   [   ] flagrantly wicked; evil; vicious

(5) nepotism   [   ] a connection, a link

(6) nirvana   [   ] the lowest point

(7) nemesis   [   ] an important or rich man

(8) nefarious   [   ] indistinct, vague

(9) nisus   [   ] an excess, a redundancy

(10) nihilism   [   ] favoritism shown a relative in hiring

(11) neophyte   [   ] a formidable and usu. victorious opponent or rival; bane

(12) nebulous   [   ] coming into existence; beginning to develop

(13) nexus   [   ] place of oblivion to pain; hoped for but unreachable goal

(1) nodus   [   ] a shade of difference; very small variation

(2) noetic   [   ] simple, artless, ingenuous; credulous

(3) nondescript   [   ] of marriageable condition or age; attractive

(4) non sequitur   [   ] a complication; difficulty

(5) nugatory   [   ] used only once or for a special occasion

(6) nuance   [   ] a process of naming; system of terms

(7) nubile   [   ] relating to or based on the intellect

(8) nonce   [   ] of no particular kind or class; not easily described

(9) nomenclature   [   ] a remark that does not follow from what has just been said

(10) naïve   [   ] of little or no consequence; without force; trifling; inoperative

QUIZ

1. On a short flight you wish to be seated next to one whose conversational pattern is:
(a) insipid   (b) jocose   (c) lachrymose   (d) laconic

2. A maître d' prefers a client known for his or her:
(a) invective   (b) levity   (c) largesse   (d) melancholy

3. The person best described as inimitable is:
(a) an ingrate   (b) a minion   (c) an ingénue   (d) a luminary

4. Most people would prefer being involved with:
(a) a jihad   (b) a junta   (c) joie de vivre (d) an injunction

5. On a long and dangerous hike one must be:
(a) insouciant   (b) intrepid   (c) loquacious   (d) irresolute

6. A student prefers a professor whose lectures and discussions are:
(a) lucid   (b) jejune   (c) nebulous   (d) inscrutable

7. The group wants someone to run a large, detailed operation whose expertise is in:
(a) litigation   (b) nihilism   (c) logistics   (d) mnemonics

8. You want any infection you may incur to be:
(a) inimical   (b) innocuous   (c) insidious   (d) latent

9. The company wants to hire someone who will:
(a) lampoon   (b) malinger   (c) infuse   (d) machinate

10. Most parents want the teacher of their small children to be:
(a) a martinet   (b) maladroit   (c) magnanimous (d) intransigent

BONUS QUIZ

The French word and meaning is given. Match the English meaning with each.

FRENCH WORD AND MEANING	ENGLISH WORD AND/OR MEANING
1. aplomb—perpendicularity, equilibrium	[ ]kind, sort; category; style (art)
2. flamboyer—to blaze, flame up; to flash	[ ]lacking social grace; crude
3. tour d'ivoire—tower of ivory	[ ]something over which one has rights or exercises control
4. de rigueur—required by fashion; proper	[ ]lighthearted; unconcerned
5. duper—to trick, fool deceive	[ ]to fake sickness or injury
6. déjà vu—already seen	[ ]self-possession; confidence
7. coup de grace—a stroke of mercy	[ ]the very best, the highest elite
8. mignon—darling; dainty	[ ]head waiter; head steward
9. fief—stronghold; private kingdom	[ ]outcome of complex events
10. genre—kind, type, sort	[ ]ivory tower
11. gauche—left, on the left	[ ]given to dashing display; showy
12. maître d'—master of house	[ ]minion - subordinate official
13. faux pas—false step	[ ]something overly familiar
14. maladroit—clumsy, awkward	[ ]required by etiquette or custom
15. malingre—sickly	[ ]to dupe – trick, fool, deceive
16. dénouement—untying	[ ]a blunder, esp. social blunder
17. in- + soucier—not + to trouble, disturb	[ ]inept; awkward
18. crème de la crème—cream of the cream	[ ]decisive finishing blow or act

SEGMENT SIX

ETYMOLOGY	OLD MEANING
WORD	**NEW MEANING**

L obdurare	to persist, stand firm; harden
obdurate	**hardened in feelings; unyielding**
L ob- + fuscus	in the way + dark, dark brown
obfuscate	**darken; make obscure; confuse**
L obicere	to throw in the way, throw against
objective	**expressing reality or facts apart from personal feelings or prejudices**
L objugare	to scold, rebuke
objurgate	**to denounce harshly; castigate**
L obliquus	slanting, downhill; sideways; askance
oblique	**not straightforward; devious, underhand**
L oblitterare	erase, cancel; consign to oblivion
obliterate	**remove from memory; destroy all trace of**
L oblivisci	to forget
oblivious	**lacking memory or attention; unaware**
L obloqui	contradict, interrupt; speak against; abuse
obloquy	**abusive language**
L obsequi	to comply with, yield to
obsequious	**showing a servile attentiveness; subservient**
L obsidere	to sit at, block; take up; guard, watch for
obsess	**to preoccupy intensely or abnormally**
L obstrepere	make a noise; shout against, cry down
obstreperous	**marked by unruly, aggressive noise; clamorous; stubbornly defiant; unruly**
L obtestari	to call to witness; beseech, entreat
obtest	**to beseech, supplicate**
L obstrudere	to force onto
obtrusive	**forward in manner, pushing; undesirably noticeable or showy**

SAMPLE SENTENCES

obdurate He was *obdurate* in his determination to get revenge. He was *hardened in feelings, unyielding,* and *stubbornly persistent in wrongdoing.*

obfuscate At the hearing the students tried to *obfuscate* the panel as to their pranks; they tried to *confuse* the panel. They tried to *obfuscate,* or *make obscure,* the details.

objective Although emotionally involved in the case, she tried to be *objective* in her analysis; that is, *expressing the facts apart from personal feelings or prejudices.*

objurgate The candidate *objurgated* his opponent's stand on the issues; he *denounced* it *harshly.* He *castigated* his opponent's position.

oblique She got an *oblique* glance from her friend, an *indirect* glance, one *not straight-forward.* He suspected they were behaving in a curiously *oblique* manner, in a *devious, underhand* way.

obliterate A success in one field of endeavor will *obliterate* all or most failures. It will *remove* them *from memory,* will *destroy all trace of* them.

oblivious The obdurate man was *oblivious* of the danger he faced. He was *lacking in memory or attention* about it. He was *unaware* of it.

obloquy The boys were fearful of the harridan's *obloquy* when their ball landed on her property. They feared her *strong, abusive language.*

obsequious Notice how *obsequious* the waiter becomes when a big spender arrives at the restaurant and on whose largesse his livelihood depends; he becomes *servilely attentive* or *subservient.*

obsess Toy trains *obsess* him. They *occupy an undue or disproportionate place in* his *mind.*

obstreperous The celebrators became more *obstreperous* as the evening progressed. The behavior was *marked by unruly, aggressive noisiness;* it was *clamorous.*

obtest Sleepy guests at the hotel tried to *obtest* the celebrators to be less obstreperous. They tried to *beseech, implore, beg,* or *supplicate* them to calm down somewhat.

obtrusive A gauche and brazen individual was *obtrusive* at the party. He was *forward in manner, forcefully and undesirably showy.*

ETYMOLOGY	OLD MEANING
WORD	**NEW MEANING**

L obtundere
obtuse
to beat against; to blunt
insensitive; dense; blunt; dull

L obviam
obviate
in the way; against
to make unnecessary; to prevent

L occludere
occlude
to shut up; to stop, to close
stop up: obstruct; hinder, prevent

L occulere
occult
to cover over; to hide
secret; abstruse; not able to be seen; esoteric; beyond human understanding

L odium
odious
hatred, dislike, displeasure; insolence
exciting or deserving hatred; hateful

L officium
officious
service; duty; sense of duty
volunteering one's services when neither asked for nor needed; meddlesome

L oleaginus
oleaginous
of the olive tree
resembling or producing oil; oily; unctuous

L olfacere
olfactory
to smell, scent
relating to the sense of smell

Sp olla
olio
a large stewing pot
a miscellaneous mixture or collection; a hodgepodge

L ominari
ominous
to forebode; prophesy
foreboding evil; threatening; fateful

Gk onkos + -ology
oncology
mass + study
the study of tumors

L onerosus
onerous
heavy, burdensome; irksome
imposing a burden; troublesome

Gk onomo + poiein
onomatopoeia
name + to make
the naming of something by its sound

SAMPLE SENTENCES

obtuse The obstreperous dolt was too *obtuse* to take a hint to simmer down. He was too *insensitive* about his own shortcomings, too *dense* to understand.

obviate In many cases e-mail can *obviate* the necessity of going to the post office. It can *make* the trip *unnecessary*; it can *prevent* the inconvenience.

occlude A rockslide threatened to *occlude* passage through the tunnel. It appeared that it might *obstruct, hinder,* or *prevent* such passage.

occult Some courses might appear to be *occult* to some students while perfectly lucid to others. To some, they are *abstruse, esoteric,* and *beyond human understanding.*

odious Every so often one sees examples of *odious* behavior, such as obtuse or careless driving. Such actions are *deserving hatred.*

officious One member of the committee was overly *officious*; she *volunteered* to vacuum the dining room during dinner, an act which was *not asked for nor needed.*

oleaginous Health experts advise against eating more than a modicum of *oleaginous* foods. They recommend only a minimum of *oily, greasy,* or *fatty* foods.

olfactory A bad cold will occlude one's *olfactory* sense. It will interfere with a person's ability *relating to the sense of smell.*

olio There was a huge *olio* of things on his desk, a *miscellaneous mixture* of items, a *hodgepodge.*

ominous The dark clouds were *ominous* for the tennis match. They were *foreboding* and *threatening.*

oncology Some medical school graduates choose a career in *oncology*, which is *the study of tumors.*

onerous Certain taxes, while beneficial to some, are *onerous* to others. Many people find them *troublesome* and *imposing a burden.*

onomatopoeia Pop, buzz, hiss, and crackle, are examples of onomatopoeia, which is *the naming of something according to its sound*, or *the use of words whose sound suggests the sense.*

| ETYMOLOGY | OLD MEANING |
WORD	NEW MEANING
L operosus	active, laborious
operose	**tedious, wearisome**
L opinari	to think, suppose, imagine
opine	**to state as an opinion; express opinions**
L optimus	best, very good; excellent
optimum	**most favorable or best possible under fixed or certain conditions**
L opulentus	rich, powerful
opulent	**wealthy, rich; luxurious**
L oraculum	prophecy
oracular	**showing great authority, knowledge and wisdom**
L ostendere	to hold out, show, display; reveal
ostensible	**seeming; apparent rather than real**
L ostentare	to hold out, exhibit; show off; boast of
ostentatious	**marked by showy display of wealth, knowledge, etc.; pretentious**
L aperire	to uncover, disclose, open; to open up
overt	**open to view; not concealed; manifest**
ME overture	*lit.,* opening
overture	**a proposal; something introductory: prelude; musical introduction**
ME overwenen	to be arrogant
overweening	**arrogant; immoderate; unrestrained; excessive; conceited; unduly confident**
Gk oxys + moros	sharp, keen + foolish
oxymoron	**a combination of contradictory or incongruous words**
L palatium	palace
palatial	**suitable to be a palace; magnificent**

SAMPLE SENTENCES

operose Some parts of any job can seem *operose* at times; e.g., onerous extra paper work can be *tedious, wearisome,* and *done with much effort.*

opine It is the expectation of each member of a jury to *opine* in an objective manner. Each juror should *state as an opinion* his or her decision in such a way.

optimum That hotel and restaurant combination was the *optimum* choice. It was the *best possible* choice *under the circumstances* (our limited funds).

opulent Since we could not afford to stay at the *opulent* Ritz, our other choice was optimum; the Ritz is *luxurious.*

oracular If you are visiting a famous museum or national landmark, it pays to have an *oracular* docent, one *showing great authority, knowledge and wisdom.*

ostensible The greeter spoke with the *ostensible* leader of the group, while the real leader was embroiled in operose details. She spoke with the *apparent rather than the real* leader.

ostentatious The new owner of the property was *ostentatious* with his recently acquired wealth; he scraped a perfectly good house in order to build a mansion, a gesture *marked by a showy display of wealth.*

overt The accounting procedure was *overt,* to the satisfaction of the bank examiner. He found that everything was *open to view* and *not concealed.*

overture The fraternity members from the university made an *overture* to the elderly widow for her classic vintage car, but she turned down the *proposal.*

overweening At the formal party an *overweening* jerk arrogated the entire bowl of shrimp for himself. He was an *arrogant, unrestrained,* and *conceited* dolt.

oxymoron A lazy factotum, kind cruelty, huge dwarf, and intelligent dolt—each is an example of an *oxymoron*. Each is a *combination of contradictory or incongruous words.*

palatial It's amazing how some interior designers can convert a plain-looking house into a *palatial* residence. They can make it a *magnificent* home, one *suited to be a palace.*

ETYMOLOGY	OLD MEANING
WORD	**NEW MEANING**

Pg palavra
palaver

word, speech
talk between people of different levels of culture or sophistication; idle talk

Gk palindromos
palindrome

running back again
a word, sentence, or number that reads the same backward or forward

LL palliare
palliate

to cloak, conceal
to abate; moderate the intensity of

L pallidus
pallid

pale; greenish; in love
lacking color or sparkle; dull

L palpare
palpable

to stroke; to coax, flatter
capable of being felt; noticeable; manifest

Gk pan- + akos
panacea

prefix for all, every + remedy
remedy for all ills or difficulties; cure-all

LL pinnaculum
panache

small wing; tuft, plume
dash; flamboyance; spirited self-confidence

Gk pandemos
pandemic

of all the people (pan- + demos = people)
occurring over a wide area affecting many

Pandora loosed a swarm of evils upon mankind when she opened the box
Pandora's box
a prolific source of troubles

Gk panegyris
panegyric

a festival assembly
formal or elaborate praise; encomium

Gk pan- + hopla
panoply

arms, armor
magnificent array; splendid display

Gk paraballein
parable

to compare
short story illustrating a moral attitude; comparison; allegory

Gk para- + deiknynai
paradigm

side by side + to show
a clear or typical example or model

SAMPLE SENTENCES

palaver There was *palaver* between the nabob who owned the boat and one of the crew members, a *talk between people of different levels of culture and sophistication.*

palindrome "Able was I ere I saw Elba," "Otto," "Yreka Bakery," and "2772"—each is an example of a *palindrome;* that is, a *word, sentence, or number that reads the same forward or backward.*

palliate The media served to *palliate* the seriousness of the crime committed by the official by making it appear to be something minor; they *moderated the intensity of* it.

pallid Extemporaneous descanting by announcers is often *pallid*. It is *lacking color or sparkle,* and *dull.*

palpable A swelling due to inflammation is *palpable*, that is, it is *capable of being felt,* is *noticeable,* and *manifest.*

panacea Beware of the politician who promises a *panacea* for all our problems. Don't fall for anyone who has a *remedy for all ills and difficulties,* or a *cure-all.*

panache The luminary aroused the crowd with his *panache*. His *dash, flamboyance,* and *spirited self-confidence* wowed those who greeted him.

pandemic The earthquake caused *pandemic* alarm. It caused a fear *occurring over a wide area affecting many* people.

Pandora's box By revealing certain information to the wrong person, he opened a *Pandora's box*. He created a *prolific source of troubles* for himself.

panegyric It seems that in order to get a *panegyric,* one must be either dead or a political nominee; in either case, one receives *formal or elaborate praise.*

panoply It is gratifying to see the *panoply* of flowers in a tropical garden, or the leaves of autumn in their glorious colors. Either is a *magnificent array,* a *splendid display.*

parable If a situation arises that needs an explanation, it is a good idea to cite or read a *parable*. Read a *short story illustrating a moral attitude,* or a *comparison.*

paradigm She is the *paradigm* of the consummate basketball coach. She is the *clear or typical example or model* of one.

ETYMOLOGY	OLD MEANING
WORD	NEW MEANING

Gk paradoxos **paradox**	contrary to expectation **something seemingly opposed to common sense but may be true**
Gk parakonan **paragon**	to sharpen **a model of excellence or perfection**
Gk para- + metron **parameter**	para- + measure **value fixed within limits; characteristic**
OFr par + amont **paramount**	by, through + above **superior to all others; supreme**
Gk paranous **paranoia**	demented **irrational suspiciousness and distrust**
Gk para- + phrazein **paraphrase**	alongside + to point out **to give the meaning of in other words**
It paro **parlay**	equal **to increase or transform into something of much greater value**
Gk para- + aidein **parody**	at the side of + to sing **comical or ridiculous imitation; caricature**
L parsimonia **parsimony**	thrift, frugality **thrift; stinginess; economy**
Fr parvenir **parvenu**	to arrive **one with new sudden wealth; upstart**
L pastor **pastoral**	herdsman; shepherd **of the countryside; pleasantly peaceful**
L patere **patent**	to be open, accessible; exposed; evident **readily visible; evident; not hidden**
Fr patois **patois**	dialect **special language of an occupation; jargon**

SAMPLE SENTENCES

paradox Good economic news often causes the market to go down, which is a *paradox*. It is *something that defies common sense, but it is the truth*.

paragon A natural wonder, such as a waterfall, a desert or ocean sunset, or a lake in a forest, is a *paragon* of beauty; it is a *model of excellence*.

parameter Political dissent is a *parameter* of modern life in a free society. It is a *characteristic element* thereof.

paramount One eccentric told the pollster that the *paramount* problem in the country is crabgrass. According to him, it was the *supreme* problem, *superior to all others*.

paranoia A person who feels constantly victimized has *paranoia;* that individual has a case of *irrational suspiciousness and distrust of others*.

paraphrase The witness could not remember someone's exact words. The attorney asked him to *paraphrase* it, that is, to *say it in his own words*.

parlay Two men *parlayed* their skill, ingenuity, and efforts from a one-car garage into a multi-billion dollar corporation that employs scores of thousands of talented, well-paid people. They *transformed it into something of much greater value*.

parody In a cartoon, play, or TV show we can expect a *parody* of some well-known person. It as a *comical or ridiculous imitation*, or *caricature*, of him or her.

parsimony Seated at the same table with the man noted for his largesse is his friend, known for his *parsimony*. The waiter nervously frets over whose turn it is to treat, hoping it's not the one recognized for his *thrift* and *stinginess*

parvenu There are tell-tale signs of a *parvenu*: new, flashy, and expensive cars, arrogant manners, and crass, unshakable habits. One can spot a *person with new sudden wealth*, an *upstart*.

pastoral Those who work in either the complaint or billing department deserve some time in a *pastoral* environment. They should have a *countryside, peaceful* experience.

patent What he tried to portray was a *patent* lie, one *readily visible* and *evident* to all.

patois He is well-versed in high-tech *patois*, but not so in the *jargon*, or *special language* of law, medicine, or music.

ETYMOLOGY WORD	OLD MEANING NEW MEANING
L patricius **patrician**	aristocrat **a person of breeding and cultivation**
L patronus **patron**	protector **supporter of the arts, institutions. or social function; customer**
L paucus **paucity**	few, little **fewness; smallness of quantity; dearth**
L peccatum **peccadillo**	mistake, fault; sin **a slight offense**
L peculatus **peculate**	embezzle **to embezzle**
Gk paidagogos **pedagogy**	slave who took children to school **he profession of teaching; education**
L paedagogare **pedantic**	to instruct **ostentatiously learned; narrowly academic**
L par **peer**	equal **a person of equal standing; a noble**
L pejor **pejorative**	worse **tending to make worse; disparaging**
L pelagius **pelagic**	of the sea **relating to the sea; oceanic**
L perlucere **pellucid**	to shine through; be transparent, intelligible **easy to understand; transparent, clear**
Fr pencher **penchant**	to incline **a strong leaning; liking**
L pendulus **pendulous**	hanging; in doubt **marked by indecision or uncertainty**

SAMPLE SENTENCES

patrician He is a true *patrician*, a *person of breeding and cultivation.*

patron He is a *patron* of the arts, a *supporter* of them. He is the maître d's favorite *patron*, his best *customer* at the restaurant.

paucity A *paucity* of essential goods will usually raise their prices, whereas a *paucity* of interest in something lowers the price. So, a *smallness of quantity,* or *dearth,* works both ways.

peccadillo In some societies a *peccadillo*, or *slight offense,* brings a major penalty.

peculate The assistant teller had hoped to replace the money he *peculated* before the bank examiner arrived. His track winnings came from the cash he *embezzled.*

pedagogy When asked about his occupation at the reception, he replied,"Pedagogy." It's the *profession of teaching,* of *education.*

pedantic Also at the reception was a *pedantic* character who liked to spout off among strangers. He was *ostentatiously learned* and *narrowly academic* in his efforts to impress.

peer In the U.S. a defendant is judged by a jury of his *peers*, or, *people of equal standing.* In England a *peer* is *one of five ranks of nobles* (duke, marquis, earl, viscount, or baron).

pejorative Bitter opponents will often make *pejorative* remarks about each other's deeds, accomplishments, or ideas. They will make *disparaging* comments and statements *tending to make worse* anything about them.

pelagic When asked to write about the summer, she indicated that her family had a great *pelagic* vacation. "What's that?" some asked. *"Relating to the sea; oceanic,"* she replied.

pellucid A good professor or lecturer is one who makes the course material *pellucid*, that is, *easy to understand, transparent,* or *clear.*

penchant She has a *penchant* for playing the piano after a certain number of guests arrive. She has a *strong leaning*, a *liking*, for it, and enjoys entertaining.

pendulous They were *pendulous* about which vacation cottage to buy – the one in the mountains, or the one by the seashore. They were so *marked by indecision or uncertainty*, that they "dug deep" and took both.

ETYMOLOGY **WORD**	OLD MEANING **NEW MEANING**
L pensare **pensive**	to weigh out; consider, judge **musingly or dreamily thoughtful**
L paenultimus **penultimate**	almost last **next to the last**
L paene + umbra **penumbra**	almost + shadow **surrounding area in which something exists in a lesser degree; fringe**
L penuria **penurious**	want, need **extremely frugal; tight with money; stingy;** *also,* **very poor**
L perambulare **perambulate**	to walk through, traverse **make an inspection; stroll leisurely**
ML per capita **per capita**	by heads **per unit of population; for each person**
L percipere **percipient**	get hold of; feel; grasp, understand **capable of perception; discerning**
L perimere **peremptory**	to destroy; prevent; kill; take entirely **expressive of urgency; imperious; haughty**
L perfungor **perfunctory**	perform; get through with; discharge **done without care; mechanical; apathetic**
L perjurus **perjury**	lying **false swearing under oath**
L permeare **permeate**	to pass through, penetrate **to spread or diffuse through**
L permutare **permute**	to change completely **to arrange in all possible ways; to change the order or arrangement of**
L pernicies **pernicious**	destruction, ruin, death **highly injurious or destructive; deadly**

SAMPLE SENTENCES

pensive It was decision time and the *pensive* coach called a time-out. He was *musingly thoughtful* about it; the risky play would be rewarding, if it worked, but the safe play avoids a possible disaster.

penultimate The foursome was to play sixteen hands of bridge. The *penultimate* hand came up, the fifteenth, or the *next to last* hand.

penumbra Although his close friend was part of the inner circle of a closely knit social club, he decided to remain on the *penumbra*, in the *outer area*, or *fringe*.

penurious "Oh, no," exclaimed the waiter, as the most *penurious* patron in the history of the restaurant arrived. He was *extremely frugal, tight with money*, or *stingy*.

perambulate His friends saw him *perambulate* up and down the hallway in the hotel. He explained that the maid was making up his room, so he *strolled leisurely*.

per capita If the dinner bill for 16 people came to $1,200, how much was the cost *per capita*? How much was it *for each person*?

percipient If you are looking for a rare bird or a golf ball in the rough, it pays to be very *percipient*. One must be *perceptive, discerning*, and *observant*.

peremptory The hostess of the big party became *peremptory* when the caterers arrived late; she was *expressive of urgency, imperious*, and even *haughty*.

perfunctory People who do the same menial work every day sooner or later do it in a *perfunctory* manner, that is, *done without care or enthusiasm*, in a *mechanical* or *apathetic* manner.

perjury The witness must be careful with his answers, since *perjury* is a serious offense. The penalty for *false swearing under oath* is severe.

permeate The aromas from the grill *permeate* the campsite; later the same evening the skunk's contribution *spreads or diffuses through* the whole general area.

permute The interior designer planned to *permute* the furniture in the room. She planned to *change the order or arrangement* of the pieces.

pernicious Driving while distracted - whether by alcohol, a cell-phone, or an attractive object off to the side—is a *pernicious* practice. It can be *highly injurious or destructive*, or *deadly*.

ETYMOLOGY	OLD MEANING
WORD	**NEW MEANING**

L perpetrare	to perform, carry out
perpetrate	**bring about, carry out; commit**
L perplexus	confused, intricate, obscure
perplex	**cause doubt and uncertainty; confuse; block clear thinking; bewilder**
L perquirere	to search for, inquire after
perquisite	**a privilege or gain besides regular pay**
L per + se	by reason of + himself, herself, itself
per se	**in itself; as such**
L perseverare	to persist; to persist in
persevere	**to hang in there against all odds; to stick with it through and through**
LL personalis	personal
personnel	**a group or body of employed persons**
L perspicere	to see through; to examine, observe
perspicacious	**of acute mental discernment; keen**
L perspicuus	transparent; clear, evident
perspicuous	**plain to the understanding due to clarity**
L pertinax	very tenacious; unyielding, stubborn
pertinacious	**adhering resolutely to a purpose; persistent**
L pertinere	to extend; lead to, concern; to apply, belong
pertinent	**decisively relevant; highly significant**
L perturbare	throw into confusion or disorder; upset
perturb	**to disquiet; make uneasy; unsettle; derange**
L per- + ME usen	thoroughly + to use
peruse	**examine in detail; study; read**
L pervadere	pass through, spread through; penetrate, reach
pervade	**to become diffused throughout every part of**

SAMPLE SENTENCES

perpetrate The dean wonders who *perpetrated* the idea of the minatory bumper sticker recently affixed to his car. Who *committed* or *carried out* this act?

perplex Variation and unpredictability in play-calling will *perplex* the opponents. The idea is to *cause doubt and uncertainty*, to *confuse* or *bewilder* them.

perquisite He has a pleasant job that includes several *perquisites*, that is, a package of *privileges or gains in addition to his regular pay*.

per se Although she was not an attorney *per se*, the file clerk came up with vital information on the case. She was not an attorney *as such*.

persevere A good student will *persevere* in the effort to learn all about an abstruse but important concept. One must *persist in the pursuit* of this goal, *hang in there*, and *stick with it* until the goal is achieved.

personnel There is hospital *personnel*, office *personnel*, and military *personnel*, among others. In each case it is *the group or body of employed persons*.

perspicacious Attempting to fool the *perspicacious* accountant with phony numbers is like trying to sneak the dawn past a rooster. He is *keen* and noted for *being of acute mental discernment*.

perspicuous In speaking or writing, especially in explanations, try to be *perspicuous*, that is, *readily understood, clear*, and *precise and intelligible in utterance*.

pertinacious During the wedding ceremony in the garden, a *pertinacious* bee harassed the groom-to-be, which subtracted substantially from the solemnity of the occasion. The bee was *hard to get rid of, persistent, unyielding*, and *holding resolutely on*.

pertinent Her remarks were *pertinent* to the discussion. They were *decisively relevant* and *highly significant*.

perturb The program planner was *perturbed* by the report of the guest of honor having a car breakdown. The news *disquieted, unsettled*, and *made* him *uneasy*.

peruse Being perspicacious, she wanted to *peruse* the contract. She planned to *read* it, to *study* it, to *examine* it *in detail*.

pervade The skunk's odor *pervaded* the campsite. It *became diffused throughout every part of* it.

ETYMOLOGY	OLD MEANING
WORD	**NEW MEANING**

L pervertere	to overturn, upset; overthrow, undo
perverse	**away from what is right; improper; corrupt; wrongheaded**
L petulans	pert, impudent
petulant	**insolent, rude; peevish; irritable**
The *Pied Piper*	
of Hamelin	hero of a Browning 1842 poem
pied piper	**a leader who makes irresponsible promises**
MDu pitte	pit of a fruit; kernel; tree pith
pith	**the essential part of something; core; substance; gist; importance, essence**
L placare	to calm, appease, reconcile
placate	**to mollify by concessions; appease**
L plagiarius	plunderer, kidnapper
plagiarism	**the taking and passing off the ideas or words of another as one's own; literary theft**
MFr plaintif	lamenting, complaining
plaintiff	**one who takes legal action; the complaining party in a litigation**
Fr plat	flat, dull
platitude	**a banal, trite, or stale remark**
L plaudere	to clap, applaud; approve, be pleased with
plaudit(s)	**round of applause; enthusiastic approval**
L plausibilis	worthy of applause; praiseworthy
plausible	**superficially fair, reasonable, or trustworthy; appearing worthy of belief**
L plebeius	of the common people; common, low
plebeian	**crude or coarse in manner or style**
L plebiscitum	decree of the people
plebiscite	**a vote by the people for or against a proposal**

SAMPLE SENTENCES

perverse The judicial system has a history of many *perverse* court decisions. They are *away from what is right, improper*, or *wrongheaded*.

petulant The larger the group on a tour, the greater the odds of a *petulant* individual in it; that is, someone who is *rude, insolent, peevish*, or *irritable over trifles*.

pied piper There is a bit of a *pied piper* in nearly every politician at election time—a *leader who makes irresponsible promises*.

pith Her analysis of the situation contained much *pith*. Her comments included the *gist* of the discussion, the *essential part*, the *substance*, the *importance* of it.

placate To pass a bill in congress, it is common practice for one party to *placate* the opposing members, that is, to *appease* them, to *mollify* them *by concessions*.

plagiarism He was expelled from the university for *plagiarism*. He was guilty of *literary theft*, or *taking and passing off the ideas and words of someone else as his own*, for his thesis.

plaintiff The *plaintiff* is the *one who takes legal action*, or the *complaining party in a law case*. The person he is taking to court, or suing, is known as the defendant.

platitude While pithy statements and even persiflage will get people's attention at a party, a *platitude* will not. People don't care for *banal, trite*, or *stale remarks*.

plaudit She received many *plaudits* for her recital, *rounds of applause* and *enthusiastic approval*.

plausible The plan had to be at least *plausible* to be considered. It had to be *appearing worthy of belief* and not something abstract or impossible.

plebian The parvenu had his private jet, drove flashy cars, and built a mansion, but his *plebian* manners gave him away; he was *crude or coarse in manner or style*.

plebiscite The type of government was determined by a *plebiscite*, that is, by a *vote of the people for or against a proposal*.

ETYMOLOGY	OLD MEANING
WORD	**NEW MEANING**

Gk plethein
plethora

to be full
superfluity, excess

L pungere
poignant

to prick, sting, pierce
deeply affecting, touching; cutting

Gk polemikos
polemic

warlike, hostile
involving disputes; controversial

Pollyanna
Pollyanna

heroine of Porter novel (1913)
**irresponsible optimist who finds
good in everything**

L pullus
poltroon

young (of animals); chicken
a thorough, spiritless coward, a craven

L pompa
pomp

procession; group of attendants
**splendor; ceremonial display;
ostentatious display, gesture, or act**

L pondus
ponderous

weight, mass; burden
heavy; clumsy; oppressively dull

L pontifex
pontificate

high priest; bishop; pope
**to deliver oracular utterances or
dogmatic opinions**

L portendere
portend

to denote, predict
give an omen or sign of; bode; indicate

L portere + folium
portfolio

to carry + leaf
the securities held by an investor

Fr pot pourri
potpourri

lit., rotten pot
miscellaneous collection; medley

Fr pour + boire
pourboire

in order to, for + to drink
a tip, gratuity

L pragmaticus
pragmatic

of affairs; skilled in law or business
matter of fact, practical, not idealistic

SAMPLE SENTENCES

plethora After a paucity of hors d'oeuvres the previous week, there was a *plethora* of them at the following tailgate picnic, an *excess, superfluity*, or *profusion* of them.

poignant Attending a funeral of a close friend is a *poignant* experience. It is a *deeply touching* one.

polemic The opposing candidates argued over *polemic* issues. They discussed heatedly *controversial, argumentative* matters.

Pollyanna The shareholder lawsuit resulted from a rosy annual report written by a *Pollyanna,* who said things were going to be great despite dismal numbers. He was an *irresponsible optimist who found good in everything, even any adversity*.

poltroon "P.G.Wodehouse, in referring to 'lily-livered *poltroons* lacking even the meager courage of a rabbit,' meant *spiritless cowards,* or *cravens*."

pomp The royal wedding procession contained much *pomp*, or *splendor*. In other news, the actress arrived with considerable *pomp*, or an *ostentatious display or gesture*.

ponderous He delivers *ponderous* speeches at the dinner table. They are *oppressively dull*.

pontificate He likes to *pontificate* to a trapped audience, e.g., at a dinner table. He likes to *deliver oracular utterances or dogmatic opinions* to the victims.

portend The appearance of seagulls inland usually *portend* rain the next day. They *give an omen or sign of* rain; they *bode* or *indicate* the coming of rain.

portfolio It pays to gradually grow and keep an eye on one's *portfolio*, which constitutes the *securities (stocks, bonds, etc.) held by an investor*.

potpourri His CD contains a *potpourri* of musical selections, a *medley* of them. In other news, his library has a *potpourri* of materials, a *miscellaneous collection* of unrelated items.

pourboire In some countries the *pourboire* is included in the price of a meal. Beyond that a taxi driver expects a *tip*, or *gratuity*, in addition to the regular fare.

pragmatic He takes a *pragmatic* approach to problem solving, not a theoretical one. He is *matter of fact*, or *practical, not idealistic,* in his way of doing things.

ETYMOLOGY WORD	OLD MEANING NEW MEANING
L prae- + ambulare **preamble**	in front (of) + to walk, go **an introductory statement**
L praecedere **precedence**	to go before; lead the way **priority of importance; preference**
L praecludere **preclude**	to close, shut; close to, impede **to shut out; make impossible; prevent**
L praecox **precocious**	early ripening; premature **showing mature qualities at an early age**
L praecurrere **precursor**	to hurry on, run before; anticipate **one that precedes and indicates the approach of another; predecessor**
L praeda **predatory**	booty, plunder; (*animal*) prey **tending to exploit others for one's own gain; living by consumption of other animals**
L praedestinare **predestine**	to predetermine **to determine or settle beforehand**
L praedicare **predicate**	to proclaim publicly; declare, assert **to assert; base (upon); affirm, declare**
L prae- + diligere **predilection**	before + to prize especially, esteem, love **an inclination, liking, preference; taste**
L prae- + emere **preempt**	before + to buy, to take **to seize upon to the exclusion of others; take the place of; replace**
L praefari **preface**	to say in advance **to give introductory remarks**
L prehendere **prehensile**	to take hold of; to seize; (*mind*) to grasp **adapted for seizing; gifted with mental grasp**
L praejudicare **prejudice**	to prejudge, decide beforehand **an adverse opinion without just grounds**

SAMPLE SENTENCES

preamble All students should study the *preamble* to the Constitution (as well as the Constitution itself). It is the *introductory statement* to it.

precedence Smart students make sure that studying for a big mid-term takes *precedence* over a night on the town. It is the wise *priority of importance* choice.

preclude The mud slide on the mountain road *precluded* our visit with friends on the other side. It *prevented,* or *made impossible,* our trip It *shut* it *out.*

precocious Mozart was an example of a *precocious* child—he was *showing mature qualities at an early age.*

precursor The sailing ship was the *precursor* to the steamship, just as the horse-drawn carriage was the *predecessor* to the automobile.

predatory Beware of the *predatory* individual. That type of person is *tending to exploit others for one's own gain.* Lions are *predatory.*

predestine How is it that the odds makers seem to *predestine* the outcome of football games so often? They somehow *determine* or *settle beforehand* the results.

predicate He *predicated* his argument on an unproven hypothesis. He *based* his entire case on it.

predilection He has a *predilection* for Camembert for the cheese course. He has an *inclination,* a *liking,* a *preference* for it. He has a *taste* for it.

preempt After they fired up the barbecue and were away setting up the table, another group *preempted* it, that is, *seized upon it to the exclusion of the first group,* or *took* it *for themselves.* Also, a baseball game *preempted* the regular program, or *took the place of* it.

preface She felt it necessary to *preface* her speech, to *give a few introductory remarks* before the main part of her address.

prehensile Students and monkeys are both *prehensile.* They are *adapted for seizing,* for example, bananas. Some are *gifted with mental grasp.*

prejudice Having a dislike for something is different from having a *prejudice,* which is an *adverse opinion without just grounds,* whereas many dislikes are justified.

Etymology	Old Meaning
Word	**New Meaning**

L praemittere **premise**	to send in advance **something assumed or taken for granted**
L praemonere **premonition**	to forewarn, foreshadow **anticipation of an event without conscious reason**
L praerogativus **prerogative**	voting first **an exclusive or special right or privilege**
L praesagus **presage**	foreboding, prophetic **to portend; foretell, predict**
L praesentire **presentiment**	to feel beforehand; to presage **a feeling that something will or is about to happen; premonition**
L praesumere **presume**	to take first; anticipate; take for granted **to accept as true without proof; to take for granted: imply**
L prae- + ML supponere **presuppose**	before + to suppose **to suppose beforehand**
L praetexere **pretext**	to weave in front; to fringe, adorn **an appearance used to cloak the real intention or situation; excuse; cover**
L praevalere **prevalent**	to be very powerful, have most influence **generally accepted; widely practiced**
L praevaricari **prevaricate**	to walk crookedly; to favor by collusion **to deviate from the truth; equivocate**
L praevenire **prevenance**	to come before; to anticipate, prevent **attentiveness to other's needs**
It prima donna **prima donna**	*lit.,* first lady **a very sensitive, vain, undisciplined person**
L prima facie **prima facie**	at first view **on the first appearance; apparent**

SAMPLE SENTENCES

premise He based his optimism on the *premise* of an expectation. He based it on *something assumed or taken for granted.*

premonition She had a *premonition* that her stock would go up, an *anticipation of it happening without conscious reason;* a *gut feeling,* or *hunch.*

prerogative According to an old adage, "It is a woman's *prerogative* to change her mind." It is her *exclusive or special right or privilege* to do so.

presage The appearance of seagulls flying inland will often *presage* rain the following day. They seem to *portend* rain, to *foretell* or *predict* it.

presentiment Awakened by heavy crepitation and seeing a moving shadow outside the open window, he had a sudden *presentiment.* He had a *feeling that something was about to happen,* a *premonition.*

presume If we see his car in the parking lot, we can *presume* he is in the area. We can *accept as true without proof* that he is somewhere in the area.

presuppose The professor *presupposes* that all the new students have fulfilled their prerequisites for his class. He *supposes beforehand* that they have.

pretext She expressed shock, horror, and deep sorrow as a *pretext* upon hearing the news of a murder she herself had committed. It was an *appearance used to cloak the real situation.*

prevalent The growing feeling that "parents know best" became *prevalent* throughout the school district after several meetings with the board. The attitude became *generally accepted* and eventually *widely practiced.*

prevaricate Politicians should know better than to *prevaricate* about their claims and accomplishments. They should not *equivocate* or *deviate from the truth.*

prevenance Good hotels, as well as good people, practice *prevenance.* They show *attentiveness to the needs of others.*

prima donna The coach looks for good team players, not hot dogs or *prima donnas.* He doesn't want *someone who shows excessive pride in himself* or *one who finds it difficult to be part of a team,* or *an undisciplined person.*

prima facie The idea was *prima facie* good. It was *on the first appearance* good. It was *prima facie* evidence. It was *apparent* evidence.

QUIZ

Match the following words with their meanings:

 (1) obdurate   [   ] marked by unruly, aggressive noise; clamorous; defiant

 (2) obfuscate   [   ] to beseech, supplicate

 (3) objective   [   ] showing a servile attentiveness; subservient

 (4) objurgate   [   ] to preoccupy intensely or abnormally

 (5) oblique   [   ] lacking memory or attention; unaware

 (6) obliterate   [   ] to darken; make obscure; confuse

 (7) obtrusive   [   ] hardened in feelings; unyielding

 (8) obtest   [   ] to denounce harshly; castigate

 (9) obsequious   [   ] not straightforward; devious, underhand

(10) oblivious   [   ] expressing reality or facts apart from personal feelings

(11) obsess   [   ] remove from memory; destroy all traces of

(12) obstreperous   [   ] forward in manner, pushing; undesirably noticeable or showy

 (1) obtuse   [   ] exciting or deserving hatred; hateful

 (2) obloquy   [   ] a miscellaneous mixture or collection; a hodgepodge

 (3) occult   [   ] foreboding evil; threatening; fateful

 (4) obviate   [   ] to state as an opinion; express opinions

 (5) odious   [   ] relating to the sense of smell

 (6) oncology   [   ] abusive language

 (7) officious   [   ] insensitive; dense; blunt; dull

 (8) opine   [   ] to stop up; obstruct; hinder, prevent

 (9) oleaginous   [   ] secret; abstruse; cannot be seen; beyond human understanding

(10) ominous   [   ] imposing a burden; troublesome

(11) occlude   [   ] to make unnecessary; to prevent

(12) olfactory   [   ] resembling or producing oil; oily

(13) onerous   [   ] volunteering one's service where it is not needed or asked for

(14) olio   [   ] the study of tumors

(1) operose   [   ] arrogant; immoderate; unrestrained; conceited; too confident

(2) optimum   [   ] seeming; apparent rather than real

(3) overture   [   ] a combination of contradictory or incongruous words

(4) opulent   [   ] open to view; not concealed; manifest

(5) oracular   [   ] suitable to be a palace; magnificent

(6) ostensible   [   ] marked by showy display of wealth or knowledge; pretentious

(7) overweening   [   ] most favorable or best possible under the circumstances

(8) oxymoron   [   ] the naming of something by its sound

(9) overt   [   ] showing great authority, knowledge, and wisdom

(10) ostentatious   [   ] wealthy; rich; luxurious

(11) palatial   [   ] tedious, wearisome

(12) onomatopoeia   [   ] a proposal; something introductory; musical introduction

(1) palaver   [   ] formal or elaborate praise

(2) paradigm   [   ] a word, sentence, or number that reads the same backwards

(3) palpable   [   ] lacking color or sparkle; dull

(4) panoply   [   ] dash; flamboyance; spirited self-confidence

(5) panacea   [   ] a prolific source of troubles

(6) parable   [   ] magnificent array; splendid display

(7) pandemic   [   ] capable of being felt; noticeable; manifest

(8) palindrome   [   ] a clear or typical example or model

(9) Pandora's box   [   ] talk between people of different cultural levels; idle talk

(10) panache   [   ] short story illustrating a moral attitude; comparison; allegory

(11) pallid   [   ] occurring over a wide area affecting many

(12) panegyric   [   ] remedy for all ills or difficulties; a cure-all

(1) paradox   [   ] comical or ridiculous imitation; caricature
(2) palliate   [   ] to increase or transform into something of
                          much greater value
(3) paramount   [   ] readily visible; evident; not hidden
(4) paragon   [   ] thrift; stinginess; economy
(5) patois   [   ] irrational suspiciousness and distrust
(6) peculate   [   ] to abate; moderate the intensity of
(7) parody   [   ] value fixed within limits; characteristic
(8) pastoral   [   ] superior to all others; supreme
(9) parlay   [   ] to give the meaning of in other words
(10) parsimony   [   ] something seemingly against common
                          sense but may be true
(11) paranoia   [   ] a model of excellence or perfection
(12) patent   [   ] of the countryside; pleasantly peaceful
(13) parameter   [   ] special language of an occupation; jargon
(14) paraphrase   [   ] to embezzle

(1) pedantic   [   ] marked by indecision or uncertainty
(2) paucity   [   ] a slight offense
(3) parvenu   [   ] a person of breeding and cultivation
(4) pejorative   [   ] easy to understand; transparent, clear
(5) pedagogy   [   ] a strong leaning; liking
(6) patron   [   ] a person of equal standing; a noble
(7) pendulous   [   ] ostentatiously learned; narrowly academic
(8) peccadillo   [   ] the profession of teaching; education
(9) patrician   [   ] one with new sudden wealth; upstart
(10) pellucid   [   ] relating to the sea; oceanic
(11) penchant   [   ] fewness; smallness of quantity; dearth
(12) peer   [   ] supporter of the arts, institutions, or social
                          functions; customer
(13) pelagic   [   ] tending to make worse; disparaging

(1) pensive   [   ] done without care; mechanical; apathetic

(2) penultimate   [   ] highly injurious or destructive; deadly

(3) perambulate   [   ] to spread or diffuse through

(4) penumbra   [   ] false swearing under oath

(5) percipient   [   ] expressive of urgency; imperious; haughty

(6) penurious   [   ] musingly or dreamily thoughtful

(7) per capita   [   ] in itself; as such

(8) permeate   [   ] to arrange in all possible ways; change the arrangement of

(9) perfunctory   [   ] capable of perception; discerning

(10) perjury   [   ] surrounding area where something is in a lesser degree; fringe

(11) pernicious   [   ] extremely frugal; tight with money; stingy; *also* very poor

(12) permute   [   ] to make an inspection; stroll leisurely

(13) peremptory   [   ] per unit of population; for each person

(14) per se   [   ] next to the last

(1) perpetrate   [   ] to disquiet; make uneasy; unsettle; derange

(2) persevere   [   ] to cause doubt and uncertainty; confuse; block clear thinking

(3) perquisite   [   ] a group or body of employed persons

(4) perspicacious   [   ] decisively relevant; highly significant

(5) pervade   [   ] to examine in detail; study; read

(6) pertinacious   [   ] plain to the understanding due to clarity

(7) personnel   [   ] a privilege or gain besides regular pay

(8) perturb   [   ] hang in there against all odds; stick with it through and through

(9) perplex   [   ] to become diffused throughout every part of

(10) pertinent   [   ] adhering resolutely to a purpose; persistent

(11) perspicuous   [   ] of acute mental discernment; keen

(12) peruse   [   ] to bring about, carry out; commit

(1) pith　　　　　　　[　] round of applause; enthusiastic approval
(2) perverse　　　　　[　] insolent, rude; peevish; irritable
(3) Pollyanna　　　　[　] a leader who makes irresponsible promises
(4) plagiarism　　　　[　] a banal, trite, or stale remark
(5) petulant　　　　　[　] crude or coarse in manner or style
(6) plaintiff　　　　　[　] irresponsible optimist who finds good in
　　　　　　　　　　　　　　everything
(7) plebiscite　　　　[　] essential part of something; gist; importance;
　　　　　　　　　　　　　　substance
(8) plausible　　　　　[　] away from what is right; improper;
　　　　　　　　　　　　　　corrupt; wrongheaded
(9) plaudit　　　　　　[　] the taking of ideas of another as one's own;
　　　　　　　　　　　　　　literary theft
(10) pied piper　　　　[　] one who takes legal action; the complaining
　　　　　　　　　　　　　　party in law
(11) plebeian　　　　　[　] superficially reasonable or fair; appearing
　　　　　　　　　　　　　　worthy of belief
(12) platitude　　　　[　] a vote by the people for or against a pro
　　　　　　　　　　　　　　posal or government

(1) plethora　　　　　[　] a miscellaneous collection; medley
(2) poignant　　　　　[　] matter of fact, practical; not idealistic
(3) placate　　　　　　[　] to deliver oracular utterances or dogmatic
　　　　　　　　　　　　　　opinions
(4) pomp　　　　　　　[　] a tip, gratuity
(5) ponderous　　　　[　] involving disputes; controversial
(6) portfolio　　　　　[　] a superfluity, excess
(7) portend　　　　　　[　] to mollify by concessions; appease
(8) pragmatic　　　　　[　] heavy; clumsy; oppressively dull
(9) potpourri　　　　　[　] splendor; ceremonial display; ostentatious
　　　　　　　　　　　　　　display or gesture
(10) polemic　　　　　[　] deeply affecting, touching; cutting
(11) pontificate　　　　[　] to give an omen or sign of; bode; indicate
(12) pourboire　　　　[　] the securities held by an investor

(1) preamble   [   ] priority of importance; preference

(2) preclude   [   ] to give introductory remarks

(3) precocious   [   ] adapted for seizing; gifted with mental grasp

(4) precursor   [   ] an inclination, liking, preference; taste

(5) preempt   [   ] to assert; base (upon); affirm, declare; to imply

(6) precedence   [   ] an adverse opinion without just grounds

(7) preface   [   ] to determine or settle beforehand

(8) predatory   [   ] showing mature qualities at an early age

(9) predilection   [   ] an introductory statement

(10) predicate   [   ] to shut out; make impossible; prevent

(11) prejudice   [   ] that which precedes and indicates the approach of another

(12) prehensile   [   ] tending to exploit others for one's own gain

(13) predestine   [   ] seize upon to the exclusion of others; take the place of; replace

(1) premise   [   ] an exclusive or special right or privilege

(2) presentiment   [   ] an appearance used to cloak the real intention or situation

(3) presage   [   ] to accept as true without proof; take for granted; imply

(4) prevalent   [   ] on the first appearance; apparent

(5) poltroon   [   ] a very sensitive, vain, undisciplined person

(6) prerogative   [   ] a feeling that something is about to happen; premonition

(7) prevaricate   [   ] to suppose beforehand

(8) prevenance   [   ] something assumed or taken for granted

(9) prima facie   [   ] generally accepted; widely practiced

(10) prima donna   [   ] a thorough, spiritless coward; a craven

(11) premonition   [   ] attentiveness to the needs of others

(12) presume   [   ] to portend, foretell; predict

(13) presuppose   [   ] to deviate from the truth; equivocate

(14) pretext   [   ] anticipation of an event without conscious reason

QUIZ

1. A pied piper is likely to offer everyone a:
(a) panegyric   (b) panacea   (c) Pandora's box   (d) parable

2. Most students would prefer a professor who is:
(a) oblique   (b) occult   (c) pellucid   (d) pallid

3. Mozart is noted for having been very:
(a) obtrusive   (b) opulent   (c) poignant   (d) precocious

4. A prima donna is recognized for being:
(a) pensive   (b) officious   (c) ostentatious   (d) obsequious

5. A waiter's favorite patron is noted for his:
(a) pourboires   (b) palaver   (c) parsimony   (d) paranoia

6. The bank manager seeks a teller who really knows how to:
(a) perplex   (b) persevere   (c) peculate   (d) prevaricate

7. At a ball game one usually prefers to sit next to someone who is:
(a) petulant   (b) polemic   (c) objective   (d) obstreperous

8. A poltroon would most likely be:
(a) plebeian   (b) pendulous   (c) overweening   (d) peremptory

9. A professor likes students whose writings consist of:
(a) obloquy   (b) pith   (c) platitudes   (d) plagiarism

10. A good student is:
(a) obdurate   (b) obtuse   (c) perspicacious   (d) pedantic

REVIEW QUIZ

Match these important words with their meanings:

(1) germane [ ] involved in the nature of; belonging by nature or habit

(2) farce [ ] oblique allusion; a hint; insinuation

(3) imply [ ] to conclude from facts or assumption

(4) infinitesimal [ ] exceeding reasonable limits; immoderate

(5) innuendo [ ] a false idea; unsound argument

(6) infer [ ] to indicate, suggest; contain potentially; express indirectly

(7) indigenous [ ] relevant and appropriate; fitting

(8 fallacy [ ] satirical comedy; empty show; mockery

(9) inordinate [ ] immeasurably small; close to zero

(10) inherent [ ] original in a region; inborn; native; innate

(1) irony [ ] a general truth; proverbial saying

(2) ostensible [ ] expressing facts apart from personal feelings or prejudices

(3) lampoon [ ] to make unnecessary; to prevent

(4) liaison [ ] a remark that does not follow from what has just been said

(5) objective [ ] best possible, most favorable, underfixed or certain conditions

(6) optimum [ ] seeming; apparent rather than real

(7) maxim [ ] something that seems to defy common sense but may be true

(8) obviate [ ] to mock or ridicule

(9) non sequitur [ ] reversal between result and expectation

(10) paradox [ ] a close connection; interrelationship

(1) pejorative [ ] done without care; mechanical; apathetic

(2) paraphrase [ ] give an omen or sign of; bode; indicate

(3) pith [ ] a banal, trite, or stale remark

(4) plausible [ ] matter of fact, practical, not idealistic

(5) preclude [ ] seize upon to the exclusion of others; take the place of

(6) perfunctory [ ] superficially reasonable; appearing worthy of belief

(7) preempt [ ] to give the meaning of in other words

(8) portend [ ] to shut out; make impossible; prevent

(9) platitude [ ] the essential part of something; substance; gist; importance

(10) pragmatic [ ] tending to make worse disparaging

SEGMENT SEVEN

ETYMOLOGY	OLD MEANING
WORD	**NEW MEANING**

L primordium	beginning, origin
primordial	**first developed; earliest; primitive**
L pristinus	former, original; of yesterday
pristine	**uncorrupted by civilization; fresh, clean**
L privatio	removal
privation	**act of taking away; lack of what is needed**
L privatus	private; not in public office
privy	**admitted as one sharing in a secret; withdrawn from common knowledge**
Fr prix fixe	fixed price
prix fixe	**the price charged for a table d'hôte meal**
L probare	to approve; to appraise
probation	**a period of testing and trial to ascertain fitness (as for a job or school)**
L probitas	goodness, honesty
probity	**adherence to the highest ideals and principles**
Gk problema + ikos	problem + ic
problematic	**puzzling; not definite or settled; doubtful**
L proclivis	downhill; prone, willing
proclivity	**inclination toward something; a leaning**
L prodigus	wasteful, lavish; generous
prodigal	**recklessly extravagant**
L prodigium	portent; unnatural deed; monster
prodigious	**causing one to marvel; extraordinary**
OFr por + offrir	forth + to offer
proffer	**to present for acceptance; to tender, offer**
L profligare	to dash to the ground; destroy; degrade
profligate	**given to dissipation; wildly extravagant**

SAMPLE SENTENCES

primodrial The tour group unexpectedly came upon a *primordial* village near the Amazon river. It was of the *earliest, primitive* kind.

pristine It is a delight to behold a *pristine* area of a forest, that is, one *untroubled by civilization,* an area that is *fresh and clean,* or *uncorrupted.*

privation The campers suffered *privation* when some bad guys committed an *act of taking away* their food and equipment, which resulted in more *privation,* or a *lack of what is needed.*

privy She was not *privy* to the conspiracy of the cabal. She was not *admitted as one sharing in the secret;* she was not *in on* the plot.

prix fixe The group agreed on the *prix fixe* dinner, or the *price charged for a table d'hôte meal.* (Fr, table d'hôte *lit.,* host's table, where a fixed price is charged)

probation The campus party boy was put on *probation* because of poor grades. A *period of testing and trial to ascertain his fitness* as a student awakened him.

probity One of the first traits people look for in an individual is *probity,* whether in a prospective employee, a blind date, or a political candidate. People hope for *adherence to the highest ideals and principles* in a person.

problematic The stability of team ratings at the start of the season is *problematic* as the season moves along. It is *puzzling, not definite or settled,* and *doubtful.*

proclivity The couple has a strong *proclivity* for photographing wild animals in their habitats. Each has an *inclination,* a *leaning toward* doing this.

prodigal The business man was worried about his *prodigal* son, who was away at school. His *recklessly extravagant* son was constantly requesting more money.

prodigious White water kayaking requires *prodigious* skill and effort. It involves *extraordinary* talent, an ability *causing one to marvel.*

proffer She was *proffered* the presidency of the sorority for the following year. The membership agreed to *present* it *for her acceptance,* to *offer* it to her.

profligate The father was upset upon learning that his son, already on probation, was *profligate* as well; he was *given to dissipation* and *wildly extravagant.*

ETYMOLOGY	OLD MEANING
WORD	**NEW MEANING**

L profundus
profound

deep, vast; high; infernal
having intellectual depth; intense of feeling; deep

L profundere
profuse

to pour out; bring forth; produce; squander
extravagant; showing great abundance

Gk prognosis
prognosticate

lit., foreknowledge
to foretell from signs or symptoms

L proletarius
proletariat

citizen of the lowest class
the lowest social or economic class

L proles
prolific

progeny, offspring; child
marked by abundant productivity

L prolixus
prolix

long, wide, spreading
unduly prolonged; long-winded

Fr promener
promenade

to take for a walk
a leisurely walk; a place for strolling

L promiscuus
promiscuous

indiscriminate; in common; open to all
not restricted to one person; casual

L propensus
propensity

inclining; inclined; well disposed
an intense, urgent natural inclination

L propinquitas
propinquity

nearness, relationship; friendship
nearness in blood; nearness in place or time

L propitius
propitiate

favorable, gracious
gain the favor of; appease, conciliate

L proponere
proponent

set forth, display; publish, declare; propose
one who argues in favor of something

L prosa
prosaic

prose
factual; dull, unimaginative; suitable for the everyday world

SAMPLE SENTENCES

profound She showed *profound* gratitude to those who rescued her from the burning building. She gave *deep* thanks to the rescuers and wanted to reward them.

profuse The university officials were *profuse* in their thanks to the alumna for her large gift. They were *extravagant* in their gratitude and praise.

prognosticate All his relatives were waiting for the doctor to *prognosticate* his case. that is, to *foretell from signs and symptoms* what the probabilities might be.

proletariat In poor countries there is a large *proletariat*, but in rich countries there exist much smaller ones. It is the *lowest social and economic class* in a country.

prolific Shakespeare, Goethe, and Hugo were *prolific* writers. Their works were *marked by abundant productivity*.

prolix His descriptions of the details of his travels were much too *prolix*. They were *unduly prolonged* and *long-winded*.

promenade It is pleasant to go on a *promenade* after dinner in the early evening. It is nice to take a crepuscular post-prandial *leisurely walk*.

promiscuous He is *promiscuous* in his relationships. He is definitely *not restricted to one class or person*; he is *indiscriminate, casual,* and *irregular* in his dealings with people.

propensity She has a *propensity* for foreign movies. She has an *intense, urgent natural inclination* to view them.

propinquity The attorney asked the heir the degree of *propinquity* between him and the deceased; he wanted to know the *kinship* between them. In other news, the two neighbors squabbled over the *propinquity* of an out-house to the property line. They argued over the *nearness* or *closeness* of it.

propitiate He decided to *propitiate* his neighbor to avoid legal action. He thought it best to *appease*, to *conciliate*, to *gain the favor of* him.

proponent He is a strong *proponent* of making changes in the school system. He is *one who argues in favor of* doing it.

prosaic His *prosaic* statements at the dinner table were about as exciting as reciting a bus schedule or the business of testing boilers. His conversation is *factual, dull,* and *unimaginative*.

Etymology	Old Meaning
Word	**New Meaning**

L proscribere
proscribe

publish in writing; advertise; confiscate
to outlaw; forbid as harmful; prohibit

Gk prot- + agonistes
protagonist

first + competitor at games; actor
leading part; leader of a cause; champion

L pro tempore
pro tem

for the time being
for the time being

Gk prot- + kollan
protocol

to glue together
a code of strict adherence to correct procedure at a formal function

L provenire
provenance

to come out, appear, arise, grow; to go on
place of origin; source

L provincia
provincial

sphere of action, duty
limited in outlook; narrow; lacking polish of city society; unsophisticated

ML proviso quod
proviso

provided that
a clause that introduces a condition

L praeponere
provost

to place in front, put first; put in charge
a high-ranking university administrator

L proximus
proximal

nearest, next
situated close to; nearest; next to

L prudens
prudent

aware, wise; skilled, versed in
wise, judicious; circumspect; discreet

L puerilis
puerile

boyish; childish, trivial
juvenile; childish, silly

L pugnare
pugnacious

to fight; to disagree; to struggle
having a belligerent nature; combative

L pulcher
pulchritude

beautiful
physical beauty

SAMPLE SENTENCES

proscribe The university decided to *proscribe* smoking in the stadium. Fans and athletes were pleased about the decision to *outlaw* it, *prohibit* it, *forbid* it *as harmful*.

protagonist She is a *protagonist* in the battle for school reform. She is the *leader of the cause*, the *champion* of it.

pro tem He was the speaker *pro tem* of the legislative body. He was the speaker *for the time being*.

protocol A buffoon is oblivious to *protocol* at a function. He is unaware of the *code of strict adherence to correct procedure at a formal function*.

provenance There is considerable discussion over the *provenance* of the zinfandel grape; many would like to know its *source*, or *place of origin*.

provincial Emma's husband, Charles Bovary, was *provincial*. He was *limited in outlook, unsophisticated*, and *lacking polish of city society*. (from *Madame Bovary*)

proviso The Wilmot *proviso* was first presented in 1846. It was an amendment containing *a clause that introduces a conditional stipulation*.

provost She was an ideal *provost* at a major university; she was a *high-ranking university administrator* who was deeply involved in all areas, including football.

proximal Hobson's choice meant taking the horse *proximal* to the door. It had to be the one *nearest*, or *next to*, the door.

prudent He is *prudent* in his choices of investments and purchases. In these matters he is *wise, judicious, circumspect*, and *discreet*.

puerile One thing that turns people off is *puerile* behavior on the part of young adults who think they are clever or funny. *Juvenile, childish*, and *silly* actions are not appreciated, nor are they amusing.

pugnacious In the old days it was common to see the *pugnacious* drunk emerge at pro football games; he would sometimes get into a fight with a similar drunk who was also *belligerent* and *combative* over a difference of opinion.

pulchritude At functions or gatherings she stood out because of her *pulchritude*. No one ignored her *physical beauty*.

ETYMOLOGY	OLD MEANING
WORD	**NEW MEANING**

| L pulmo | lung |
| **pulmonary** | **relating to the lungs** |

| Skt pundita | learned, wise |
| **pundit** | **critic; one who gives opinions in an authoritative manner; authority** |

| ME purloinen | to put away, render ineffectual |
| **purloin** | **to appropriate wrongfully; to steal** |

| OFr porporter | to convey |
| **purport** | **to have the appearance of being or claiming something; to profess** |

| AF purveu (est) | it is provided (opening phrase of a statute) |
| **purview** | **the range or limit of authority, concern, competence, or responsibility** |

| L punctum | point, dot; moment |
| **punctilious** | **careful, exact; paying strict attention to details of codes or conventions** |

| L pusillus + animus | very little; petty; paltry + spirit |
| **pusillanimous** | **lacking courage and resolution; cowardly; contemptibly timid** |

| L putare | to think, suppose; think over; reckon |
| **putative** | **commonly accepted or supposed; assumed to exist** |

| Pyrrhus | king of Epirus who sustained heavy losses in defeating the Romans |
| **Pyrrhic victory** | **a victory won at excessive cost** |

| L quassare | to shake; to shatter, damage |
| **quash** | **to nullify; suppress, extinguish completely** |

SAMPLE SENTENCES

pulmonary Pneumonia is a *pulmonary* disease; it is a disease *of the lungs*. In other news, the *pulmonary* artery goes from the heart to the *lungs*, and the *pulmonary* vein goes from the lungs back to the heart, carrying fresh oxygenated blood.

pundit Whenever there are events or probabilities coming up, *pundits* abound. They are *those who give opinions in an authoritative manner* about things.

purloin While no one was watching the barbecue being set up in the park, someone *purloined* all the T-bone steaks. The thief *wrongfully appropriated*, or *stole*, them.

purport The analysis by some pundits *purported* to express public opinion, but it turned out not to be the case. It *had the appearance of claiming* to reflect public opinion; it *professed* that it would.

purview To make a medical diagnosis, or offer an opinion as to the cause of death, is beyond the *purview* of park rangers. It is beyond their *range or limit of concern, authority, competence, or responsibility*.

punctilious Some institutions are more *punctilious* than others; they are more *careful* and *exact*, as well as *paying strict attention to details of codes or convention*.

pusillanimous One can be a bit chary or circumspect without being *pusillanimous* when facing challenges. Who wants to be *cowardly, craven, lacking courage or resolution*, or *contemptibly timid?*

putative According to the pundits, one team emerged as the *putative* leader. It is the *commonly accepted or supposed* top team, the one *assumed to be* the best.

Pyrrhic victory In mid-season the team won a crucial game, but it was a *Pyrrhic victory*; five star players were lost for the season with injuries. It was a *victory won at excessive cost*.

quash The mob was able to *quash* the speech of someone with whom they disagreed by drowning him out, to the detriment of those who invited him and wanted to hear what he had to say. The mob planned to *nullify* the speech, to *suppress* it, to *extinguish* it *completely* with its tactics.

ETYMOLOGY	OLD MEANING
WORD	NEW MEANING

L cauda
queue

tail
a waiting line of persons or cars

L quid nonc
quidnunc

what now?
one who seeks the latest gossip; busybody

NL quid pro quo
quid pro quo

something for something
something given or received for something else

quiescere
quiescent

to keep quiet or neutral; be at peace
at rest, inactive; causing no trouble

L quinta + essentia
quintessence

lit., fifth essence
the most typical example

Don Quixote
quixotic

hero of Cervantes novel, (1605, 1615)
idealistic to an impractical degree extravagantly chivalrous or romantic

L cottidianus
quotidian

daily; everyday, ordinary
everyday; ordinary, commonplace

MFr railler
raillery

to mock
good-natured ridicule; banter; jest

Fr raison d'être
raison d'être

reason for being
reason or justification for existence

L apportare
rapport

to bring, carry to
relation marked by harmony or accord

L raptare
rapt

to seize and carry off; drag away; plunder
wholly absorbed; engrossed

L ruptus
rapture

carrying off, abduction; plundering
expression of ecstasy or passion; great joy

L rara avis
rara avis

rare bird
a rare person or thing; rarity

SAMPLE SENTENCES

queue Casual in starting out on time, the football fans found a long *queue* at the will-call booth. They were at the tail end of a long *waiting line of people.*

quidnunc Most of those at the reception recognized the *quidnunc* of the group; she is the *one who seeks all the latest gossip,* the *busybody.*

quid pro quo The police offered the gunman his *safety for* his *testimony.* Both sides thought this to be a favorable *quid pro quo,* or *something for something.*

quiescent The reporters sensed the *quiescent* gloom and bitterness of the locker room after the game. The room was *quiet* and *motionless.*

quintessence He was the *quintessence* of frugality, the *most typical example* of a being a tightwad.

quixotic He was able to beguile some of the ladies at the party with his *quixotic* gestures. He charmed them with his *extravagantly chivalrous or romantic* ways.

quotidian His job was not very exciting; it was a *quotidian* routine. It consisted of an *everyday, commonplace,* and *ordinary* occupation.

raillery At a "roast" the guest of honor is the recipient of much *raillery;* he gets his share of *good natured ridicule, banter,* and *jest.*

raison d'être A field of endeavor for a committed individual is his or her *raison d'être.* It is the *reason or justification for existence* of the person.

rapport In a team effort it is important that each individual has good *rapport* with all the other teammates. *Relation marked by harmony and accord* is necessary.

rapt He was so *rapt* in his project that he was oblivious to everything else. He was *wholly absorbed* in it, *totally engrossed.*

rapture The home crowd expressed *rapture* when the team scored the winning touchdown in the waning moments of the game. The fans expressed *ecstasy, passion,* and *great joy.*

rara avis He was considered the local *rara avis* of politics, the disinterested man. He was indeed a *rare person,* or *rarity,* in this regard.

ETYMOLOGY	OLD MEANING
WORD	**NEW MEANING**

| MFr rocquet | head of a lance |
| **ratchet** | **to allow motion in one direction only** |

| L ratus | fixed, settled; sure; determined |
| **ratify** | **to approve formally; confirm** |

| L rationalis | having reason or understanding |
| **rationale** | **an underlying reason; basis** |

| L raucus | hoarse; harsh |
| **raucous** | **boisterously disorderly** |

| OFr reboter | to butt against |
| **rebut** | **to oppose in argument; disprove** |

| L recalcitrare | to kick back |
| **recalcitrant** | **defiant of authority; difficult to handle** |

| L recantare | to charm away |
| **recant** | **to make an open confession of error** |

| LL recapitulare | to restate by heads; sum up |
| **recapitulate** | **to repeat the main points of; summarize** |

| L recedere | to move back, withdraw; recede |
| **recession** | **a period of reduced economic activity** |

| Fr rechercher | to seek out |
| **recherché** | **exquisite; rare; choice; overly refined; affected; overblown, pretentious** |

| L reciprocare | move to and fro (ship); rise and fall (tide) |
| **reciprocate** | **give and take mutually; make a return for something; return in kind** |

| L re + claudere | re- + to close |
| **recluse** | **shut off from society or the world** |

| L reconciliare | to win back again, restore |
| **reconcile** | **restore to friendship; settle, resolve** |

Sample Sentences

ratchet Some people feel that taxes and expenses tend to *ratchet* up, while income does not. The former are *allowed to go in one direction only*: up

ratify In order to enact an amendment to the U.S. constitution, the legislatures of three fourths of the states must *ratify* it.; that is, they must *approve* it *formerly*.

rationale What was Isaac Newton's *rationale* for having a large hole cut in the door for the mother cat and a much smaller one cut next to it for the baby kittens? What was his *underlying reason* or *basis* for it?

raucous It was near midnight when *raucous* whoops of delight erupted from the fraternity house next door, as a fresh keg of beer arrived. It was a *boisterously disorderly* outburst.

rebut After one guy presents his argument in a debate, the opponent will get a chance to *rebut*; that is, *to oppose in argument*, or *disprove*, what he had to say.

recalcitrant The old gal was very *recalcitrant* in the hospital ward. She was very *defiant, resistant,* and *difficult to handle*.

recant New evidence made him realize he made a false accusation, and he came to *recant*. He came to *make an open confession of error*.

recapitulate Near the end of the hour the professor decided to *recapitulate* his lecture. He decided to *repeat the main points* of it, to *summarize* it.

recession A *recession* is not good for those in business. It is a *period of reduced economic activity*, which slows business down.

recherché The connoisseur sought only *recherché* items for his collection. He wanted *rare, choice, elegant,* and *carefully sought out* items.

reciprocate After having been invited to the magnificent dinner by their new friends, the couple decided to *reciprocate*. They decided to *return* the invitation.

recluse The hermit, *recluse* all his life, was recalcitrant about going on stage. All his life he was *shut off from society* and *from the world,* for that matter.

reconcile The mutually hostile neighbors decided to *reconcile* their differences. They planned to *settle*, or *resolve,* their differences.

ETYMOLOGY	OLD MEANING
WORD	**NEW MEANING**

L recondere	to store or hide away; to bury
recondite	**profound; hard to understand; obscure**

Fr recouper	to cut back
recoup	**make up for something lost; regain**

L criminari	to accuse; complain of; charge with
recrimination	**accusing in return; counter accusation**

L recumbere	to lie down, recline
recumbent	**leaning, resting; lying down**

L recusare	to refuse, decline; be reluctant; object
recuse	**to disqualify oneself as a judge**

L redigere	to bring back; to reduce; bring
redact	**to edit; adapt for publication**

L redolere	to give out a smell; smell of, smack of
redolent	**evocative; suggesting thoughts or feelings**

MFr redouter	to dread
redoubtable	**causing fear; formidable; worthy of awe**

OFr re- + drecier	to make straight
redress	**compensation for wrong or loss**

LL reductio ad absurdum	reduction to the absurd
reductio ad absurdum	**disproof of idea by showing absurdity to which it leads**

L redundare	to overflow; abound; be in excess
redundant	**repetitive; more than normal; not needed**

L referre	to refer to, trace back to; to reckon amongst
referendum	**a vote by a legislature or by the people**

L refragari	to oppose, thwart
refractory	**unruly; stubborn; unresponsive to stimuli**

SAMPLE SENTENCES

recondite The subject matter of an advanced course will be *recondite* for a student who did not take the prerequisite courses. It will be *profound, hard to understand.*

recoup It is a habit of many gamblers to try to *recoup* their losses by continuing to play. They think they can *make up for what they lost*, or *regain* what they lost.

recrimination As the accusations and *recriminations* grew louder, the police were called in. Each accusation resulted in a loud *counter accusation.*

recumbent Taking a break from their promenade, the couple sat on a branch of a *recumbent* tree that had fallen across the stream. The tree was *resting.*

recuse The umpire had to *recuse* himself from the game because his son played on one of the teams. He decided to *disqualify himself as an umpire* in order to prevent any conflict of interest during the game.

redact They wanted to wait until all the facts were in before they could *redact* the story. They needed accurate information with which to *edit* the story.

redolent The skyline of Vancouver, British Columbia, is *redolent* of the skyline of San Francisco. One is *evocative* of the other.

redoubtable The hikers stopped at the wildly-raging, *redoubtable* white-water stream they must cross. One false step means one is history; it was *formidable, reason for fear,* and *worthy of awe.*

redress He sought *redress* after paying too much in taxes. He appealed to the agency for *compensation for wrong or loss.*

reductio ad absurdum He quickly noted the *reductio ad absurdum* in his opponent's argument. He stated the *disproof of his proposition by showing the absurdity to which it leads.*

redundant He wanted to get the point across without seeming *redundant.* He decided to paraphrase without being *repetitive* or emphasizing *more than normal.*

referendum If a legislature fails to respond to local needs, the people can petition for a *referendum,* which in this case is a *vote by the people.*

refractory The police had difficulty with the *refractory* suspect. He was *unruly, stubborn, and hard to handle.* In other news, a traffic light undergoes a *refractory* period, during which it is *unresponsive to a stimulus.*

ETYMOLOGY	OLD MEANING
WORD	**NEW MEANING**

L refutare
refute

to check, repress; disprove
to prove wrong; deny the truth

Fr régaler
regale

to treat to a delicious meal
entertain richly; indulge oneself

L regimen
regimen

guiding, steering; rule, command
a systematic plan; regular course

MFr rejoindre
rejoinder

to answer, reply
a reply: an answer to a reply

L relegare
relegate

send away, out of the way; banish
consign to insignificance; demote

L relentescere
relent

to slacken off
become less severe; let up; yield

L relevare
relevant

to lift up, lighten; relieve, ease
connected with the matter at hand

L relinquere
relinquish

leave, leave behind; abandon, forsake
give up; stop holding; release; yield

LL remandare
remand

to send back word
to order back to another court (a case)

L remittere
remiss

to send back; relax; slacken, loosen
negligent, careless; inattentive, lax

L remittere
remit

to send back
to send money, as in a payment

L re- + monstrare
remonstrate

to show, inform; instruct; denounce
to protest; expostulate; to object

L remordere
remorse

to worry; torment; to bite again
distress from sense of guilt; self-blame

SAMPLE SENTENCES

refute He was able to *refute* his opponent's argument, to *prove* it *wrong*. Elsewhere, she *refuted* the election returns which showed her the loser. She *denied the truth*.

regale Some people often *regale* in celebration of a momentous event. They like to *entertain* their friends *richly*.

regimen She started a *regimen* of diet and exercise that paid off. It was a *systematic plan*, a *regular course*, that was very beneficial.

rejoinder His recrimination was met with a sharp *rejoinder* from another member of the panel discussion. It was an *answer to* his *reply* to a question.

relegate Instead of having a role in the school play, he was *relegated* to the job of backstage maintenance. He was *consigned to insignificance*, i.e., *demoted*.

relent Angry at first, the host *relented* when he found his dog hiding after having snitched an hors d'oeuvre from the tray. He *became less severe* over the matter.

relevant Her questions were *relevant* to the discussion. They were very much *connected with the matter at hand*.

relinquish The wire-haired terrier would not *relinquish* his grip on the guest's trousers. No one could get him to *stop holding* or *release* his firm grip.

remand The high court decided to *remand* the case to the lower court, that is, to *order the case back to the other court* for reconsideration.

remiss The professor said he would be *remiss* if he did not post the examination schedule on the bulletin board. He did not wish to be *negligent, careless, inattentive*, or *lax* about any aspect of his course.

remit The company allowed the customer 90 days in which to *remit* the first payment. He had 90 days in which to *send the money, as in a payment*.

remonstrate The tenor who was relegated to maintenance duties in the auditorium *remonstrated* with the choir director. He *protested, expostulated,* and *objected* to being consigned to oblivion instead of being in the choir.

remorse Already 20 miles out of town, he felt great *remorse* for forgetting to pay at the restaurant for his lunch. He felt *distress from a sense of guilt* and *self-blame* for being so remiss.

ETYMOLOGY	OLD MEANING
WORD	**NEW MEANING**

L remunerari	to repay, reward
remunerate	**to pay an equivalent for; recompense**

MFr renaistre	to be born again
renaissance	**rebirth, revival (of an activity)**

Fr rendre	to give back, return, bring back
render	**deliver; yield; cause to be; impart**

MFr rendez vous	present yourselves
rendezvous	**a place appointed for a meeting**

L re- + negare	to deny
renege	**go back on a promise; back out**

L renuntiare	to announce; refuse, call off
renounce	**to refuse to follow or recognize further**

L reparare	to retrieve, recover; restore; repair
reparation	**compensation for a wrong; payment of damages**

Fr repartir	to retort, reply, answer back
repartee	**quick, witty reply; cleverness in reply**

L repercutere	drive back; make rebound; reflect, echo
repercussion	**action or effect given in return; unforeseen effect**

Fr répertoire	index notebook; list; catalogue
repertoire	**list or supply of skills or devices used**

L re- + plenus	full, filled
replenish	**to fill or build up again**

L reprehendere	to hold back, catch; restrain; to blame
reprehensible	**worthy of censure; culpable**

L reprimere	to keep back, force back; to check
reprimand	**a severe or formal criticism for a fault**

SAMPLE SENTENCES

remunerate The boss wanted to *remunerate* the man for a job well done plus expenses. He planned to *pay* him *an equivalent amount for* all he had done.

renaissance There are signs of a *renaissance* of individualism in the society. Signs of a *rebirth*, or *revival* of it, are evidenced by increasing entrepreneurship.

render The surprise arrival of the police, who surrounded the building, was enough to *render* the gunman powerless. The maneuver *caused* him *to be* powerless; it *left* or *made* him powerless.

rendezvous In order to go over their confidential plans, they agreed to meet at a secret *rendezvous* in a run-down section of the city. It was a well hidden *place appointed for the meeting*.

renege It was considered very unwise to *renege* on "The Boss." He paid big money for tough assignments, but it was curtains to *go back on a promise* or *back out of* a *deal* with "The Boss."

renounce He decided to *renounce* the political party for drifting too far from his beliefs. He *refused to follow or recognize* it *further*.

reparation She sought *reparation* from the dolt who rammed her car. She threatened to sue for *payment of damages*.

repartee The two jokers amused the others with their *repartee*. Each was capable of *quick, witty reply* or *cleverness in reply*.

repercussion No one could tell what the *repercussion* might be when the popular coach was fired. The administration was worried about the *unforeseen effect*.

repertoire He has an amazing *repertoire* of jokes designed to amuse the guys. He has quite a *list or supply of skills* when it comes to humor.

replenish The hiker's canteen was almost out of water, and he wished to *replenish* it. He hoped to *fill* it *up again*, and soon.

reprehensible Her abasement of him in front of his new friend was *reprehensible*. It was *worthy of censure*, or *culpable*.

reprimand The attorney got a *reprimand* from the judge for allowing his client to get out of hand. He received a *severe, formal criticism for the fault*.

ETYMOLOGY	OLD MEANING
WORD	**NEW MEANING**

L reprehendere
reprisal

to hold back; seize, catch
act of getting even against someone

OFr reprochier
reproach

to blame, censure
cause of blame; disgrace; disapproval

L repudiare
repudiate

to reject, refuse, scorn; to divorce
**refuse to accept or acknowledge;
reject as untrue or unjust**

L repugnare
repugnant

to fight against; oppose, resist; disagree
causing distaste or aversion; unlikable

L reputare
repute

to count back; think over, consider
one's character or status

L requirere
requisite

look for, search for; inquire after
essential, necessary

ME quiten
requite

quit
make a return for, repay; get even, avenge

L rescindere
rescind

cut back, cut open; annul
take back, annul, cancel; to void, repeal

Fr resentir
resent

to be emotionally sensitive of
to express annoyance or ill will at

MF reserver
reservation

to reserve
a limiting condition; specific objection

L resilire
resilient

to jump back; to recoil, rebound
**able to withstand shock or adjust to bad
luck**

L resolvere
resolute

to unfasten, loosen, open, release
determined; bold, firm, steady

L respectus
respite

act of looking back; refuge
temporary delay; interval of rest or relief

SAMPLE SENTENCES

reprisal Before committing a *reprisal* against someone, consider other means of dealing with him. Give him a chance to atone rather then doing an *act of getting even.*

reproach As the membership committee filed out of the room, two of them seemed to look at him with *reproach*. They had a look of *disapproval* toward him.

repudiate Half of the crowd *repudiated* the speaker's statements. That group *refused to accept* his ideas and *rejected* them *as untrue.*

repugnant The drunk's *repugnant* actions at the game got him escorted from the arena. His loud swearing and other behavior was *distasteful, objectionable*, and *highly unlikable.*

repute The attorney asserted that his client was a man of high *repute*, and that bail should be set at a low figure. He was of high *character and status* in the community.

requisite He has the skills and tools *requisite* for the position. He has the ability and talent *necessary* for the job.

requite It is natural to *requite* kindness with kindness. People tend to *repay*, or *make a return for*, whatever is offered.

rescind The city council decided not to *rescind* the ordinance against leaf-blowers. The council voted not to *annul, cancel,* or *repeal* it.

resent He *resented* the unkind remark made about his friend. He *expressed annoyance* and *ill will at* it.

reservation The admissions dean had some *reservation* about the application of the superstar athlete. She set a *limiting condition* on its consideration.

resilient To become a good camper one must learn to be *resilient*. One must be *able to withstand shock or adjust to bad luck,* come what may.

resolute If she starts a project, she will finish it. She is *resolute*. She is *determined, bold, firm,* and *steady,* in the pursuit of her goals.

respite The boss offered his beleaguered clerk a *respite* in the coffee lounge by filling in for him. It was a welcome *interval of rest or relief* for the busy clerk.

ETYMOLOGY	OLD MEANING
WORD	**NEW MEANING**

L restituere — to replace, restore; rebuild; give back
restitution — **a making good for any loss**

MFr rester — to stop behind; remain
restive — **balky; restless, fidgety**

L resurgere — to rise again, revive
resurgent — **rising again into life, activity, or prominence**

L talion — punishment in kind
retaliate — **to repay in kind; to get revenge; requite**

L reticere — to be silent, say nothing; to keep secret
reticent — **inclined to be silent; restrained in expression**

L retorquere — to turn back; twist
retort — **a quick, witty, or cutting reply**

L retrahere — to draw back, drag back; withdraw, remove
retract — **take back, withdraw; disavow; recant**

L retribuere — to restore, repay
retribution — **reward; punishment as recompense**

MFr reviler — to despise
revile — **to use abusive language; rail**

L revocare — to call back, recall; to invite in return
revoke — **to annul by taking back; rescind**

L revellere — to pull out, tear off; to remove
revulsion — **a sense of utter distaste or repugnance**

Gk rhaptein + aiden — to sew together + to sing
rhapsody — **ecstasy, rapture**

Gk rhetorike — *lit.,* art of oratory
rhetoric — **skill in the effective use of speech**

SAMPLE SENTENCES

restitution If a golf ball goes through a window, the golfer should make *restitution* for the damage. He should be responsible for *making good for any loss.*

restive The substitue rider became *restive* at the sight of the brahma bull that only a championship cowboy should try. He was *balky, restless* and *fidgety.*

resurgent After a period of lassitude and mediocrity, he burst forth with a *resurgent* effort that won him great acclaim. It was an effort *rising again into activity, life, and prominence.*

retaliate Officials often call penalties against players who *retaliate* against players who started things. To *get revenge* for a wrong is what the officials see.

reticent He was *reticent* about the two-year hiatus in his résumé during the job interview. He was *inclined to be silent* about it.

retort The jury's laughter at the *retort* by the witness during the cross-examination disconcerted the district attorney; the *quick, witty reply* clearly upset the D.A.

retract Sometimes it is too late to *retract* a slip of the tongue. It can be embarrassing to have to *take back, disavow,* or *recant* an invidious remark.

retribution The iconoclast's *retribution* was a month in jail for vandalism. It was a fitting *punishment as recompense* (for what he did).

revile The light fine which caused him to *revile* was increased as retribution for doing so. It is not good policy to *use abusive language* or *rail* in a court of law.

revoke After a third conviction for drunk driving, it was time to *revoke* his license. The DMV did right to *annul* the license *by taking* it *back*, i.e., to *rescind* it.

revulsion His *revulsion* about being around cadavers ended his interest in medical school. He had a *sense of utter distaste and repugnance* for them..

rhapsody The rise of his stocks and the lowering of his golf score sent him into *rhapsody*. He had a feeling of *ecstasy* or *rapture.*

rhetoric Her *rhetoric*—not the issues—won her the debating society's top award. It was her *skill in the effective use of speech* that got her the top prize.

ETYMOLOGY WORD	OLD MEANING NEW MEANING
OFr ribauld **ribald**	unruly, befitting the rabble, low **crude, offensive; coarse**
ON rifr **rife**	abundant **increasing in degree; widespread**
MFr rifler **rifle**	to scratch, file; plunder **to ransack with intent to steal**
L rigor **rigor**	stiffness, hardness, numbness **severity; strictness; austerity; exactness**
It riposta **riposte**	*lit.,* answer **a retaliatory verbal quip; a retort**
L risus **risible**	laughter, laugh; laughing stock **arousing or provoking laughter; funny**
Fr risquer **risqué**	to risk **approaching impropriety; daring; off-color**
ME rubrike **rubric**	heading in red letters of part of a book **title; concept; class, category; custom**
L rudimentum **rudimentary**	first attempt, beginning **of a primitive kind; elementary**
OHG hriuwan **rue**	to regret **to feel sorrow, remorse, or regret for**
L ruminare **ruminate**	to chew the cud **go over in the mind; reflect, ponder**
Fr ruser **ruse**	to dodge, deceive **a crafty, clever deception or scheme; trick**

SAMPLE SENTENCES

ribald The intoxicated, loud, and *ribald* patron was regarded with revulsion by everyone else in the restaurant. This *crude, offensive, and coarse* man was asked to leave.

rife The campus was *rife* with rumors surrounding the new president. They were *widespread* and increasing in degree.

rifle The burglar *rifled* through every room of the house in search of valuables. He *ransacked with intent to steal.*

rigor The Donner Party faced many *rigors* while crossing the Sierra Nevada in heavy snow. They faced extreme *severity* and *austerity.*

riposte The *riposte* given by the debater left his opponent stunned. The *retaliatory verbal quip* left him abashed.

risible The final scene of the episode was *risible.* It was *funny.*

risqué Certain cocktail dresses can seem somewhat *risqué.* They can be somewhat *daring* and *approaching impropriety.*

rubric The teacher created a *rubric* which her students were to use toward the completion of a writing assignment. It was a *custom* to follow while writing.

rudimentary While traveling through the jungle we encountered *rudimentary* living conditions. The dwellings were *of a primitive* kind.

rue He *rued* the day he became involved with the wrong crowd. He *regretted* having associated with that group.

ruminate They *ruminated* on their plans to travel around the world in a hot air balloon. They *pondered* the idea.

ruse The embezzler used a *ruse* to avoid detection at the airport. He used a *clever deception* or *scheme* to elude the police.

QUIZ

Match the following words with their meanings:

(1) primordial   [   ] puzzling; not definite or settled; doubtful
(2) privation   [   ] inclination toward something; a leaning
(3) pristine   [   ] causing one to marvel; extraordinary
(4) prix fixe   [   ] a period of testing and trial to ascertain fitness
(5) privy   [   ] given to dissipation; wildly extravagant
(6) problematic   [   ] recklessly extravagant
(7) proclivity   [   ] adherence to the highest ideals and principles
(8) prodigal   [   ] first developed; earliest; primitive
(9) probation   [   ] the price charged for a table d'hôte meal
(10) prodigious   [   ] admitted as one sharing in a secret; in on
(11) probity   [   ] act of taking away; lack of what is needed
(12) profligate   [   ] uncorrupted by civilization; fresh, clean

(1) profound   [   ] unduly prolonged; long-winded
(2) promenade   [   ] an intense, urgent natural inclination
(3) profuse   [   ] not restricted to one person; casual
(4) proffer   [   ] to gain the favor of; appease, conciliate
(5) proletariat   [   ] one who argues in favor of something
(6) prosaic   [   ] marked by abundant productivity
(7) propinquity   [   ] a leisurely walk; a place for strolling
(8) promiscuous   [   ] having intellectual depth; intense of feeling; deep
(9) propitiate   [   ] to present for acceptance; to tender, offer
(10) proponent   [   ] the lowest social or economic class
(11) prolix   [   ] extravagant; showing great abundance
(12) propensity   [   ] nearness in blood relation, space, or time
(13) prolific   [   ] factual; dull; of the everyday world

(1) pro tem   [   ] situated close to; nearest; next to
(2) protocol   [   ] a clause that introduces a condition
(3) prognosticate   [   ] to outlaw; forbid as harmful; prohibit
(4) provincial   [   ] wise, judicious; circumspect; discreet
(5) protagonist   [   ] a high-ranking university administrator
(6) provenance   [   ] physical beauty
(7) puerile   [   ] for the time being
(8) proximal   [   ] having a belligerent nature; combative
(9) proscribe   [   ] to foretell from signs or symptoms
(10) prudent   [   ] juvenile; childish, silly
(11) pugnacious   [   ] narrow; lacking polish; unsophisticated
(12) proviso   [   ] place of origin; source
(13) provost   [   ] leader of a cause; champion; a leading part
(14) pulchritude   [   ] adherence to procedure at a formal function

(1) purview [ ] good-natured ridicule; banter; jest
(2) pulmonary [ ] careful, exact; paying strict attention to details
(3) quintessence [ ] reason or justification for existence
(4) pusillanimous [ ] commonly accepted or supposed; assumed to exist
(5) Pyrrhic victory [ ] expression of ecstasy or passion; great joy
(6) raillery [ ] range of authority, concern, competence, or responsibility
(7) punctilious [ ] lacking courage and resolution; cowardly; contemptibly timid
(8) rapture [ ] the most typical example
(9) putative [ ] relating to the lungs
(10) raison d'être [ ] a victory won at excessive cost

(1) quiescent [ ] everyday; ordinary; commonplace
(2) pundit [ ] one who seeks the latest gossip; busybody
(3) purport [ ] to nullify; suppress; extinguish completely
(4) quixotic [ ] wholly absorbed; engrossed
(5) rara avis [ ] critic; one who gives opinions in an authoritative manner
(6) quotidian [ ] idealistic to an impractical degree; ; extravagantly chivalrous
(7) queue [ ] relation marked by harmony and accord
(8) quidnunc [ ] a rare person or thing; rarity
(9) rapt [ ] at rest; inactive; causing no trouble
(10) quash [ ] to have the appearance of being something; to profess
(11) rapport [ ] a waiting line of persons or cars

(1) ratchet [ ] to oppose in argument; oppose
(2) raucous [ ] exquisite; rare; choice; overly refined; affected; pretentious
(3) ratify [ ] restore to friendship; settle, resolve
(4) rationale [ ] a period of reduced economic activity
(5) recant [ ] give and take mutually; return in kind
(6) recalcitrant [ ] shut off from society or the world
(7) recapitulate [ ] to allow motion in one direction only
(8) reconcile [ ] to approve formally; confirm
(9) recherché [ ] defiant of authority; difficult to handle
(10) rebut [ ] to repeat the main points of; to summarize
(11) recession [ ] an underlying reason; basis
(12) recluse [ ] boisterously disorderly
(13) reciprocate [ ] to make an open confession of error

(1) recondite   [   ] evocative; suggestion thoughts or feelings
(2) recrimination   [   ] disproof of idea by showing absurdity to
                         which it leads
(3) recoup   [   ] to disqualify oneself as a judge
(4) recumbent   [   ] repetitive; more than normal; not needed
(5) redress   [   ] a vote by a legislature or by the people
(6) redolent   [   ] unruly; stubborn; unresponsive to stimuli
(7) recuse   [   ] to edit; adapt for publication
(8) redoubtable   [   ] profound; hard to understand; obscure
(9) referendum   [   ] an accusing in return; counter accusation
(10) refractory   [   ] leaning, resting; lying down
(11) redact   [   ] make up for something lost; regain
(12) reductio ad absurdum
                     [   ] compensation for a wrong or loss
(13) redundant   [   ] causing fear; formidable; worth of awe

(1) refute   [   ] to entertain richly; indulge oneself
(2) relegate   [   ] to become less severe; let up; yield
(3) regimen   [   ] a reply; an answer to a reply
(4) relinquish   [   ] to order (a case) back to another court
(5) relevant   [   ] negligent, careless; inattentive, lax
(6) remit   [   ] to protest; expostulate; to object
(7) remorse   [   ] a systematic plan; regular course
(8) regale   [   ] to consign to insignificance; to demote
(9) relent   [   ] to prove wrong; deny the truth
(10) remiss   [   ] connected with the matter at hand
(11) rejoinder   [   ] distress from sense of guilt; self-blame
(12) remand   [   ] to send money, as in a payment
(13) remonstrate   [   ] to give up; stop holding; release; yield

(1) renaissance   [   ] a place appointed for a meeting
(2) remunerate   [   ] deliver; yield; cause to be; impart
(3) reparation   [   ] action or effect given in return; unforeseen
                         effect
(4) renounce   [   ] to fill up again; to build up again
(5) repartee   [   ] a severe or formal criticism for a fault
(6) rendezvous   [   ] a list or supply of skills or devices used
(7) renege   [   ] to pay an equivalent for; recompense
(8) repercussion   [   ] a rebirth, revival (of an activity)
(9) render   [   ] to refuse to follow or recognize further
(10) reprimand   [   ] compensation for a wrong; payment of damages
(11) replenish   [   ] to go back on a promise; to back out
(12) repertoire   [   ] a quick, witty reply; cleverness in reply

(1) reprisal   [ ] cause of blame; disgrace; disapproval
(2) reprehensible   [ ] essential, necessary
(3) repudiate   [ ] make a return for; repay; get even, avenge
(4) repute   [ ] temporary delay; interval of rest or relief
(5) repugnant   [ ] able to withstand shock or adjust to bad luck
(6) requite   [ ] to take back, annul, cancel; to void, repeal
(7) reproach   [ ] a limiting condition; specific objection
(8) requisite   [ ] worthy of censure; culpable
(9) resent   [ ] to refuse to accept or acknowledge; reject
                           as untrue or unjust
(10) respite   [ ] act of getting even against someone
(11) resilient   [ ] causing distaste or aversion; unlikable
(12) rescind   [ ] to express annoyance or ill will at
(13) reservation   [ ] one's character or status

(1) resolute   [ ] inclined to be silent; restrained in expression
(2) restitution   [ ] reward; punishment as recompense
(3) restive   [ ] crude, offensive; coarse
(4) retract   [ ] to use abusive language; rail
(5) retort   [ ] ecstasy, rapture
(6) reticent   [ ] rising again into life, activity, or prominence
(7) retribution   [ ] a sense of utter distaste or repugnance
(8) retaliate   [ ] to annul by taking back; rescind
(9) resurgent   [ ] determined; bold, firm, steady
(10) rhetoric   [ ] a quick, witty, or cutting reply
(11) ribald   [ ] balky; restless, fidgety
(12) revoke   [ ] to take back (what was said), withdraw;
                           disavow; recant
(13) rhapsody   [ ] skill in the effective use of speech
(14) revile   [ ] to repay in kind; to get revenge; to requite

(1) rife   [ ] arousing or provoking laughter; funny
(2) rigor   [ ] a title; concept; class, category; custom
(3) rifle   [ ] to feel sorrow, remorse, or regret for
(4) risible   [ ] approaching impropriety; daring; off-color
(5) ruse   [ ] a retaliatory verbal quip; a retort
(6) ruminate   [ ] to ransack with intent to steal
(7) rudimentary   [ ] increasing in degree; widespread
(8) rubric   [ ] a crafty, clever deception or scheme; a trick
(9) rue   [ ] to go over in the mind; reflect, ponder
(10) riposte   [ ] severity; strictness; austerity; exactness
(11) risqué   [ ] of a primitive kind; elementary

QUIZ

1. The person on campus holding the widest purview is a:
(a) protagonist   (b) quidnunc   (c) provost   (d) pundit

2. When the business owner sends out the bill, he hopes his customer will:
(a) regale   (b) remit   (c) renege   (d) ruminate

3. Most people enjoy talking with someone who is:
(a) raucous   (b) ribald   (c) recluse   (d) prudent

4. A store manager prefers a clerk known for his:
(a) probity   (b) ruses   (c) ripostes   (d) rejoinders

5. One usually enjoys a speech which is:
(a) prosaic   (b) recondite   (c) risible   (d) prolix

6. If something is resurgent, it is undergoing a:
(a) repercussion   (b) Pyrrhic victory   (c) renaissance   (d) referendum

7. When facing the rigors of rugged terrain and bad weather, the lost hikers should be:
(a) puerile   (b) resilient   (c) restive   (d) prodigal

8. Most people would prefer a neighbor who is known for his or her:
(a) recriminations   (b) reprisals   (c) rapport   (d) probation

9. Anyone would prefer a dentist who is:
(a) problematic   (b) promiscuous   (c) remiss   (d) punctilious

10. Couples usually like friends who are likely to:
(a) refute   (b) revile   (c) rifle   (d) reciprocate

BONUS QUIZ

The Latin word and meaning are given. Match the English word with each.

LATIN WORD	MEANING	ENGLISH WORD
1. primordium	beginning, origin	[ ] profound
2. pristinus	former, original; of yesterday	[ ] relevant
3. privatio	removal	[ ] queue
4. privatus	private; not in public office	[ ] resilient
5. probare	to approve; to appraise	[ ] proclivity
6. profundus	deep, vast; high	[ ] profligate
7. proles	progeny, offspring; child	[ ] primordial
8. redundare	to overflow, abound; be in excess	[ ] prodigious
9. relegare	send away, out of the way; banish	[ ] proscribe
10. relevare	lift up, lighten; relieve, ease	[ ] promiscuous
11. resilire	to jump back; recoil, rebound	[ ] pristine
12. ruminare	to chew the cud	[ ] relegate
13. cauda	tail	[ ] rapport
14. proclivis	downhill; prone, willing	[ ] privation
15. prodigium	portent; unnatural deed; monster	[ ] privy
16. proscribere	publish; advertise; confiscate	[ ] ruminate
17. profligare	to dash to the ground; extravagant	[ ] prolific
18. promiscuous	indiscriminate; open to all	[ ] redundant
19. apportare	to bring, carry to	[ ] probation

SEGMENT EIGHT

ETYMOLOGY	OLD MEANING
WORD	**NEW MEANING**

ON saga
saga
story, legend; history
a long detailed narrative or account

L sagire
sagacious
to perceive keenly
of keen judgment; discerning

L sapere
sage
to taste, have good taste; be wise
wise

L salire
salient
to leap, spring; to throb
standing out conspicuously; striking

L sal
saline
salt, brine; sea
containing salt; salty

L salire
sally
to leap, spring; to throb
a witty saying; bright retort; quip

L saltare
saltatory
to dance
by leaps rather than gradual; discontinuous

L salubris
salubrious
health-giving; wholesome; healthy, sound
promoting health or well-being

L salutaris
salutary
wholesome, healthy; beneficial
curative; producing a beneficial effect

L sanctus
sanctimonious
sacred, holy
hypocritically devout; assuming holiness

L sanctus
sanction
sacred, holy
authorized approval; economic coercive measure

L sanctus
sanctuary
sacred, holy
a place of refuge and protection

Fr sang-froid
sang-froid
lit, cold blood
self-possession under strain; equanimity

SAMPLE SENTENCES

saga The class reviewed the *saga* of the American farm—from feeding the family to feeding the world. They traced the *long detailed account* of American farm history.

sagacious Sometime after the founder died, the family business started to fall apart, so the heirs sought a *sagacious* outsider to turn things around. They wanted someone *of keen judgment* to run things.

sage Everyone in the village recognized the *sage* leader, but could they distinguish between a *wise* man and a *wise* guy?

salient Two students who spent the day at the beach asked friends to give them the *salient* features of the lecture they missed. They sought the *striking* parts of it, the parts *standing out conspicuously.*

saline As an eye-wash, a *saline* solution is better than pure water. Use sterile *salty* water.

sally "No, I'm not a career girl; are you a career boy?", came her *sally* in response to the guy's question. It was a *bright retort*, a good *quip.*

saltatory He worked on his project in a *saltatory* manner—by *leaps rather than steady* or *gradual* progress. His efforts were *discontinuous.*

salubrious Low-fat diets, enjoyable exercises, and serendipity can have a *salubrious* effect. Seek a regimen *promoting health and well-being.*

salutary Fresh air, good friends, and a large inheritance had a *salutary* effect on him. The combination was *curative* and *productive of a beneficial result.*

sanctimonious In order to gain the family's trust, the agent was *sanctimonious* at the funeral. He was *hypocritically devout* at the affair.

sanction He got a *sanction* from the city to build a tennis court, an *authorized approval.* In other news, the nations imposed a *sanction* on the dictatorship, an *economic coercive measure*, until it demonstrated much greater civility.

sanctuary To "get away from it all," he built a private den, all his own, which became his *sanctuary.* It was his *place of refuge and protection* from outside influences.

sang-froid The new pitcher showed plenty of *sang-froid* with the bases loaded, no outs, and before a hostile crowd. He demonstrated great *self-possession under stress* and *equanimity.*

ETYMOLOGY	OLD MEANING
WORD	**NEW MEANING**

L sanguis	blood, bloodshed; family; offspring, life
sanguine	**of blood; hopeful; optimistic**

L sapere	to have a taste; to have sense, be wise
sapid	**having agreeable flavor; palatable**

L sapient	to taste; be wise
sapient	**possessing great sagacity; wise, sage**

Gk sarkazein	to tear flesh like dogs; sneer
sarcasm	**caustic language meant to hurt**

Gk sardanios	derisive
sardonic	**derisively mocking; disdainfully humorous; scornful; cynical; sarcastic**

L sartus	patched, mended; repaired
sartorial	**of a tailor or tailored clothes**

L satis	enough, sufficient
satiate	**to satisfy a desire or appetite fully**

L satura	full plate, mixed dish
satire	**cutting wit or irony used to expose vice**

OPer xshathrapavan	*lit.*, protector of the dominion
satrap	**a subordinate official; henchman**

L Saturnus	Saturn, god of sowing, ruler of the Golden Age
saturnine	**slow to act; gloomy; of sardonic disposition**

Fr savoir	to know
savant	**a man of learning, *esp.* one of detailed knowledge in some specialized field**

Fr savoir-faire	*lit.*, knowing how to do
savoir-faire	**knowledge of just what to do (e.g., socially)**

L scaena	stage; stage setting; outward appearance
scenario	**an account of a course of action or events**

SAMPLE SENTENCES

sanguine After greeting a highly regarded recruiting class, the coach was *sanguine* about the prospects for the next season. He was very *hopeful* and *optimistic*.

sapid It was more than savoir-faire when he complimented the hostess for her *sapid* dinner. It was a *flavorful, palatable* meal, very *tasty*.

sapient Upperclassmen can often give *sapient* advice to incoming freshmen. Such *wise* or *sage* counsel can be of great help.

sarcasm The imperious writer was known for her *sarcasm*, stating that an acquaintance was sweet but had popcorn for brains. It was *caustic language meant to hurt*.

sardonic Political cartoonists are often *sardonic* in their portrayals of anyone with whom they disagree. They are *derisively mocking, disdainfully humorous*, and *cynical*.

sartorial He was a true dude—always arriving at parties in *sartorial* splendor. He was fastidious *about* his *tailored clothes*.

satiate Sometimes it takes a nimiety of something to *satiate* a person. Peanuts, chips, or chocolates in excess will *satisfy a desire or appetite fully*.

satire Several great writers are known for good *satire* in their essays. Their *cutting wit* or *irony used to attack or expose vice, corruption, etc.*, helped make needed changes.

satrap Governments are loaded with *satraps* when one considers all the fiefdoms involved. There are many *subordinate officials*, or *henchmen*, in a government.

saturnine The customs agent at the border was *saturnine* that day. He was *gloomy* and was *of sardonic disposition*.

savant A *savant* makes a good consultant. He is a *man of learning, especially one of detailed knowledge in a specialized field*.

savoir-faire He has plenty of *savoir-faire* at social functions. He has *knowledge of just what to do*, or a great deal of *tact*.

scenario She was asked to describe the *scenario* of the strange case, from the beginning to the denouement. They wanted her to give an *account of a course of events*.

ETYMOLOGY	OLD MEANING
WORD	**NEW MEANING**

Gk schizein	to split
schism	**division, separation; discord, disharmony**
L scintilla	spark
scintilla	**the slightest particle or trace**
L scire	to know
sciolism	**a superficial show of learning**
OHG chinan	to sprout
scion	**a descendant, a child**
Dan skof + law	jest, mockery + law
scofflaw	**a contemptuous law violator**
It scopo	purpose, goal
scope	**range of activity, influence, or operation**
OFr escorgier	to whip
scourge	**a cause of great affliction**
L scriba	clerk, writer
scribe	**public secretary; author, journalist**
Sw skrympa	to shrink
scrimp	**to be stingy in providing for; be frugal**
L scrupulus	small sharp stone; uneasiness, doubt
scruple	**ethical principle that inhibits action; qualm**
L scrutari	to search, examine; find out, probe into
scrutiny	**an inquiry; close watch; examination**
L scurra	jester, buffoon
scurrilous	**using coarse, vulgar, obscene, abusive language**
Fr seoir	to sit
séance	**a meeting for receiving spirit communications**

SAMPLE SENTENCES

schism A *schism* in the club resulted after a heated disagreement at the meeting. It was a *division of the club into two discordant groups.*

scintilla The defense attorney averred there was not a *scintilla* of evidence that showed any wrongdoing on the part of his client. He claimed there was not the *slightest trace* of evidence.

sciolism In a classroom or tour group it is fairly common to detect *sciolism* by someone. There is now and then someone who renders *a superficial display of learning.*

scion The heir to the estate is usually a *scion* of the founder, that is, a *descendant* of him.

scofflaw A *scofflaw* runs stop-signs, double parks, ignores ordinances, etc. He is a *contemptuous law violator.*

scope The chemistry professor told the student that labor policy was beyond the *scope* of class discussion when the matter of unionized particles arose. It was well beyond the *range of activity, purpose,* or *influence* of the field of chemistry.

scourge AIDS is a major *scourge* in many parts of the world. It is a *cause of great affliction* for many.

scribe She is a noted *scribe* for the newspaper, a well known *writer* or *journalist.*

scrimp Some students have to *scrimp* while going through college. They must *be frugal in providing for* themselves.

scruple Moral people have *scruples* about what they do, that is, they have *qualms* or *ethical principles that inhibit actions* of harmful or questionable nature. Others, however, have no *scruples* at all, which is unfortunate.

scrutiny The records of anyone who applies for a sensitive position of great responsibility must undergo close *scrutiny.* A *searching inquiry* is needed. In other news, a private eye must maintain a *close watch,* or *surveillance,* on a suspect.

scurrilous Some scribes have no scruples about their *scurrilous* attacks against those who disagree with their viewpoints. They have no qualms about using *coarse, vulgar, obscene,* or *abusive language.*

séance In the darkened room the group held a *séance,* which is a *meeting for receiving spirit communications,* i.e., a *session for talking with the dead.*

ETYMOLOGY	OLD MEANING
WORD	NEW MEANING

L secedere	to withdraw, retire; revolt
secede	**to withdraw from an organization**
L secludere	to shut off; to separate, remove
seclude	**to remove from outside influence**
L sedatus	calm, quiet, composed
sedate	**quiet, steady in attitude or pace; unruffled**
L sedentarius	sitting
sedentary	**stationary, settled; doing much sitting**
L seditio	separation; mutiny
sedition	**incitement to resistance to the law**
L seducere	to take away, withdraw; to divide
seduce	**to lead away by persuasion or false promises; to attract, to lure**
L sedulus	busy, diligent, assiduous; officious
sedulous	**diligent in application or pursuit; busy**
It segue	there follows
segue	**proceed to what follows without pause**
Gk semantikos	significant
semantics	**the study of meanings; meaning of signs**
L semen	seed
seminal	**contributing the seeds of later development; creative, original**
L seminarium	a nursery, seed plot
seminar	**a meeting for giving and discussing information**
L senilis	of an old person
senile	**showing loss of mental faculties with old age**
L sentire	to feel; experience; observe; think
sentient	**responsive; aware; finely sensitive in feeling**

SAMPLE SENTENCES

secede If the schism between the discordant factions gets too wide, one of them is likely to *secede*. It will *withdraw from the organization*, which, in the case of the Civil War, meant *withdrawing from the Union*.

seclude Once in a while it is good to *seclude* oneself from the busy activity all around. It is good to have a sanctuary, and thus *remove* oneself *from outside influence*.

sedate Despite all the distractions, she was able to remain *sedate*, that is, *unruffled, quiet,* and *steady in attitude or pace*.

sedentary He had a *sedentary* occupation, one that was *stationary, settled,* and involved *doing much sitting*.

sedition During periods of massive protest, the government has a hard time enforcing anti-*sedition* laws. These are laws against the *incitement to resistance to the law*.

seduce The wrong crowd tried to *seduce* the honest young merchant away from his business and clients. It tried to *lure* him *away by false promises* of fast money.

sedulous He is *sedulous* in his studies and other obligations and goals. He is *diligent in application or pursuit* of whatever he sets out to do.

segue The orchestra *segued* from one musical composition into another. It *proceeded to what followed without pause*.

semantics She was deeply involved with *semantics*, that is, the *study of meanings.* as well as the *study of the changes in meanings of words*.

seminal He is a truly *seminal* thinker. His ideas are *creative* and *original*; they influence other ideas, and thus are *contributing the seeds of later development*.

seminar Attending a *seminar* is often very beneficial. A *meeting for giving and discussing information* is both enjoyable and especially helpful.

senile People become *senile* at various ages, and some seem to never become *senile*. It is a condition *showing loss of mental faculties with old age*.

sentient A group leader must always be *sentient* of her surroundings and responsibilities. She must be *responsive, sensitive,* and *aware* of things that may happen.

ETYMOLOGY	OLD MEANING
WORD	**NEW MEANING**

L sequi	to follow; come after
sequacious	**intellectually servile; imitative, obsequious**

L sequi	to follow; come next
sequel	**consequence, result; subsequent development; next installment**

LL sequestrare	to set apart for safekeeping
sequester	**set apart, segregate; seclude, withdraw**

from Three Princes of Serendip (Ceylon, now Sri Lanka), Horace Walpole, ca. 1754	
serendipity	**luck in finding good things accidentally**

L serra	a saw
serrate	**notched or toothed on the edge**

L servus	slave, servant
servile	**of a menial position; cravenly submissive**

L separare	to part, separate, divide; to distinguish
sever	**keep apart; remove by cutting; separate**

ME shrewe	an evil or scolding person
shrew	**an ill-tempered scolding woman**

ME shrewe + -ed	causing trouble; mischievous; naughty
shrewd	**clever, keen, astute; tricky, crafty**

L sibilare	to hiss, whistle; to hiss at
sibilant	**having the sound of *s* or *sh* in *sash***

L sic	so, thus, this way
sic	**intentionally so written**

ME sidling	side
sidle	**to move sideways, esp. in a furtive advance**

L significare	to indicate, show; to mean
signify	**to mean, denote; imply; to matter**

SAMPLE SENTENCES

sequacious Dictators and other powerful politicians are strengthened by *sequacious* populations, the *intellectually servile, obsequious,* and *imitative* masses who recite clichés and mantras given to them from above.

sequel Higher prices come as a *sequel* to higher production costs, or the *result* thereof. "The Marriage of Figaro" is the *sequel* to "The Barber of Seville." It is the *subsequent development*, or the *next literary installment,* of the latter.

sequester When the wolves are on the prowl, it is time to *sequester* the sheep. We must *seclude* or *withdraw* them. Also, one might *set apart* the good lumber *for a special purpose.*

serendipity The discovery of the cave at Lascaux was an example of *serendipity.* The boys experienced *luck in finding a good thing accidentally.*

serrate In the forest the hikers found an old double-edged bayonet, sharp and smooth on one side and *serrate* on the other, that is, *notched or toothed on the edge.*

servile For some reason he always acted in a *servile* manner around only certain people. His behavior was *menial (humble)* and *cravenly submissive* around them.

sever The widening schism between the two discordant factions caused them to *sever* all relations. They decided to *keep apart* from each other, to *cutting off* relationships.

shrew When some fans set on a tailgate on her lawn, the *shrew*, an *ill-tempered scolding woman,* turned on the sprinkling system.

shrewd He was no patsy or sucker; in fact, he was very *shrewd* in his business dealings. He was *clever, keen,* and *astute*, and at times *tricky* and *crafty* as well.

sibilant While resting momentarily on some rocks at the bottom of a cliff, the hikers were suddenly concerned about a *sibilant* noise, one *having the sound of s or sh in sash.*

sic The expression *sic* usually points out an apparent error, a misprint, typo, or intentional original by the writer and not the publisher, and is surrounded by parentheses. Examples: "He said he seed (sic) it all." "All that glisters (sic) is not gold." "The capital of the United States is Washingtown (sic)."

sidle On group trips it is usually the fat balding guy who manages to *sidle* up to the pretty tour guide. He will *move sideways in a furtive advance* toward her.

signify What does his gesture *signify?* What does it *mean* or *imply?*

ETYMOLOGY	OLD MEANING
WORD	**NEW MEANING**

L similitudo	likeness; imitation; analogy; monotony
similitude	**image, likeness; imaginative comparison**

L sympathia	sympathy
simpatico	**congenial, likable**

Dan simper	affected, coy
simper	**to smile in a silly manner; smirk**

L simulare	to copy, imitate; feign; impersonate; pretend
simulate	**to give the appearance of, usu. to deceive**

ML sine cura	without cure of souls
sinecure	**extremely easy job that provides an income**

LL sine qua non	*lit.,* without which not
sine qua non	**an absolutely essential thing**

L sinister	on the left side; unfavorable; unlucky
sinister	**left; presaging ill-fortune, trouble, or disaster**

L from Gk Sisyphean	of the labors of Sisyphus
Sisyphean	**requiring continual but ineffective effort (rolling repeatedly a heavy stone uphill)**

Gk skeptikos	thoughtful, reflective
skeptic	**one disposed to doubt, uncertainty, or incredulity**

ON skiota	to shoot
skittish	**easily frightened; restive; coy, shy; cautious, wary**

Dan skulke	to shirk, play truant
skulk	**move furtively; hide oneself out of fear; to hide with sinister intent; lurk**

LL scandalum	stumbling block, offence
slander	**false, defamatory statements about a person**

ME slouthe	slow
sloth	**aversion to action or labor; laziness**

SAMPLE SENTENCES

similitude The defense attorney averred that the witness has his client confused with a *similitude*. He claimed she saw an *image,* or *double,* of his client.

simpatico They were pleased that the new neighbors seemed to be *simpatico*, especially after the harridan moved out. The new people were *congenial* and *likable*.

simper She will *simper* every time she thinks she has won a point in a controversial discussion. She will *smile in a silly manner,* or *smirk.* every time.

simulate With the recording of the violin solo safely behind a screen, he *simulated* the playing of it. He *gave the appearance of* playing it, to impress his new friends.

sinecure Some appointments are *sinecures*, such as director of flood control in a dry region. This is a *very easy job, involving little or no work, that provides income.*

sine qua non A passport is a *sine qua non* for an international tourist. It is the *one thing necessary,* the *absolutely essential thing* he must have while on the trip.

sinister Oculus *sinister,* or o.s., as seen on prescriptions, means *left* eye. In other news, the *sinister* expressions of the jurors as they filed in made the defendant uneasy. Their looks were *presaging ill-fortune, trouble, or disaster.*

Sisyphean Recounting the votes seemed to be a *Sisyphean* task. It turned out to be a job *requiring continual and ineffective effort.*

skeptic A *skeptic* poses a serious challenge to a pied piper, promoter, or salesman. He is a *person disposed to doubt, uncertainty, or disbelief.*

skittish She was *skittish* about committing her limited resources to the "get rich quick" proposal. She had reason to be *shy, cautious, and wary* about it.

skulk The dog *skulked* in the bushes until the right moment to grab the steak by the barbecue; he *hid with sinister intent.* Then he *skulked* in the bushes again. This time he *hid himself out of fear* of his master.

slander The politician was accused of *slander* by the supporters of his opponent. They cited him for *false, defamatory statements about their man.*

sloth The odd jobs around the house never got completed because of his *sloth*. His *aversion to action or labor* on weekends held him back. It was just plain *laziness.*

Etymology	Old Meaning
Word	**New Meaning**

ON slean
sly

to strike, beat
clever; furtive; crafty; tricky; dissembling

OE smerian
smirk

to laugh
to smile in an affected manner; simper

L sobrius
sobriety

sober; temperate, moderate; sane, sensible
state of being sober

Fr sobriquet
sobriquet

familiar name; nickname
nickname

L socius
socialist

companion, friend; partner, ally
**advocate of state-run businesses
and no private property**

L socius
socialite

companion, friend; partner, ally
a socially prominent person

Fr soi-disant
soi-disant

lit., saying oneself
**so-called; would-be; supposedly
(used disparagingly)**

Fr soigner
soigné

to take care of
elegantly maintained; well-groomed, sleek

Fr soirée
soirée

an evening period
an evening party or reception

L sub + LL diurnum
sojourn

under, during + day
a temporary stay; a stop

L solacium
solace

comfort, consolation, relief
alleviation of grief or anxiety

L soloecismus
solecism

grammatical mistake
speech blunder; breach of etiquette

L sollicitus
solicit

disturbed; troubled, worried; anxious
**to plea; strongly urge; entice, lure; ask,
invite**

SAMPLE SENTENCES

sly The *sly* party-crasher sidled his way into the reception line at the inaugural ball. To do this, he had to be *clever, furtive,* and *crafty.*

smirk Several guests saw the party-crasher *smirk,* and suspicions grew as nobody could identify him. They saw him *smile in an affected manner,* like the proverbial "cat who swallowed the canary."

sobriety On holidays the highway patrol will conduct *sobriety* tests on questionable drivers. The police want to check the *state of being sober* of such a motorist.

sobriquet A colorful, famous, or well-liked person will often have a *sobriquet.* It can be a descriptive term or a brief modification of a real name. It is a *nickname.*

socialist A *socialist* is an *advocate of government, or state, ownership of property, state operation of all businesses, and no private property or enterprises.*

socialite A *socialite* is a *socially prominent person,* often active and fairly wealthy.

soi-disant He is a *soi-disant* connoisseur of fine art and of wines. Beyond distinguishing between a red and a white, this *so-called* expert knows little about wines.

soigné The dude was always *soigné* at social gatherings. He was *well-groomed* and *sleek.*

soirée At a *soirée* it is often de rigueur to be soigné. At *an evening party or reception* one is expected to be well groomed or elegantly dressed.

sojourn On their way to Africa they spent a pleasant *sojourn* in London. It was a nice *temporary stay* in the city.

solace The doctor's encouraging words were *solace* to the worried parents. The good prognosis of their son's illness was *alleviation of grief or anxiety* to them.

solecism If a politician commits a *solecism,* the media are quick to jump on it. Everyone hopes to avoid a *speech blunder* or a *breach of etiquette.*

solicit The hawkers at a fair or bazaar will *solicit* the tourists to buy their wares. They will *strongly urge, entice, plea,* or *lure* the tourists to shop.

ETYMOLOGY	OLD MEANING
WORD	**NEW MEANING**
L sollicitus	agitated, disturbed; worried; careful
solicitous	**full of fears or anxiety; eager; careful**
L solus + loqui	alone + to speak
soliloquy	**act of talking to oneself; monologue**
L solvere	to loosen; to free, release; dissolve
solvent	**able to pay all debts; able to dissolve**
OFr saumalier	pack animal driver
sommelier	**one in charge of wines and their service**
L somnus + ambulare	sleep, sloth + to walk
somnambulist	**one who walks while asleep; sleepwalker**
L somnus	sleep
somnolent	**of a kind likely to induce sleep; drowsy**
L sonus	sound, noise
sonorous	**loud, noisy; full, clear, rich in tone**
Gk sophos	clever, wise
sophist	**philosopher, thinker; fallacious reasoner**
L sophisticus	sophistic
sophisticated	**complex; worldly-wise, knowing; finely aware; intellectually appealing**
Gk sophos + moros	wise + foolish
sophomore	**a student in his second year at college or secondary school**
Gk sophos + moros	wise + foolish
sophomoric	**conceited and overconfident of knowledge but poorly informed and immature**
L sopor	sleep; apathy
soporific	**tending to cause sleep or dull alertness**
L sordidus	dirty, squalid; shabby; in mourning; poor
sordid	**dirty, filthy; wretched; vile; mean**

SAMPLE SENTENCES

solicitous Both couples were *solicitous* about trying white-water kayaking. One was *full of fears or anxiety*, while the other was *eager* to try it.

soliloquy Hamlet's famous *soliloquy* provides much food for thought. It is a *monologue*, or an *act of talking to oneself.*

solvent Her father wanted to make sure her boyfriend was *solvent* before getting serious about matrimony. He needed to know if he was *able to pay all* his *debts.*

sommelier A fine restaurant usually has a *sommelier*, that is, *someone in charge of wines and their service.*

somnambulist The night watchman saw a *somnambulist* walking across the campus. He saw a *sleepwalker* ambulating past the library during the night.

somnolent The lengthy discussion of the by-laws resulted in a *somnolent* experience. It was a meeting *of a kind likely to induce sleep.*

sonorous A shy, soft-spoken potential actor should develop a *sonorous* speech delivery. His words should be *full, clear,* and *rich in tone.*

sophist Any professor should be a *sophist* in the sense of a *philosopher* or *thinker*. But beware the *one who uses fallacious reasoning for purposes of deceiving.*

sophisticated They are a *sophisticated* couple. They are *worldly-wise, knowing,* and *finely aware and experienced.* They are not naïve or simple-minded.

sophomore Having survived freshman year, he is now a *sophomore*. He is now a *student in his second year at the university.*

sophomoric A student should avoid *sophomoric* tendencies. To be *conceited and over-confident but poorly informed and immature* in the presence of true sophists or sophisticated persons can be embarrassing.

soporific Smart students regard the subject matter in class as the most important part of their lives for the 50-minute duration, and never allow it to be *soporific.* Class topics must not be guilty of *tending to cause sleep or dull alertness.*

sordid There is a tendency among sophisticated people to improve the *sordid* conditions of the world's poorest. The latter live in *filthy, wretched* circumstances, but they have an instinctive resistance to outsiders, which perpetuates the problem.

ETYMOLOGY	OLD MEANING
WORD	**NEW MEANING**
Fr sous + chef	under, beneath + chef
sous-chef	**a chef's assistant**
OFr soverain	super, over, above
sovereign	**independent, self-governing**
L speciosus	showy, beautiful; plausible
specious	**having false look of truth or genuineness; having deceptive attractiveness**
L specere	to look, look at
specter or spectre	**ghost; something that haunts the mind**
L spectrum	appearance
spectrum	**continuous sequence or range**
L splen	spleen
splenetic	**marked by bad temper, malevolence, or spite**
L spondere	to promise, pledge, or vow; put up bail for
sponsor	**one who takes responsibility for or pays for a project**
L sponte	voluntarily; of one's own free will
spontaneous	**self-acting; developing without external cause**
Gk sporaden	here and there
sporadic	**occurring occasionally; infrequent**
L spurius	of illegitimate birth
spurious	**false; forged; of a deceitful quality or nature**
L squalidus	rough; neglected; filthy; unpolished
squalid	**filthy; degraded by neglect or poverty; sordid**
OE staelwierthe	serviceable
stalwart	**one of great strength of body and spirit; an unwavering partisan**
L status quo	state in which
status quo	**the existing state of affairs**

SAMPLE SENTENCES

sous-chef Fortunate is the *sous-chef* who works with and learns from a great chef. Some day he or she will no longer be a *chef's assistant* but a full-fledged chef.

sovereign Many a colony would prefer to be a *sovereign* nation. They would rather be *independent, self-governing* countries.

specious One must be on the lookout for *specious* reasoning. One must be prepared to recognize claims *having the false look of truth or genuineness.*

specter The *specter* of the near accident makes him extra cautious. It is the *one thing that haunts his mind* every now and then.

spectrum Some politicians try to appeal to all factions of the political *spectrum* while others try to focus on the middle of the *range* of ideology.

splenetic A highly successful coach can be considered controversial if he is *splenetic* with reporters after a tough loss. His words are *marked by bad temper.*

sponsor He became the *sponsor* of the local Little League team. He was the *one who took responsibility for and paid for all the team's expenses.*

spontaneous What was intended to be a serious statement drew a *spontaneous* burst of laughter when everyone picked up the inadvertent double meaning. It was a *self-acting* reaction, one *developing without external cause.*

sporadic The success in catching fish that day was *sporadic* at best. It was *infrequent, occurring occasionally.*

spurious The jury saw through the *spurious* testimony of the witness. All the members of the panel agreed it was *false* and *of a deceitful nature.*

squalid The tourists were shocked to see the *squalid* living conditions of the local inhabitants. They were *filthy, degraded by neglect and poverty,* and *sordid.*

stalwart The practice-field *stalwart* is the truly dedicated football fan. He may or may not be *one of great strength of body* but is *one of spirit* and an *unwavering partisan.*

status quo The iconoclast tries to change the *status quo*, while others wish to preserve it. Many are generally satisfied with the *existing state of affairs.*

ETYMOLOGY	OLD MEANING
WORD	**NEW MEANING**

OFr estancher	to make watertight
staunch	**substantial; steadfast in loyalty or principle**

OE stelan	to steal
stealth	**act of moving furtively or secretly; slyness**

L stella	star
stellar	**astral; of a film star; leading; outstanding**

L stigma	brand
stigma	**a mark of shame or discredit: stain**

L stipendium	soldier's pay
stipend	**fixed sum of money paid periodically**

L stipulari	to demand a formal promise
stipulate	**to specify as a condition of an agreement**

Gk stoikos	of the portico at Athens where Zeno taught
stoic	**person indifferent to pleasure or pain**

L stolidus	dull, stupid
stolid	**having little or no sensibility; unemotional**

Gk strategein	to be a general, maneuver
stratagem	**a clever trick or scheme; skill in ruses**

L stringere	to draw tight, bind tight
stricture	**narrowed part; adverse criticism: censure; animadversion**

L stridere	to creak, hiss, shriek, whistle
strident	**harsh, insistent, and discordant in sound; commanding attention in a loud way**

L stringere	to draw tight, bind tight
stringent	**rigid, strict, or severe with regard to rule**

L stultus	foolish, silly
stultify	**to impair or frustrate by repressive influence**

SAMPLE SENTENCES

staunch He is a *staunch* supporter of the school's athletic program and its high academic standards. He is an *unwavering, steadfast in loyalty and principle.* type of fan.

stealth The spy worked his way by *stealth* past the agents in the crowded airport. He used a *maneuver of moving furtively, silently, and secretly* around the police.

stellar She gave a *stellar* performance of the piano concerto. It was *outstanding.*

stigma Hanging out with the wrong crowd can put a social *stigma* on one's reputation. Bad companions can put a *mark of shame or discredit,* or a *stain,* on one's repute.

stipend In olden times a star athlete would receive a *stipend* for very little work effort, e.g., carrying a few books into the library every Thursday. He would get a *fixed sum of money paid periodically* for his job, a true sinecure.

stipulate Because of the short cut-off time, the teams *stipulated* that if the score goes to 3-all, they will play a tie breaker. They *specified* that *as a condition of the deal.*

stoic Everyone but him was jumping for joy and ecstasy at the winning basket at the buzzer, and he didn't flinch when someone accidentally spilled hot coffee on him in all the excitement. He was a *stoic,* a *person indifferent to pleasure or pain.*

stolid No matter how hard the coach ranted and screamed at him, the referee remained *stolid.* He was *having little or no sensibility;* i.e., was *unemotional.*

stratagem The embezzler used a *stratagem* by hiring a double to lure the cops off in the wrong direction at the airport. It was a *clever trick,* or quite a *scheme.*

stricture Because he screwed up once, he became the victim of one *stricture* after another. Despite impeccable behavior since, he got repeated *adverse criticism.*

strident The larger the group, the more *strident* the tour leader's voice must be. His announcements must be *commanding attention in a loud way.*

stringent Some schools are lax, while others are *stringent* in policy. The latter are *rigid, strict, or severe with regard to rules.*

stultify Where there is no diversity of ideas, there is a policy to *stultify* free inquiry. With monolithic dogma goes the policy to *impair or frustrate* independent ideas *by repressive influence.*

ETYMOLOGY	OLD MEANING
WORD	**NEW MEANING**

L suavis
suave

sweet, pleasant, delightful
smooth, affable, and polite, often insincerely; superficially gracious in manner

L subicere
subjective

lit., to throw under; put under; expose
of individual bias or personal views

L sublimis
sublime

high, raised high, lifted up; elevated
awe-inspiring because of elevated quality

L subornare
suborn

to equip, furnish; instigate secretly
induce secretly to do an unlawful thing or commit perjury

L sub poena
subpoena

under penalty
writ commanding a person to appear in court under penalty for failure to do so

L subsidium
subsidiary

reserve troops
furnishing aid, auxiliary; of secondary importance

L subsistere
subsist

to stand still; make a stand; halt; hold out
persist, continue; get maintenance; live; hold true

L subterfugere
subterfuge

to escape from; evade
deception by artifice to hide or evade; a stratagem

L subtilis
subtle

finely woven; slender, fine
elusive; hard to distinguish; ingenious; artful, crafty; skillful; operating insidiously

L subvertere
subversion

to turn upside down; upset
an attempt to overthrow a government

L succingere
succinct

to gird up, tuck up
brief in expression without wasted words; concise

L succorrere
succor

come quickly up; run to the help of
relief; aid, help; something that furnishes relief

L sucus
succulent

juice, sap; flavor; strength, vigor
juicy; full of vitality, freshness, or richness

SAMPLE SENTENCES

suave The *suave* party crasher easily befriended several guests at the large reception. He was *smooth, affable, and polite;* he was also *superficially gracious in manner.*

subjective Party stalwarts and partisan fans usually see things in a *subjective* sense. They opine in a manner *of individual bias or personal views* and not objectively.

sublime It was a *sublime* evening—the stars were out with fragrance and music in the air, and he had won the lottery. The night was *awe-inspiring due to its high quality.*

suborn He was accused of trying to *suborn* a witness. He was cited for attempting to *secretly induce* the witness *to do the unlawful thing of committing perjury.*

subpoena He was issued a *subpoena* just before attempting to abscond with a suitcase full of fifty-dollar bills. The *writ commanding him to appear in court under a penalty for failure* to do so frustrated his plans.

subsidiary He was relegated to a *subsidiary* role in the school play, in which his friend was the star. His role was one *of secondary importance.*

subsist The lost patrol had to *subsist* on very little, as supplies were getting very low. It had to *get maintenance*, or *live*, off the land, until the rescue team found them.

subterfuge The smart embezzler avoided getting a subpoena by *subterfuge.* He used *deception by artifice to hide or evade* those looking for him. It was a *stratagem.*

subtle A politician often gives *subtle* answers to questions. He or she will offer *elusive, hard to distinguish, crafty, or artful* responses, rather than reply in no uncertain terms or with blunt answers.

subversion There are always small dissident groups who favor *subversion*, or an *attempt to overthrow the government.*

succinct Interrogators usually prefer *succinct* responses to their questions. They like *concise* replies or answers *brief in expression without wasted words.*

succor The lost patrol suddenly realized that *succor* was on the way when they spotted the helicopters coming towards them. *Relief* and *help* were about to arrive.

succulent The succor for the lost patrol included *succulent* meats and fruits. The foods were *juicy* and *full of vitality, freshness, or richness.*

ETYMOLOGY	OLD MEANING
WORD	**NEW MEANING**

L succumbere	to fall, sink under; submit, surrender
succumb	**to yield to overpowering appeal or desire; be brought to an end by destructive forces**

L solus	only, alone; lonely, deserted
sullen	**gloomily or resentfully silent; dismal**

L sumptus	expense, cost
sumptuary	**designed to regulate spending and stop extravagance**

L sumptuosus	expensive, lavish, extravagant
sumptuous	**excessively costly, rich, luxurious, or magnificent**

ME sundry	different for each
sundry	**miscellaneous, various**

L supercilium	eyebrow; brow; arrogance
supercilious	**coolly and patronizingly haughty; proud**

L superficies	top, surface
superficial	**cursory; lacking in depth of intellect; not far-reaching**

L superfluere	to overflow
superfluous	**exceeding what is enough or necessary; extra**

L super- + numerus	above + number
supernumerary	**exceeding the usual number; more than needed**

L supersedere	to be superior to; refrain from, desist
supersede	**take the place of by being better suited for; supplant**

L supplantare	to trip up; overthrow by tripping up
supplant	**replace and substitute for by being superior; supersede by force or trickery**

L supplere	to fill up, make good, complete
supplement	**something that completes or adds to**

L supplicare	to entreat, pray to, worship
supplicate	**to ask or ask for humbly and earnestly; to beg**

SAMPLE SENTENCES

succumb Despite his modest income, he *succumbed* to the urge to buy an expensive new car. He *yielded to overpowering appeal or desire* to do so.

sullen A month later he was *sullen* because the monthly payments ate up most of his income. He was *gloomily or resentfully silent*, indeed *dismal*, because his life style was now drastically curtailed.

sumptuary He should have sought stringent *sumptuary* advice instead of the dulcet words of the suave salesman. He needed advice *designed to regulate spending and stop extravagance.*

sumptuous He joined a club that had many wealthy members, but he has no intention of trying to emulate their *sumptuous* lifestyles. Their *excessively costly, rich,* or *luxurious* ways of life were beyond his means.

sundry The agenda contained *sundry* topics. It had *miscellaneous* or *various* items to be considered.

supercilious She has a *supercilious* attitude. She is *coolly and patronizingly haughty.*

superficial The dilettante's knowledge in widely sundry areas of interest is *superficial.* His interest is *cursory, lacking in depth,* and *not far-reaching.*

superfluous Why are there *superfluous* carrot sticks among the hors d'oeuvres, but a shortage of meatballs, shrimp, and crab cakes? The carrot sticks always seem to be *exceeding what is enough or necessary,* or *extra,* in supply.

supernumerary Three volunteers were needed to serve food at the picnic, but five showed up. Two were *supernumerary,* that is, *more than were needed.*

supersede The incandescent lamp *superseded* the kerosene lantern, just as the automobile *took the place of* the horse-drawn buggy *by being better suited for* its purpose.

supplant Cassettes *supplanted* LP's, and CD's *replaced and substituted for* cassettes *by being superior* for sound and longevity.

supplement Her part-time specialized teaching at the school is a *supplement* to the regular courses. Her specialty is *something that adds to* regular education.

supplicate He *supplicated* the intransigent cop not to give him a speeding ticket. He *asked* him *humbly and earnestly,* indeed *begged* him, not to write a ticket.

QUIZ

Match the following words with their meanings:

 (1) sagacious   [ ] by leaps rather than gradual; discontinuous
 (2) salutary   [ ] containing salt; salty
 (3) saga   [ ] a place of refuge and protection
 (4) salient   [ ] hypocritically devout; assuming holiness
 (5) sally   [ ] authorized approval; economic coercive
                            measure
 (6) salubrious   [ ] of keen judgment; discerning
 (7) sang-froid   [ ] a long detailed account or narrative
 (8) saltatory   [ ] wise
 (9) sanctuary   [ ] a witty saying; bright retort; quip
(10) saline   [ ] standing out conspicuously; striking
(11) sanction   [ ] self-possession under strain; equanimity
(12) sanctimonious   [ ] promoting health or well-being
(13) sage   [ ] curative; producing a beneficial effect

 (1) sanguine   [ ] having agreeable flavor; palatable
 (2) sarcasm   [ ] knowledge of just what to do (socially)
 (3) satrap   [ ] a man of learning, *esp.,* one of detailed
                            pecialized knowledge
 (4) satiate   [ ] to be stingy in providing for; be frugal
 (5) sapient   [ ] derisively mocking; disdainfully humorous;
                            scornful; cynical
 (6) scenario   [ ] cutting wit; irony used to expose vice
 (7) scion   [ ] a subordinate official; a henchman
 (8) scrimp   [ ] to satisfy a desire or appetite fully
 (9) sardonic   [ ] of blood; hopeful; optimistic
(10) savoir-faire   [ ] an account of a course of action or events
(11) savant   [ ] a descendant; a child
(12) sapid   [ ] possessing great sagacity; wise, sage
(13) satire   [ ] caustic language meant to hurt

(1) schism   [   ] the slightest particle or trace

(2) sciolism   [   ] ethical principle that inhibits action; qualm

(3) sartorial   [   ] using coarse, vulgar, obscene, or abusive language

(4) scribe   [   ] a contemptuous law violator

(5) scope   [   ] a cause of great affliction

(6) séance   [   ] an inquiry; close watch; examination

(7) saturnine   [   ] of a tailor or tailored clothes

(8) scintilla   [   ] range of activity, influence, or operation

(9) scofflaw   [   ] public secretary; author; journalist

(10) scruple   [   ] division, separation; discord, disharmony

(11) scurrilous   [   ] slow to act; gloomy; of sardonic disposition

(12) scourge   [   ] a meeting for receiving spirit communications

(13) scrutiny   [   ] a superficial show of learning

(1) sedate   [   ] responsive; aware; finely sensitive in feeling

(2) secede   [   ] proceed to what follows without pause

(3) sedition   [   ] a meeting for giving and discussing information

(4) sedentary   [   ] showing loss of mental qualities with old age

(5) sedulous   [   ] contributing the seeds of later development; creative; original

(6) seduce   [   ] to remove from outside influence

(7) semantics   [   ] incitement to resistance to the law

(8) sentient   [   ] diligent in application or pursuit; busy

(9) segue   [   ] to lead away by persuasion or false promises; to attract, lure

(10) senile   [   ] stationary; settled; doing much sitting

(11) seminar   [   ] the study of meanings; meaning of signs

(12) seclude   [   ] to withdraw from an organization

(13) seminal   [   ] quiet, steady in attitude or pace; unruffled

(1) sequacious   [   ] clever, keen, astute; tricky, crafty

(2) sequester   [   ] to move sideways, *esp.,* in a furtive advance

(3) sequel   [   ] luck in finding things accidentally

(4) serrate   [   ] intentionally so written

(5) servile   [   ] having the sound of *s* or *sh* in *sash*

(6) signify   [   ] to set apart, segregate; seclude, withdraw

(7) serendipity   [   ] image, likeness; imaginative comparison

(8) shrewd   [   ] of a menial position; cravenly submissive

(9) sidle   [   ] keep apart; remove by cutting; to separate

(10) sic   [   ] intellectually servile; imitative; obsequious

(11) similitude   [   ] consequence, result; subsequent development; next installment

(12) sever   [   ] to mean, denote; imply; to matter

(13) sibilant   [   ] notched or toothed on the edge

(1) simpatico   [   ] left; presaging ill-fortune, trouble, or disaster

(2) sinecure   [   ] aversion to action or labor; laziness

(3) simper   [   ] to give the appearance of, *usually* to deceive

(4) shrew   [   ] one disposed to doubt, uncertainty, or incredulity

(5) sinister   [   ] requiring continual but ineffective effort

(6) sine qua non   [   ] false, defamatory statements about a person

(7) simulate   [   ] move furtively; lurk; hide out of fear or with sinister intent

(8) skeptic   [   ] an ill-tempered scolding woman

(9) skittish   [   ] congenial, likable

(10) slander   [   ] an extremely easy job that provides an income

(11) skulk   [   ] to smile in a silly manner; smirk

(12) Sisyphean   [   ] easily frightened; restive; coy, shy; cautious, wary

(13) sloth   [   ] an absolutely essential thing

(1) sly   [ ] able to pay all debts; able to dissolve
(2) sobriety   [ ] an evening party or reception
(3) smirk   [ ] to plea; strongly urge; entice, lure; ask, invite
(4) soi-disant   [ ] full of fears or anxiety; eager; careful
(5) socialist   [ ] a socially prominent person
(6) sobriquet   [ ] state of being sober
(7) soigné   [ ] clever; furtive; crafty; tricky; dissembling
(8) soirée   [ ] a temporary stay; a stop
(9) solicit   [ ] to smile in an affected manner; simper
(10) socialite   [ ] advocate of state-run businesses and no
                          private property
(11) solicitous   [ ] elegantly maintained; well-groomed, sleek
(12) sojourn   [ ] nickname
(13) solvent   [ ] so-called; would-be; supposedly

(1) somnolent   [ ] loud, noisy; full, clear, rich in tone
(2) sommelier   [ ] one who walks while asleep; a sleepwalker
(3) solace   [ ] speech blunder; breach of etiquette
(4) sophisticated   [ ] overconfident of knowledge but poorly
                          informed and immature
(5) somnambulist   [ ] a student in his second year of high school
                          or college
(6) sonorous   [ ] tending to cause sleep or dull alertness
(7) soliloquy   [ ] alleviation of grief or anxiety
(8) sophist   [ ] one in charge of wines and their services
(9) sordid   [ ] of a kind likely to induce sleep; drowsy
(10) sophomoric   [ ] complex; worldly-wise, knowing; finely
                          aware and experienced
(11) solecism   [ ] act of talking to oneself; monologue
(12) soporific   [ ] dirty, filthy; wretched; vile; mean
(13) sophomore   [ ] a philosopher, thinker; fallacious reasoner

(1) sovereign   [   ] occurring occasionally; infrequent
(2) sous-chef   [   ] a person indifferent to pleasure or pain
(3) specter   [   ] the existing state of affairs
(4) specious   [   ] self-acting; developing without external
                            cause
(5) splenetic   [   ] independent, self-governing
(6) sponsor   [   ] one of great strength of body and spirit; an
                            unwavering partisan
(7) spectrum   [   ] a ghost; something that haunts the mind
(8) sporadic   [   ] having false look of truth; having deceptive
                            attractiveness
(9) spontaneous   [   ] false; forged; of a deceitful quality or nature
(10) stoic   [   ] one who takes responsibility for or pays for
                            a project
(11) status quo   [   ] a continuous sequence or range
(12) spurious   [   ] marked by bad temper, malevolence, or
                            spite
(13) stalwart   [   ] a chef's assistant

(1) squalid   [   ] substantial; steadfast in loyalty or principle
(2) stealth   [   ] a mark of shame or discredit; stain (on a
                            reputation)
(3) stellar   [   ] having little or no sensibility; unemotional
(4) stipulate   [   ] to impair or frustrate be repressive influence
(5) stipend   [   ] narrowed part; adverse criticism; censure;
                            animadversion
(6) staunch   [   ] harsh, insistent, and discordant; loud in
                            commanding attention
(7) stigma   [   ] a clever trick or scheme; skill in ruses
(8) stringent   [   ] filthy; degraded by neglect or poverty; sordid
(9) stultify   [   ] to specify as a condition of an agreement
(10) stolid   [   ] of a film star; leading; outstanding
(11) stricture   [   ] act of moving furtively or secretly; slyness
(12) strident   [   ] rigid, strict, or severe with regard to rule
(13) stratagem   [   ] a fixed sum of money paid periodically

(1) suave [ ] brief in expression without wasted words; concise

(2) subjective [ ] elusive; hard to distinguish; artful; crafty; operating insidiously

(3) subpoena [ ] relief; aid, help; something that furnishes relief

(4) sublimate [ ] to induce secretly to do an unlawful thing or commit perjury

(5) succulent [ ] gloomily or resentfully silent; dismal

(6) subsidiary [ ] of individual bias or personal views

(7) subterfuge [ ] writ commanding person to appear in court

(8) subsist [ ] to divert primitive energy to a higher cultural aim

(9) subtle [ ] juicy; full of vitality, freshness, or richness

(10) sullen [ ] smooth, affable, gracious, and polite, *often* insincerely

(11) succor [ ] deception by artifice to hide or evade; a stratagem

(12) suborn [ ] persist; get maintenance; hold true; support with provisions

(13) succinct [ ] furnishing aid, auxiliary; of secondary importance

(1) sumptuary [ ] exceeding what is enough or necessary; extra

(2) supercilious [ ] exceeding the usual number; more than needed

(3) succumb [ ] take the place of by being better suited for; supplant

(4) subversion [ ] something that completes or adds to

(5) superficial [ ] excessively costly, rich, luxurious, or magnificent

(6) supplicate [ ] replace and substitute for by being superior; supersede by force

(7) sundry [ ] coolly and patronizingly haughty; proud

(8) superfluous [ ] designed to regulate spending and stop extravagance

(9) supercede [ ] to yield to overpowering appeal or desire

(10) sumptuous [ ] cursory; lacking intellectual depth; not far-reaching

(11) supplement [ ] an attempt to overthrow a government

(12) supplant [ ] to ask or ask for humbly and earnestly; to beg

(13) supernumerary [ ] miscellaneous, various

QUIZ

1. Most people would prefer holding a conversation with a:
(a) shrew   (b) socialite   (c) stoic   (d) somnambulist

2. The embezzler who absconded would be most comfortable at a:
(a) soirée   (b) seminar   (c) sanctuary   (d) séance

3. The father of the debutante prefers that her escort be:
(a) subtle   (b) sly   (c) suave   (d) solvent

4. The young lady herself prefers an escort who is:
(a) simpatico   (b) sardonic   (c) senile   (d) sophomoric

5. The store owner wishes to hire a manager who is:
(a) splenetic   (b) sullen   (c) sedulous   (d) saturnine

6. A sophisticated person at a social function is probably noted for his/her:
(a) solecisms   (b) savoir-faire (c) slander   (d) sarcasm

7. The sine qua non for an alleged scofflaw is:
(a) scrutiny   (b) a subpoena (c) succor   (d) a sobriquet

8. Most students like a professor whose lectures are:
(a) specious   (b) superficial (c) soporific   (d) stellar

9. Most young students want teachers who are:
(a) stolid   (b) strident   (c) sentient   (d) stringent

10. You wish to hire a contractor who can reliably be characterized by his:
(a) stealth   (b) sobriety   (c) stigma   (d) sloth

BONUS QUIZ

The etymology word and old meaning are given. Enter a word derived from each set.

ETYMOLOGY	OLD MEANING	WORD
L inflatus	blown up, swollen	
L inhaerere	cling to; to be always in	
L insidiari	to lie in ambush; plot against	
L. intrinsicus	on the inside	
L itineris	journey, way; route, road	
L levis	light; slight, trivial; fickle	
L loqui	to speak, talk, say; talk about	
L malignus	unkind, ill-natured, spiteful	
L mandatus	command	
L manifestare	to disclose	
Gk melan + chole	black + bile	
L minutus	small; paltry	
L mitigare	to ripen, soften; to calm, pacify	
L nepos	grandson; nephew	
L nasci	to be born, originate; be produced	
L nullus	no, none; not, not at all; non-existent	
L nihil	nothing	
L limbus	fringe, hem; edge, border	
L litigare	to quarrel; to go to law	
L littera	letter	

SEGMENT NINE

ETYMOLOGY	OLD MEANING
WORD	**NEW MEANING**
L supponere	to put under; substitute, falsify
supposititious	**spurious; fraudulently substituted**
MFr surfaire	to overdo
surfeit	**overabundant supply; excess**
ME sirly	lordly, imperious
surly	**irritably sullen; threatening in appearance**
ME surmisen	to accuse
surmise	**to imagine or infer on slight grounds**
MF sur- + monter	on + to mount
surmount	**overcome; climb; stand at the top of**
Fr sur- + réalisme	over, super, above, up + realism
surrealism	**practice of producing fantastic imagery in art, literature, or theater**
L surrupticius	taken away secretly; stolen
surreptitious	**done by stealth; clandestine; secret**
L surrogare	to choose in place of another; substitute
surrogate	**a person to act in place of another; deputy**
Fr surveiller	to watch over
surveillance	**close watch kept over someone or something**
L suscipere	to take up, admit; undertake; receive
susceptible	**open or subject to some influence**
L suspicere	look up at, look up to; admire, respect; mistrust
suspect	**to distrust; imagine to be true or probable**
L sustinere	to hold up, support; uphold, maintain; bear, suffer
sustain	**prolong; bear up under; suffer, undergo; support; allow or admit as valid**
It svellere	to pluck out
svelte	**slender, lithe; having clean lines, sleek; suave**

SAMPLE SENTENCES

supposititious When confronted by the fundraiser, he made *supposititious* claims of poverty. He made *spurious* or *fraudulent* claims of hard times.

surfeit The popular girl ended up with a *surfeit* of Valentine candies from several people. She shared the *overabundant supply*, or *excess*, with friends in the dormitory.

surly The *surly* customs official had all the personality of a North Korean prison camp guard. He was *irritably sullen* and *threatening in appearance*.

surmise One could only *surmise* what is plans were. He gave hardly a clue what his intentions were, so we had to *imagine or infer on slight grounds*.

surmount The hikers faced a nodus, indeed a seeming Gordian knot, which they had to *surmount* before darkness settled in. They had to *overcome* the problem soon.

surrealism The art museum had several paintings depicting examples of *surrealism*. Each showed the *practice of producing fantastic imagery by means of unnatural juxtapositions and combinations*.

surreptitious A spy or private investigator operates in a *surreptitious* manner. One must function in a *clandestine* way, or use a method *done by stealth*.

surrogate A celebrated history professor, an ardent football fan, offered to serve as a *surrogate* for the hospitalized head coach. He would be willing to be the *person to act in place of* the coach, or be his *deputy*.

surveillance Working in a surreptitious manner, the police kept the building under *surveillance*. They also conducted a *close watch over* suspicious persons.

susceptible Referees and umpires are often *susceptible* to criticism by home-team fans. They are *open or subject to the influence* created by their decisions.

suspect The members *suspect* the new arrival for his motives. They *distrust* him. In other news, many *suspect* a lower turnout for the game if it rains; that is, they *imagine* a lower attendance *to be true or possible*.

sustain The star player *sustained* an ankle injury; he *suffered* the injury in practice. In another case, the judge *sustained* an objection by the prosecutor, that is, he *allowed* it *as valid*.

svelte His sobriquet had been "Butterball," but with a good diet and exercise program, he is now *svelte*, that is, *slender* and *lithe*.

ETYMOLOGY	OLD MEANING
WORD	**NEW MEANING**

L sycophanta
sycophant
swindler, slanderer, cheat; informer
a servile self-seeking flatterer; toady

L sylva
sylvan
wood
relating to the woods or forest

Gk symbios
symbiosis
living together
a mutually beneficial living together

Gk sympinein
symposium
to drink together
a meeting for the exchange of ideas

Gk symptoma
symptom
happening, attribute
something that indicates a bodily disorder

Gk synopsis
synposis
lit., comprehensive view
a brief outline; a summary

Gk syntassein
syntax
to arrange together
the way words form sentences

Gk syntithenai
synthesis
to put together
combination of parts so as to form a whole

L tabula rasa
tabula rasa
smoothed or erased tablet or blank slate
empty mind ready to receive impressions

L tacitus
tacit
silent, quiet; unmentioned
expressed or implied without words or speech

L taciturnus
taciturn
silent, quiet
temperamentally disinclined to talk

L tactus
tact
touch, handling; sense of touch
a keen sense of what to do or say in order to maintain good relations

L tactus
tactile
touch, handling; sense of touch
perceptible by touch; of the sense of touch

SAMPLE SENTENCES

sycophant The tactics of the bureaucratic *sycophant* were disdained by others in the office. He was a *servile self-seeking flatterer* of those above him, a *toady*.

sylvan The *sylvan* atmosphere always soothed his frayed nerves. The fragrances and dulcet stillness *of the woods* calmed him down.

symbiosis A happy situation is when one member's skills and contributions complement those of another, or *symbiosis*, that is, *a mutually beneficial cohabitation*.

symposium Attending the *symposium* on metaphysics helped to elucidate some concepts. It was a profitable *meeting for the exchange of ideas*.

symptom A *symptom* can show up during a medical examination. Yellowish pigmentation of the skin, for example, can be *something that indicates a bodily disorder*, such as jaundice.

synopsis Before attending the opera, he peruses a *synopsis* of it. He goes over a *brief outline*, or *summary*, of the story.

syntax Before turning in a paper, the student should review the *syntax*. He/she should go over the *way words form sentences*.

synthesis The *synthesis* of a new chemical compound is necessary before testing it. The team of scientists determine the *combination of parts so as to form a whole*.

tabula rasa When encountering a totally new concept, one should be in a state of *tabula rasa*, free of preconceived notions, and like a baby, have an *empty mind ready to receive impressions*.

tacit He was *tacit* about what he wanted done, but everyone understood. His wishes were *implied without words or speech*.

taciturn The coach was *taciturn* with reporters after the bitter loss. His mood made him *temperamentally disinclined to talk*.

tact The diplomat showed a lot of *tact* with the foreign dignitaries. She had a *keen sense of what to do or say in order to maintain good relations*, or *savoir-faire*.

tactile Not only are substantive objects visible, they are also *tactile*. Things like fabrics, sandpaper, or the Venus de Milo in the Louvre, are *perceptible by touch*, although the sign says, in the case of the latter, "Priere de ne toucher pas." (Please do not touch).

ETYMOLOGY	OLD MEANING
WORD	**NEW MEANING**

L tingere	to dip; to dye, color
taint	**to affect slightly with something bad**
L tangere	to touch, handle
tangible	**palpable, tactile; substantially real**
L tantus	so great, so little; to be worth so much
tantamount	**equivalent in value, significance, or effect**
MFr tenter	to try, tempt
taunt	**challenge in a mocking manner; jeer at**
Gk taut + legein	tight, tense, high-strung
tautology	**needless repetition of an idea or word**
MFr tanner	to tan
tawny	**of a warm sandy color**
Gk tekton	builder
tectonics	**science or art of construction**
L taedium	weariness, loathing
tedious	**tiresome due to length or dullness; boring**
L temeritas	chance, rashness, thoughtlessness
temerity	**foolhardy contempt of danger**
L temperantia	moderation, self-control
temperance	**restraint; abstinence from alcohol**
OL tempestus	season, weather, storm
tempestuous	**of a violent storm; turbulent, stormy**
L tenere	to hold, to keep
tenable	**maintainable; defensible, reasonable**
L tenax	gripping; sticky; firm, persistent, stubborn
tenacious	**tending to cling to; persistent in holding on**

SAMPLE SENTENCES

taint He wanted nothing that might *taint* his character to be made public. The last thing he wanted was anything that might *affect slightly* his reputation *with something bad.*   .

tangible Most small children prefer something *tangible*, e.g., candy now, rather than tax-free municipal bonds in the future. They want something *substantially real* now.

tantamount His abstention from voting on the proposal was *tanta-mount* to voting against it. His non-vote was *equivalent in effect* to voting against it.

taunt Obstreperous dissidents tried to *taunt* the guest speaker. Their plan was to *mock* or *jeer at* him.

tautology Some of the dinner guests suffered ennui, while others grew restive because of the immoderate *tautology* of the grandiloquent, soi-disant orator. The latter belabored *needless repetition of his ideas.*

tawny While several antelopes were peacefully drinking water, a large *tawny* cat crept in the tall grass in a stealthy manner. The former then fled from the lion *of a warm sandy color.*

tectonics She planned to study *tectonics*, that is, the *science or art of construction.*

tedious If a person is stuck in a *tedious* job, sooner or later the work will be done in a perfunctory manner. This is caused be *boring* work, which is *tiresome due to length or dullness.*

temerity Because of his tedious steady work, he found more exciting odd jobs in his spare time, e.g., high-wire acts and transferring alliga-tors. People admired his *temerity*, or his *foolhardy contempt of danger.*

temperance After regaling at Saturday night parties, every Sunday morning he was ready to join a *temperance* union, which advocates an *abstinence from alcohol.*

tempestuous The overflow crowd witnessed a *tempestuous* meeting of the city council. It was *stormy* debate involving accusations and recriminations over issues.

tenable Each side claimed its argument was *tenable*, that is, *defensible* and *reasonable.*

tenacious The wire-haired terrier had a *tenacious* grip on the man's trousers. He was *persistent in holding on.*

ETYMOLOGY	OLD MEANING
WORD	**NEW MEANING**

| L tendere | to stretch; aim; bend; direct |
| **tendentious** | **favoring a particular viewpoint; biased** |

| L tenebrosus | dark, gloomy |
| **tenebrous** | **shut off from light; obscure; causing gloom** |

| L temptare | to feel, test by touching; to try |
| **tentative** | **not fully worked out; hesitant, uncertain** |

| L tenuis | thin, fine; small, shallow |
| **tenuous** | **slender; of little substance; flimsy, weak** |

| L tenere | to hold, keep, occupy |
| **tenure** | **a status protecting a teacher from dismissal** |

| L tepidus | warm, lukewarm |
| **tepid** | **lukewarm; lacking enthusiasm or conviction** |

| L tergiversari | to turn the back; to hedge, be evasive |
| **tergiversate** | **to apostatize; to equivocate** |

| ME Termagant | imaginary boisterous deity in medieval plays |
| **termagant** | **overbearing or nagging woman; shrew** |

| L tersus | clean, neat |
| **terse** | **devoid of superfluity; concise** |

| L tertius | third |
| **tertiary** | **of third rank; being (in) a third stage** |

| L testimonium | evidence, proof |
| **testimony** | **a declaration made under oath** |

| Gk theorein | to look at |
| **theory** | **ideal set of facts; unproved assumption** |

| OE threa | threat, pang |
| **throe** | *pl:* **a hard or painful struggle** |

SAMPLE SENTENCES

tendentious Ideally, the front page is for objective reporting, while the editorial page is for *tendentious* commentary. The op-ed page is for *biased* material, that which is *favoring a particular viewpoint.*

tenebrous His car ran out of gas on a deserted *tenebrous* street. Without a phone, he was uncertain which way to walk along the unfamiliar *dark, obscure* street.

tentative He made a *tentative* plan to go fishing, contingent on certain circumstances. His plan was *not fully worked out*; it was *uncertain.*

tenuous In the waning moments of the game the team was clinging to a *tenuous* lead. Playing not to lose rather than to win, the lead became even more *flimsy.*

tenure The good teacher had *tenure*, which warded off the complaints of a few whiners who thought him too strict. He had *a status protecting him from dismissal.*

tepid The majority of the group was *tepid* regarding the compromise decision of the committee. The feeling was *lukewarm*, i.e., *lacking enthusiasm or conviction.*

tergiversate He claims he did not *tergiversate* , but that he could no longer support the cause financially. He did not *apostatize*, or *defect*, from it; he was broke.

termagant When the baseball bounced off her porch, the neighborhood *termagant* went on the warpath. She was a *shrew*, an *overbearing, nagging woman.*

terse The security agent was *terse* in his responses. He was *concise*, or, *devoid of superfluity.*

tertiary In the middle of a tough mid-term examination, thoughts of extraneous matters are hardly of *tertiary* significance. Of primary concern are the questions and the time remaining; of secondary concern is comfort and state of health; all other matters are *of tertiary*, i.e., *of third rank* or beyond in importance.

testimony The witness was nervous in his *testimony*. i.e., a *declaration made under oath.*

theory Quite often the facts conflict with someone's *theory*, which is an *ideal set of facts*, rather than a real set of facts. A *theory* is an *unproved assumption.*

throe(s) He convinced the potential assailants that his mother, two ex-wives, and several bartenders would have to undergo the *throes* of poverty if they did him in. Each would undergo a *hard or painful struggle* without him.

ETYMOLOGY	OLD MEANING
WORD	**NEW MEANING**

L torquere	to twist
thwart	**oppose successfully; defeat the hopes of**

L timor	fear, alarm; a terror
timorous	**fearful; expressing timidity**

L tinnitus	ringing, jingle
tinnitus	**sensation of ringing or roaring**

L titillare	to tickle
titillate	**to stimulate or excite agreeably**

L titulus	label, title of honor; pretext
titular	**having the title but without duties of**

L torpere	to be stiff, be numb; to be stupefied
torpid	**dormant; sluggish; apathetic, dull**

L torquere	to turn, twist, bend
tort	**wrongful act calling for civil action**

L torquere	to turn, twist, bend
tortuous	**full of twists; crooked, tricky; circuitous**

Fr toucher	to touch
touché	**a remark after a successful witty point**

Fr tour de force	*(the same as in English)*
tour de force	**a feat of strength, skill, or ingenuity**

ME tuten	to peer
tout	**one who gives tips or bets on a horse**

ME to witen	*lit.,* to know
to wit	**that is to say; namely**

L tractare	to maul; to handle, deal with, manage
tractable	**easily led, controlled, or managed; docile**

SAMPLE SENTENCES

thwart Incessant nearby chattering *thwarted* his efforts to listen to salient points of the lecture. The noise *defeated his hopes of* hearing what the professor had to say.

timorous The young playwright became *timorous* with the arrival of a noted critic, whose opinion could make or break his career. He was *fearful* and *expressing timidity.*

tinnitus A large dose of aspirin can cause *tinnitus*, a *sensation of ringing* in the ears.

titillate A visit to the art museum *titillated* the pragmatist's interest in fine arts. It seemed to *stimulate or excite* him *agreeably.*

titular The popular celebrity was the *titular* head of the organization. He was noted for *having the title but without the duties of* the chief functionary.

torpid Certain ailments, e.g., flu, can render even an active person *torpid.* They can make anyone *dormant, sluggish, apathetic,* or *dull.*

tort He was suspected of committing a *tort*, which is a *wrongful act calling for civil action.* It is a *civil wrong not arising from a contract.*

tortuous The hikers followed a *tortuous* path. It was *full of twists.* In other news, the witness resorted to a *tortuous* expatiation in his testimony, or one which was *crooked, tricky,* and *circuitous.*

touché The repartee elicited a *"touché!"* from the group. It was a fitting *remark after a successful witty point.*

tour de force In many sports and under certain urgent circumstances, one can sometimes witness a *tour de force.* It is thrilling to see *a feat of strength, skill, or ingenuity.*

tout It is common to encounter a *tout* at a racetrack. He is *one who gives tips on a horse* as well as *one who bets on a horse.*

to wit When someone says or writes, *"to wit,"* it means *"that is to say,"* or *"namely."* The expression is usually used to introduce lists.

tractable Is a *tractable* population healthy for a democracy? Is a *docile* population, one which is *easily led, controlled, or managed,* good for freedom?

ETYMOLOGY	OLD MEANING
WORD	**NEW MEANING**

| L traducere | to lead across; transfer; make an exhibition of |
| **traduce** | **to falsely blame or shame; violate, betray** |

| L transcendere | to pass or climb over; overstep; surpass |
| **transcend** | **rise above or go beyond the limits of** |

| L transcendere | to pass or climb over; overstep; surpass |
| **transcendent** | **exceeding usual limits; beyond comprehension** |

| L transcendere | to pass or climb over; overstep; surpass |
| **transcendental** | **transcending experience but not knowledge** |

| L transfigere | to pierce; to thrust through |
| **transfix** | **to hold motionless as if by piercing** |

| L transire | to go across, pass over |
| **transient** | **lasting only a short time** |

| L transire | to go across, pass over |
| **transition** | **passage from one stage to another; change** |

| L transire | to go across, pass over |
| **transitory** | **not persistent; of brief duration; transient** |

| L transponere | carry across; change the position of |
| **transpose** | **to shift; alter normal order or sequence of** |

| OFr travaillier | to torture |
| **travail** | **painful work; task; agony, torment; exertion** |

| Fr travestir | to disguise |
| **travesty** | **a grossly inferior imitation of; distortion** |

| L tremulus | trembling, shivering |
| **tremulous** | **affected with trembling or timidity; easily shaken** |

| MF trenchier | to cut |
| **trenchant** | **sharp; caustic; vigorously articulate; clear-cut** |

SAMPLE SENTENCES

traduce To declare someone guilty of a crime before a fair trial is to *traduce* the principle that one is innocent until proven guilty; it is to *betray*, or *violate*, that principle.

transcend Games such as chess and tennis, music, and art, *transcend* national boundaries and language barriers. They *go over and beyond* those limits to be understood.

transcendent His tour de force in crossing that formidable stream appeared *transcendent* to everyone. It seemed to be *exceeding* the *usual limits* of human endeavor. Also, something *transcendent* can mean it is *beyond comprehension*.

transcendental Mathematics can be defined as *transcendental*. It is an example of something *transcending experience but not knowledge*.

transfix The man was *transfixed* as he suddenly met his similitude in the narrow aisle. Then his counterpart was likewise *held motionless as if by piercing*.

transient Waiting in line for ten minutes seems very long, but when one is late or in a hurry, ten minutes is *transient*, i.e., a period *lasting only a short time*.

transition The building is undergoing a *transition* from a casino to a bank. It will undergo a *passage from one stage to another*, or a *change*. From then on, the money you leave there will still be yours.

transitory In some places, the transition from winter to spring is *transitory*, that is, *not persistent, of brief duration*, or *transient*.

transpose At times it is fun to *transpose* the letters of a word or name to see the result. To *alter* the *normal order or sequence of* the letters can produce amusement.

travail A person holding a sinecure wants no part of any *travail*. He will avoid any *hard task, painful work, agony, torment*, or *exertion*.

travesty To pay a heavy fine for a minor offense seems to many a *travesty* of justice. Also, to exculpate a felon from a major crime on a technicality is viewed as a *grossly inferior imitation of* justice, or a *distortion* thereof.

tremulous The diffident ingénue was *tremulous* when asked to give a synopsis and an analysis of the book assigned to her in front of the class. She was *affected with timidity* and *easily shaken*.

trenchant Bystanders were awed by his *trenchant* response to the innuendo. It was *sharp* and *caustic*. In other news, the new dean was *trenchant* in his outlining of the rules on campus; he was *vigorously articulate and clear-cut* on the matter.

ETYMOLOGY	OLD MEANING
WORD	**NEW MEANING**

ME trencher	knife; wooden platter for cutting meat
trencherman	**a hearty eater, gourmand**
L trepidus	agitated, restless; anxious; alarming
trepidation	**timorous uncertainty; apprehension; fear**
L tribulare	to press; oppress
tribulation	**distress from oppression; a trying experience**
L tribunal	platform; judgment seat
tribunal	**judge's seat; a court; something that decides**
AFr trové	found
trove	**discovery; valuable collection; haul**
ME truant	vagabond, idler
truant	**one who stays out of school without permission**
L truculentus	ferocious, grim, wild
truculent	**scathingly harsh; self-assertive; belligerent**
OFr triste	watch post
tryst	**agreement to meet; appointed meeting place**
L tumidus	swollen, swelling; puffed up; bombastic
tumid	**swollen, enlarged; bulging; bombastic**
L tumultus	commotion, uproar; storm; disorder
tumult	**commotion; riot; din; violent outburst**
L turba	disorder, riot; brawl; mob
turbulent	**causing unrest; tempestuous**
L turgidus	swollen, distended; bombastic
turgid	**swollen, tumid; bombastic, pompous**
L tutela	protection, guardian
tutelage	**guardianship; hegemony; guiding influence**

Sample Sentences

trencherman The fastidious hostess was unaware that two *trenchermen* were among the guests, leaving her short of food. They were *hearty eaters*, or *gourmands*.

trepidation The golfer approached his ball in the rough with *trepidation*, as there was a twelve-foot alligator asleep between him and the ball. He was overcome by *timorous uncertainty, apprehension*, and *fear*.

tribulation Being a substitute umpire for a Little League championship game turned out to be a *tribulation* for him. The threats and invectives from splenetic parents and other rabid partisans proved to be a *trying experience* for him.

tribunal He was brought before a *tribunal,* that is, he stood trial before a *court*.

trove In a case of serendipity, Felix Mendelssohn came across a treasure *trove*—the complete works of Johann Sebastian Bach—in an attic. It was a great *discovery*, as well as a *valuable collection* of musical works of genius.

truant The boy was a capricious and frequent *truant*. He was *one who stayed out of school without permission*.

truculent After several swigs from his concealed bottle, the *truculent* fan had to be led from the arena. He was *scathingly harsh, self-assertive,* and *belligerent*.

tryst Romeo and Juliet made a *tryst*, or, an *agreement to meet*. They met at the *tryst*, which was the *appointed meeting place (as between lovers)*.

tumid After the injury, her ankle became *tumid*, that is, *swollen, enlarged,* and *bulging*.

tumult There was *tumult* at the city council meeting as protagonists and opponents of a controversial issue took turns speaking. There was *din, commotion, a near-riot,* and an occasional *violent outburst*.

turbulent They were awakened by a *turbulent* argument next door. The accusations, followed by recriminations, were *stormy* or *tempestuous*.

turgid After the fall, his wrist was *turgid*, which means *swollen* or *tumid*. In other news, the speech consisted of *turgid* jargon, *bombastic* or *pompous* language.

tutelage He became an excellent student under the *tutelage* of an outstanding, superb teacher. Her *guiding influence* sublimated his habits to a higher level.

ETYMOLOGY	OLD MEANING
WORD	**NEW MEANING**

| OE twegen | two |
| **twain** | **two; couple, pair** |

| OE aet + witan | at + to reproach |
| **twit** | **subject to light ridicule; taunt** |

| Chin ta + chün | great + ruler |
| **tycoon** | **businessman of great wealth and power** |

| L tyrannus | ruler, king; despot |
| **tyranny** | **oppressive power** |

| L tiro | young soldier, recruit, beginner |
| **tyro** | **beginner in learning; novice** |

| L ubique | everywhere, anywhere |
| **ubiquitous** | **being everywhere at the same time; constantly encountered; widespread** |

| Russ ukazat | to show, order |
| **ukase** | **proclamation with force of law; edict** |

| MFr eullage | act of filling a cask |
| **ullage** | **amount that a tank lacks of being full** |

| L ulterior | farther, beyond, more remote |
| **ulterior** | **beyond what is said or proper** |

| L ultimus | farthest; most remote; the end of; last |
| **ultimate** | **last in a series; eventual; utmost** |

| ML ultimatus | final |
| **ultimatum** | **a final proposition, condition, or demand** |

| L ululare | to shriek, yell, howl; cry out to |
| **ululate** | **to howl, wail** |

| L umbra | shade, shadow; uninvited guest |
| **umbrage** | **foliage; feeling of resentment; offense** |

SAMPLE SENTENCES

twain "and never the *twain* shall meet" is an expression meaning that the *two*, or *pair*, of entities referred to will not come together or encounter each other.

twit One object of a roast is to *twit* the honoree, i.e., to *taunt* him, or *subject him to light ridicule.*

tycoon One must often be a *tycoon* first in order to be in a position to be a philanthropist. The latter is usually a *businessman of great wealth and power.*

tyranny By definition, there is no *tyranny* in a free society. The converse is true: if there is *tyranny*, or *oppressive power*, there is no free society.

tyro In a case of nepotism, the boss put his nephew, a *tyro*, in charge of part of the operation, which he later regretted. The nephew, a *novice*, or *beginner in learning*, was nowhere close to being suited for the job.

ubiquitous Tourists from free countries are *ubiquitous* throughout the world. They are *everywhere at the same time* and *constantly encountered.*

ukase The *ukase* of the board to ban smoking in the stadium won the plaudits of many. It was an *edict*, or *proclamation with the force of law.*

ullage Is the tank half empty or half full? Ask instead, "What is the *ullage?*" That is the *amount that a tank lacks of being full.*

ulterior Several relatives suddenly showed up to shower the aging and ailing tycoon with adulation and kindness. Some were genuine in their feelings, while others had *ulterior* motives, i.e., intentions *beyond what is said or demonstrated.*

ultimate While playing bridge with his wife, whom he loves, he secretly looked forward to the *ultimate* hand, or the *last*, each time they played. In other news, the man's hubris led to his *ultimate* downfall. It resulted in his *eventual* retribution.

ultimatum "You have two minutes to come out with your hands up, or we're coming in after you," was the *ultimatum* over the police bullhorn to the alleged criminal inside the building. It was the *final demand* to the suspect to give it up.

ululate The campers could hear the wolves *ululate* at night. They could hear them *howl.*

umbrage He took *umbrage* at the remark about his sister. He had a *feeling of resentment* to it; he took *offense* at the statement.

ETYMOLOGY	OLD MEANING
WORD	**NEW MEANING**

L unus + animus
one + mind
unanimous
of one mind; having agreement of all

L unctus
oiled; greasy; rich, sumptuous
unctuous
oily; marked by smug, false earnestness

L unda
wave
undulating
rising and falling; like a wave; rolling

L unicus
one and only; sole; unparalleled
unique
being the only one; without equal; very rare, uncommon; very unusual

L uni- + sonus
one + sound
unison
harmonious agreement or union

ME kemben
to comb
unkempt
not combed or neat; rough, unpolished

OE upbregdan
move suddenly; snatch; weave together
upbraid
find fault with; scold vehemently

OE up + hreran
up + to stir
uproar
commotion or violent disturbance

L urbs
city
urban
of, or characteristic of, a city

L urbanus
refined, polite; witty, humorous; impertinent
urbane
notably polite; polished; suave

L usurpare
lit., take possession of by use
usurp
to seize and hold without right or by force

L usura
use, enjoyment; interest
usury
interest charged far beyond the legal rate

L utilis
useful, expedient, fit (for)
utilize
to make use of

SAMPLE SENTENCES

unanimous The measure passed by a *unanimous* vote of the committee, 7 to 0. It was a vote *having the agreement of all*, i.e., having no dissenters.

unctuous The candidate gave an *unctuous* speech. It was *marked by smug and false earnestness.*

undulating Seeing the *undulating* hillocks elevate in the direction of larger hills made the returning alumnus joyful. He was overcome with happiness upon seeing where the *rolling* foothills rise up towards mountains higher.

unique Since no two people are exactly alike, it can be said that every person is *unique*. Each individual is *without equal*, or as *being the only one.*

unison The throng shouted its unanimous agreement in *unison*. It let its view be known to be in *harmonious agreement.*

unkempt The fastidious mother looked askance when her daughter's *unkempt* escort arrived. He explained that his hair was *not combed or neat* because of the wind created while driving his new convertible.

upbraid The termagant *upbraided* the boy whose dog caused her cat to stay high in the tree for almost ten hours. She *found fault with* and *scolded* him *vehemently.*

uproar There was a loud *uproar* in the stands when the officials ignored a flagrant foul. It was a great *commotion.*

urban She preferred an *urban* lifestyle, while he liked a rural setting. She liked the bright lights *of the city*, whereas he longed for the dulcet life in the country.

urbane A person can be *urbane* without being unctuous at social functions. One can be *notably polite, polished*, or even *suave*, and without affectations.

usurp Sometimes the president will try to *usurp* functions of the legislature, and vice versa. Each will try to *seize and hold without right or by force* the functions and duties of the other; each will try to *supplant* the other.

usury He accused the loan shark of *usury*, which is *lending money to individuals at exorbitant rates of interest*, or *interest charged far beyond the legal rate.*

utilize Everyone should *utilize* time to good advantage. One must *make* good *use of* it.

Etymology	Old Meaning
Word	**New Meaning**

Gk ou + topos	not + place; imaginary and ideal place
utopia	**impractical scheme for social improvement**
L uxor	wife
uxorious	**excessively fond of a wife**
	excessively submissive to a wife
L vacillare	to stagger, totter; to waver, be unreliable
vacillate	**waver; hesitate in choice of opinions**
L vacuus	empty, void; vacant; worthless
vacuous	**stupid, inane; devoid of seriousness**
L vagari	to wander, rove, go far afield
vagary	**erratic, unpredictable manifestation**
	or action; caprice
OFr wacrer	to roll, wander
vagrant	**homeless person; idle wanderer; rover**
L vagus	wandering, unsettled; fickle
vague	**indefinite; unclear; not specific; hazy**
L vanus	empty, idle, useless; false; conceited
vain	**futile; unsuccessful; foolish; conceited**
L vanus + gloria	vain + glory, fame, pride
vainglorious	**excessively proud; boastful**
L vale + dicere	goodbye, farewell + to say
valedictory	**an address or statement of farewell**
L valere	to be strong
valiant	**having strength of spirit; courageous**
L valere	to be strong
valid	**having legal force; well-grounded**
L valere	to be strong
valor	**strength to meet danger with firmness**

SAMPLE SENTENCES

utopia Coming up with a *utopia* is like waving a magic wand. It is an *impractical scheme for social improvement.*

uxorious At the office he is a martinet, imperious and peremptory; but at home he is *uxorious.* He is *excessively fond of his wife*, and *submissive to her* as well.

vacillate Overwhelmed by so many choices, the couple began to *vacillate* on what they wanted. They began to *waver*, to *hesitate in* their *choice of options.*

vacuous Newspapers amazingly print many *vacuous* letters to the editor, e.g., those advocating some kind of utopia. They are *inane,* or *devoid of seriousness.*

vagary The *vagaries* of the weather and the stock market are phenomena over which we have no control. They are *erratic* and *unpredictable manifestations.*

vagrant One *vagrant* made $40,000 in one year while obtesting for cash from passers-by. With no mailing address, this *homeless person,* this *idle wanderer,* had no overhead and didn't even think about income taxes or the IRS.

vague The unprepared student gave *vague* answers to the examination questions. His responses were *indefinite, unclear, not specific*, and *hazy.*

vain The student made a *vain* effort to persuade the professor to reconsider his grade. It was a *futile,* or *unsuccessful* try. In other news, the "Dapper Dan" of the campus was *vain* about his appearance, indeed, very *foolish* or *conceited* about it.

vainglorious If there is anything that would sink a candidate's hopes, it would be a bombastic and *vainglorious* speech. An *excessively proud,* or *boastful* oration about his accomplishments would finish his aspirations.

valedictory The top student in the graduating class gave the *valedictory*, which is an *address or statement of farewell* to his or her classmates at the commencement program.

valiant Although injured, he gave it his all, a truly *valiant* effort. It was a *courageous* endeavor, one *having strength of spirit.*

valid She has a *valid* parking sticker on the windshield; it is recognized for *having legal force.* Also, that the earth goes around the sun is a *valid* theory. It is *well-grounded.*

valor He displayed *valor* while maneuvering the kayak through the raging whitewater ordeal. He showed *strength to meet danger with firmness.*

ETYMOLOGY **WORD**	OLD MEANING **NEW MEANING**
L vanitas **vanity**	emptiness; falsehood, worthlessness **inflated pride in oneself; conceit**
L vincere **vanquish**	to conquer, defeat, subdue **to defeat in battle or contest**
L vappa **vapid**	wine that has gone flat **lacking force; flat, uninteresting**
L varius **variegated**	colored, spotted; diverse **varied; having different colors**
L vaticinari **vaticinate**	to prophesy; to rant, rave **to prophesy, predict**
L vanitas **vaunt**	emptiness; falsehood, worthlessness **to brag; call attention to boastfully**
ML vegatare **vegetate**	to grow **to lead a passive, effortless existence**
L vehemens **vehement**	impetuous, violent; powerful, strong **impassioned; forcibly expressed**
L velle **velleity**	to wish, want; to be willing **lowest degree of volition; slight wish**
L venalis **venal**	for sale; bribable **open to corruption, *esp.* bribery**
L vendere **vend**	to sell **to sell, hawk, peddle**
It vendetta **vendetta**	*lit.* revenge **prolonged feud with bitter hostility**
L venerari **venerate**	to worship, revere, pray to; to honor **regard with admiring respect or esteem**

Sample Sentences

vanity His *vanity* did not go over well with others on the trip. His *inflated pride in himself,* his *conceit,* elicited general disapproval.

vanquish He *vanquished* all comers in ping-pong at the language school, but failed to earn a diploma. He *defeated* everyone *in the contest,* winning the championship.

vapid Listening to his *vapid* desultory descanting had a soporific effect. His *flat, uninteresting* descriptions of prosaic details would put most people to sleep.

variegated The band arrived in *variegated* costumes. It was a *motley* group, that is, *having different colors.*

vaticinate When barbers and cab drivers attempt to *vaticinate* the direction of the stock market, prepare for the opposite, one tycoon advised. Trying to *prophesy,* or *predict,* the vagaries of the market is beyond the purview of tyros.

vaunt He would *vaunt* every little accomplishment at every opportunity. Every time he did something he would *call attention to* it *boastfully.*

vegetate After months of hectic work, they liked to *vegetate* on the beach for a couple of weeks. It was nice to lay back and *lead a passive and effortless existence* before going back to the rat race.

vehement The choleric coach yelled at the obdurate official in a *vehement* manner after a call he didn't like. His words were *impassioned* and *forcibly expressed.*

velleity Playing tennis was to him a *velleity;* he would just as soon paint the kitchen or pull weeds. To him it was only a *slight wish,* or, the *lowest form of volition.*

venal It is unfortunate when a *venal* official is elected, that is, one *open to corruption, especially bribery.*

vend Before big games it is common to see scalpers trying to *vend* tickets at high prices. They try to *sell, hawk,* or *peddle* tickets before the start of the game.

vendetta Legend has it that the Hatfields and the McCoys had a *vendetta* against each other. They conducted a *prolonged feud with bitter hostility.*

venerate Many former students came to *venerate* their favorite professor at his retirement ceremony and reception. They came to *regard* him *with admiring respect or esteem..*

ETYMOLOGY	OLD MEANING
WORD	**NEW MEANING**

L vindicare	to lay claim to; to avenge
vengeance	**punishment in retaliation; retribution**

L venia	favor, indulgence, kindness; pardon
venial	**forgivable, pardonable; excusable**

L ventus	wind
vent	**give vigorous or emotional expression to**

L venire	to come
venue	**the place of the jury and trial**

L verax	truthful
veracity	**truthfulness; something true; truth**

L verbum	word
verbatim	**in the exact words: word for word**

L verbum	word
verbose	**wordy; given to or impaired by wordiness**

L viridis	green
verdant	**green in color, experience, or judgment**

L verus	true, real, actual; right, reasonable
verdict	**the finding or decision of a jury; judgment**

L verus	true
verify	**establish the truth, accuracy, or reality of**

L veri similis	like the truth; probable
verisimilitude	**probability; statement apparently true**

L verus	true
veritable	**being in fact the thing named; authentic**

L vernaculus	of home-born slaves; native
vernacular	**of a substandard language or dialect**

SAMPLE SENTENCES

vengeance What kind of *vengeance* should be carried out against an overweening, ribald man who poured a pitcher of beer over someone's head at the picnic? Should there be any *retribution*, or *punishment in retaliation?*

venial The car behind him nudged his bumper. He jumped out, as did the other driver, a beautiful young lady. He then considered the matter *venial*, that is, *forgivable.*

vent In a similar situation, the other driver was a somewhat obnoxious-looking guy, Our man this time *vented* his anger on him. He *gave vigorous expression to* his wrath.

venue A murder case required a change of *venue.* The case had to be heard in a new *place of a jury and trial,* in order to have a more objective and less subjective atmosphere for the trial.

veracity Each witness must strive for *veracity* in order to avoid a charge of perjury. He or she must say the *truth*, or *something true.*

verbatim One does not have to repeat *verbatim* what he heard said; to paraphrase will suffice. To say *in the exact words*, or *word for word*, is not necessary.

verbose In many restaurants the odds favor the presence of a *verbose* orator at a nearby table. Only the arrival of the main course will quiet the *wordy* speaker down.

verdant Behold the *verdant* hills in spring! How *green* they are! In a case of nepotism reversal, the CEO fired his *verdant* nephew; he was too *green in experience.*

verdict The moment was tense as the judge asked the jury if it has reached a *verdict.* The defendant and his attorney nervously awaited the *decision of the jury.*

verify The interested parties asked an arbitrator to *verify* the authenticity of the will. His job is to *establish the truth, accuracy, or reality* of it.

verisimilitude Is his evaluation of the property a veracity or a *verisimilitude?* Is the claim an absolute truth, or a *probability*, an *apparently true statement?*

veritable The second half of the game was played in a *veritable* mud bath. The churned-up field during the rain resulted in an *authentic* sea of mud, it *being in fact the thing named.*

vernacular The *vernacular* speech of local yokels often bemuse visiting foreigners. The use of expressions *of a substandard language or dialect* confuses them.

QUIZ

Match the following words with their meanings:

(1) supposititious   [ ] done by stealth; clandestine, secret
(2) symbiosis   [ ] practice of producing fantastic imagery in art
(3) surmise   [ ] to distrust; imagine to be true or probable
(4) surly   [ ] slender, lithe; having clean lines, sleek; suave
(5) surfeit   [ ] a close watch kept over something or someone
(6) surmount   [ ] to prolong; bear up under; support; allow as valid
(7) susceptible   [ ] spurious; fraudulently substituted
(8) surrealism   [ ] overabundant supply; excess
(9) suspect   [ ] to overcome; climb; stand at the top of
(10) svelte   [ ] open or subject to some influence
(11) surveillance   [ ] a mutually beneficial living together
(12) sustain   [ ] to imaging or infer on slight grounds
(13) surreptitious   [ ] irritably sullen; threatening in appearance

(1) symposium   [ ] a brief outline; a summary
(2) sylvan   [ ] perceptible by touch; of the sense of touch
(3) symptom   [ ] combination of parts so as to form a whole
(4) tacit   [ ] temperamentally disinclined to talk
(5) synopsis   [ ] a keen sense of what to do or say
(6) tactile   [ ] equivalent in value, significance, or effect
(7) syntax   [ ] something that indicates a bodily disorder
(8) tangible   [ ] expressed or implied without words or speech
(9) tabula rasa   [ ] a meeting for the exchange of ideas
(10) taciturn   [ ] relating to the woods or forest
(11) synthesis   [ ] the way words for sentences
(12) tantamount   [ ] palpable, tactile; substantially real
(13) tact   [ ] an empty mind ready to receive impressions

(1) tawny   [ ] tending to cling to; persistent in holding on
(2) tautology   [ ] the science or art of construction
(3) surrogate   [ ] a servile self-seeking flatterer; a toady
(4) tedious   [ ] of a violent storm; turbulent, stormy
(5) temperance   [ ] a foolhardy contempt of danger
(6) tenable   [ ] favoring a particular viewpoint; biased
(7) sycophant   [ ] an overbearing or nagging woman; a shrew
(8) tenacious   [ ] of a warm sandy color
(9) tectonics   [ ] restraint; abstinence from alcohol
(10) tempestuous   [ ] maintainable; defensible, reasonable
(11) termagant   [ ] a person to act in place of another; deputy
(12) temerity   [ ] needless repetition of an idea or word
(13 tendentious   [ ] tiresome due to length or dullness; boring

(1) tenebrous   [ ] slender; of little substance; flimsy, weak
(2) tenure   [ ] ideal set of facts; unproved assumption
(3) taint   [ ] to apostatize; to equivocate
(4) tepid   [ ] devoid of superfluity; concise
(5) testimony   [ ] a hard or painful struggle
(6) tertiary   [ ] not fully worked out; hesitant, uncertain
(7) tergiversate   [ ] to challenge in a mocking manner; jeer at
(8) tenuous   [ ] of third rank; being in a third stage
(9) theory   [ ] status protecting a teacher from dismissal
(10) terse   [ ] shut off from light; obscure; causing gloom
(11) taunt   [ ] to affect slightly with something bad
(12) throe   [ ] a declaration made under oath
(13) tentative   [ ] lukewarm; lacking enthusiasm or conviction

(1) timorous   [ ] dormant; sluggish; apathetic, dull
(2) tinnitus   [ ] wrongful act calling for civil action
(3) thwart   [ ] to stimulate or excite agreeably
(4) titular   [ ] easily led, controlled, or managed; docile
(5) tour de force   [ ] sensation of ringing or roaring
(6) to wit   [ ] full of twists; crooked, tricky; circuitous
(7) traduce   [ ] oppose successfully; defeat the hopes of
(8) torpid   [ ] having the title but without the duties of
(9) touché   [ ] a feat of strength, skill, or ingenuity
(10) tractable   [ ] fearful; expressing timidity
(11) titillate   [ ] to falsely blame or shame; violate, betray
(12) tort   [ ] a remark after a successful witty point
(13) tortuous   [ ] that is to say; namely

(1) transcendent   [ ] not persistent; of brief duration; transient
(2) transition   [ ] painful work; task; agony, torment; exertion
(3) transcend   [ ] to hold motionless as if by piercing
(4) tout   [ ] a hearty eater; gourmand
(5) transcendental   [ ] lasting only a short time
(6) travail   [ ] a grossly inferior imitation of; distortion
(7) transfix   [ ] to shift; alter the normal order or sequence of
(8) trencherman   [ ] one who stays out of school without
                            permission
(9) transient   [ ] exceeding usual limits; beyond comprehension
(10) travesty   [ ] passage from one stage to another; a change
(11) transpose   [ ] to rise above or go beyond the limits of
(12) truant   [ ] one who gives tips or bets on a horse
(13) transitory   [ ] transcending experience but not knowledge

(1) trepidation   [   ] commotion; riot; din; violent outburst
(2) tremulous   [   ] sharp; caustic; vigorously articulate; clear-cut
(3) tribulation   [   ] judge's seat; a court; something that decides
(4) truculent   [   ] causing unrest; tempestuous
(5) trove   [   ] agreement to meet; appointed meeting place
(6) tumid, turgid   [   ] affected with trembling or timidity; easily
                          shaken
(7) tutelage   [   ] timorous uncertainty; apprehension; fear
(8) trenchant   [   ] scathingly harsh; self-assertive; belligerent
(9) tribunal   [   ] discovery; valuable collection
(10) turbulent   [   ] swollen, enlarged; bulging; bombastic,
                          pompous
(11) tryst   [   ] distress from oppression; a trying experience
(12) tumult   [   ] guardianship; hegemony; guiding influence

(1) twain   [   ] amount that a tank lacks of being full
(2) ubiquitous   [   ] beyond what is said or proper
(3) tyranny   [   ] a proclamation with force of law; edict
(4) twit   [   ] to howl, wail
(5) unanimous   [   ] last in a series; eventual; utmost
(6) ultimatum   [   ] feeling of resentment; offense; foliage
(7) unctuous   [   ] being everywhere at the same time;
                          constantly encountered
(8) ukase   [   ] two; a couple, pair
(9) ululate   [   ] to subject to light ridicule; taunt
(10) ullage   [   ] a final proposition, condition, or demand
(11) ulterior   [   ] of one mind; having agreement of all
(12) umbrage   [   ] oppressive power
(13) ultimate   [   ] oily; marked by smug, false earnestness

(1) undulating   [   ] not combed or neat; rough; unpolished
(2) unison   [   ] commotion or violent disturbance
(3) upbraid   [   ] to seize and hold without right or by force
(4) tycoon   [   ] a beginner in learning; a novice
(5) unique   [   ] rising and falling like a wave; rolling
(6) uproar   [   ] interest charged far beyond legal rate
(7) usurp   [   ] to make use of
(8) tyro   [   ] homeless person; idle wanderer; rover
(9) unkempt   [   ] of, or characteristic of a city
(10) usury   [   ] harmonious agreement or union
(11) utilize   [   ] find fault with; scold vehemently
(12) vagrant   [   ] businessman of great wealth and power
(13) urban   [   ] being the only one; without equal; very
                          unusual

(1) urbane   [   ] futile; unsuccessful; foolish; conceited
(2) utopia   [   ] an erratic, unpredictable manifestation or action; caprice
(3) vacillate   [   ] to prophesy, predict
(4) vague   [   ] excessively proud; boastful
(5) valedictory   [   ] strength to meet danger with firmness
(6) vacuous   [   ] notably polite; polished; suave
(7) vanquish   [   ] to waver; hesitate in choice of opinions
(8) vagary   [   ] an address or statement of farewell
(9) uxorious   [   ] stupid, inane; devoid of seriousness
(10) vaticinate   [   ] to defeat in battle or contest
(11) vainglorious   [   ] indefinite; unclear; not specific; hazy
(12) valor   [   ] an impractical scheme for social improvement
(13) vain   [   ] excessively fond of or submissive to a wife

(1) valiant   [   ] open to corruption, especially bribery
(2) vaunt   [   ] to lead a passive, effortless existence
(3) vanity   [   ] lowest degree of volition; slight wish
(4) valid   [   ] impassioned; forcibly expressed
(5) variegated   [   ] lacking force; flat, uninteresting
(6) vegetate   [   ] to regard with admiring respect or esteem
(7) vendetta   [   ] inflated pride in oneself; conceit
(8) venal   [   ] having legal force; well-grounded
(9) vend   [   ] to brag; call attention to boastfully
(10) vapid   [   ] varied; having different colors
(11) vehement   [   ] having strength of spirit; courageous
(12) velleity   [   ] prolonged feud with bitter hostility
(13) venerate   [   ] to sell, hawk, peddle

(1) venial   [   ] being in fact the thing named; authentic
(2) vengeance   [   ] the place of a jury and trial
(3) verbatim   [   ] wordy; given to or impaired by wordiness
(4) vent   [   ] to establish the truth, accuracy, or reality of
(5) veracity   [   ] probability; statement apparently true
(6) verdant   [   ] forgivable, pardonable, excusable
(7) venue   [   ] the finding or decision of a jury; judgment
(8) veritable   [   ] of a substandard language
(9) verisimilitude [   ] punishment in retaliation; retribution
(10) verify   [   ] to give vigorous or emotional expression to
(11) verbose   [   ] green in color, experience, or judgment
(12) verdict   [   ] truthfulness; something true; truth
(13) vernacular   [   ] in the exact words; word for word

QUIZ

1. A fund raiser is most likely to solicit a:
(a) tout   (b) tyro   (c) tycoon   (d) vagrant

2. A private investigator should be astute and assiduous in the field of:
(a) tectonics   (b) surrealism   (c) tutelage   (d) surveillance

3. On a first date or job interview, it is wise to appear:
(a) unctuous   (b) urbane   (c) unkempt   (d) tremulous

4. A restaurant owner wishes to hire a maître d' who is noted for his:
(a) tact   (b) trysts   (c) umbrage   (d) vernacular

5. A club prefers its next new member to be:
(a) surly   (b) taciturn   (c) valiant   (d) truculent

6. At a retirement ceremony people come to ~ the guest of honor:
(a) taint   (b) taunt   (c) upbraid   (d) venerate

7. An exercise class prefers an instructor who is:
(a) torpid   (b) svelte   (c) vague   (d) timorous

8. An audience likes a speaker who:
(a) titillates   (b) vents   (c) ululates   (d) tergiversates

9. The hikers want their leader to be a person characterized by his/her:
(a) vanity   (b) temerity   (c) valor   (d) trepidation

10. You wish to hire a contractor who can be characterized by his/her:
(a) theories   (b) veracity   (c) vendettas   (d) vagaries

BONUS QUIZ

The etymology word and old meaning are given. Enter a word derived from each set.

ETYMOLOGY	OLD MEANING	WORD
ME surmisen	to accuse	
MF sur- + monter	on, upon + to mount	
Fr sur- + réalism	over, above + realism	
L surrogare	to choose in place of another; substitute	
Fr surveiller	to watch over	
Gk syntithenai	to put together	
L tacitus	silent, quiet; unmentioned	
L tactus	touch, handling; sense of touch	
L tangere	to touch, handle	
L tenere	to hold, keep; occupy	
L temptare	to feel, test by touching; to try	
Gk theorein	to look at	
L transcendere	to pass or climb over; overstep; surpass	
L trepidus	agitated, restless, anxious; alarming	
L tyrannus	ruler, king; despot	
L ulterior	farther, beyond; more remote	
L ultimus	farthest; most remote; the end of; last	
L unus + animus	one + mind	
L unicus	one and only; without equal; very unusual	
L verbum	word	

SEGMENT TEN

ETYMOLOGY	OLD MEANING
WORD	**NEW MEANING**

L ver **vernal**	spring **relating to spring; fresh or new**
L versatilis **versatile**	turning easily; revolving **changing readily; turning with ease** **from one thing to another**
L vertigo **vertiginous**	turning around; dizziness **dizzy; tending to cause dizziness**
Fr verve **verve**	fantasy, caprice; animation **spirit, enthusiasm, vivacity; energy**
L vestigium **vestige**	footstep, footprint; trace, sign **trace of something lost; tiny remaining amount**
Brit vet **vet**	to subject to examination or appraisal **to subject to expert appraisal or correction**
L vetare **veto**	to forbid, prohibit, oppose; protest **to refuse to admit, approve, or assent to**
L vexare **vex**	to shake, trouble, distress, injure, attack **to irritate, annoy, harass; to baffle, puzzle**
L via **via**	road, street, way; passage; method; the right way **by way of; by means of**
Fr vie **viable**	life **capable of existence and development** **as an independent unit**
L vicarius **vicarious**	substituted; substitute, proxy **imagined through the experience of another**
L vicissitudo **vicissitude**	interchange, alternation **a shift of luck, vagary of chance; difficulty**
L vigilare **vigilant**	to remain awake; keep watch **alertly watchful, *esp.* to avoid danger**

SAMPLE SENTENCES

vernal Besides the *vernal* equinox, we get *spring* sunshine, *spring* blossoms, *spring* fever, *spring* practice, and allergies. Everything is *fresh or new*, it seems.

versatile He is a *versatile* athlete. In sports action he is seen as *changing readily* in moves and direction, and even *turning with ease from one sport to another*.

vertiginous Washing the outside windows of say the 66th floor of an office building would be a *vertiginous* experience for most people. Looking down would be *tending to cause dizziness*; it would make most people *dizzy*.

verve The group planning the new annex to the library showed great *verve* upon receipt of the tycoon's large donation. The committee showed *spirit, enthusiasm, energy*, and *vivacity* in its undertaking.

vestige The team of students dug with verve upon finding what was thought to be a *vestige* of an early civilization. It was perhaps a *trace* or *tiny remaining amount*.

vet Before buying a costly item about which you know little, it's a good idea to find an expert to *vet* the object. He or she can *subject* it *to expert appraisal*.

veto If a president does not like a bill sent to him, he can *veto* it; that is, he can *refuse to approve or assent to* it.

vex Sometimes barking dogs would *vex* him late at night, at other times it was the stench of a skunk that seemed to *irritate, annoy, or harass* him while he tried to sleep.

via He arrived in Rio *via* a tortuous route. He got there *by way of* a roundabout way. She gets information *via* the internet, that is, *by means of* the internet.

viable Entrepreneurship and adequate cash made the business a *viable* enterprise. It was then *capable of existence and development as an independent unit*.

vicarious He got a *vicarious* thrill out of watching the star player hitting a home run. His thrill was *imagined through the experience of the star* as if he hit the homer.

vicissitude Through assiduous effort he surmounted the *vicissitudes* one encounters. He overcame the *shifts of luck*, the *vagaries of chance*, the *ups and downs*, and the *difficulties*.

vigilant He was *vigilant* as he led the group through the jungle. He was *alertly watchful, especially to avoid danger*.

ETYMOLOGY	OLD MEANING
WORD	**NEW MEANING**

L vilis	cheap; worthless, poor, mean, common
vile	**morally despicable; repulsive; obnoxious**
L vilis	cheap, worthless, poor, mean, common
vilify	**to slander, defame, malign**
L viliv + pendere	of small worth + to weigh, estimate
vilipend	**contemn; express low opinion of; disparage**
L vindicare	to lay claim to; avenge
vindicate	**to confirm; justify; defend**
L vindicta	defense; revenge, punishment
vindictive	**disposed to seek revenge; vengeful; spiteful**
L virago	heroine, warrior maid
virago	**a loud overbearing woman; termagant**
L virilis	male; manly, brave, bold
virile	**energetic, vigorous; masculine; forceful**
L virtus	strength, worth, virtue
virtual	**being such in effect but not actual**
L virtus	strength, worth, virtue
virtuoso	**savant; one skilled in fine arts, esp. music**
L virus	slime, poison
virulent	**able to overcome bodily defensive mechanisms; very poisonous; objectionably harsh**
L visus	sight; a sight, vision
visage	**the face or countenance of a person**
Fr vis-à-vis	*lit.,* face to face
vis-à-vis	**face to face with; in relation to; as compared with**
L visceratio	public distribution of meat
visceral	**instinctive; emotionally elemental; earthy**

SAMPLE SENTENCES

vile He was expelled from the school for *vile* behavior. His actions were morally *despicable, repulsive,* and *obnoxious.*

vilify If some people can't win the battle of ideas, they find it expedient to *vilify* their opponents, that is, to *slander, defame,* or *malign* them.

vilipend It is bad form to *vilipend* the deeds or accomplishments of a competitor. To *express a low opinion of* what he has achieved is not kind.

vindicate To persevere when at the moment everything looks abject will often *vindicate* one's hopes. To hang in there against all odds may *confirm* or *justify* one's sanguine convictions.

vindictive A driver barely aced out another car for the last available parking space. The other driver became *vindictive* in a fit of parking-lot rage. He was *disposed to seek revenge;* he was *vengeful* and *spiteful* as he vilified the first driver.

virago The local people tended to eschew the neighborhood *virago;* they regarded the *loud, overbearing termagant* with apprehension.

virile It takes a versatile and *virile* athlete to perform a tour de force. To do that requires an *energetic* and *vigorous* competitor, or true jock.

virtual While the insouciant appointee was the titular head of the group, the virile athlete was the *virtual* leader. He was *in effect the leader but not the actual* one.

virtuoso The violin tyro got a vicarious thrill out of watching the *virtuoso* play. If only he could emulate the *one skilled in music,* or, the *savant!*

virulent Fortunately she was not infected by a *virulent* organism, that is, one *able to overcome the bodily defense mechanisms* or an *extremely poisonous* one.

visage The defendant had an ominous feeling as he studied the *visage* of each juror as he or she filed in. The *face or countenance* of each one terrified him.

vis-à-vis The discussion was about oil exploration *vis-à-vis* the environment, that is, one *in relation to* the other. Also discussed was the relative amount of freedom in a democratic society *vis-à-vis* a statist one, that is, *as compared with* statism.

visceral Even scholarly, analytical types can be quite partisan and *visceral* at athletic contests, especially football and basketball games. They can be very *instinctive, emotionally elemental,* and downright *earthy.*

ETYMOLOGY	OLD MEANING
WORD	**NEW MEANING**
L visus	sight; a sight, vision
visualize	**to see or form a mental image of**
L vita	life; livelihood; way of life
vital	**of the utmost importance; essential**
L vitium	fault, flaw, defect
vitiate	**to make defective, impair; spoil; weaken; make faulty by adding something that impairs**
L vitis + E culture	vine, vine branch + culture
viticulture	**the cultivation or culture of grapes**
L vitreus	glass, glassy
vitriolic	**caustic; virulent of feeling or speech**
L vituperare	to find fault with; disparage
vituperate	**to censure abusively; berate; to scold harshly**
L vivax	long-lived, lasting
vivacious	**lively in temper or conduct**
L vivere	to live, be alive; enjoy life
vivid	**producing distinct mental images; acting clearly and vigorously**
L vivus	alive, living
vivify	**endue with life, animate; impart vitality to**
OE fyxe	*fem. of* fox
vixen	**a shrewish ill-tempered woman**
L vociferari	to cry out loud; shout
vociferous	**marked by vehement insistent outcry**
MF vogue	act of rowing, course, fashion
vogue	**popularity; one that is in fashion at the time**
L vacuus	empty, wanting; vacant; free from
void	**containing nothing; vain, useless; null**

SAMPLE SENTENCES

visualize He tried to *visualize* the dénouement if everything went according to his plans. He tried to *see or form a mental image of* the outcome if all went well.

vital Unlike the repairman, it is *vital* to the salesman to be on time for an appointment. Never keep a customer waiting! It is *of the utmost importance* to him to be on time.

vitiate Addiction to television or video games can *vitiate* the educational process. Too much distraction can *impair, weaken,* or *make defective* attempts to educate.

viticulture Some tycoons, seeking a change of pace or lifestyle, take up *viticulture*, or the *cultivation of grapes*.

vitriolic The op-ed pages of many newspapers contain frequent *vitriolic* letters or columns. They are *caustic*, or *virulent of feeling*.

vituperate It is generally not good policy for a coach to *vituperate* a player in front of the team. There are better ways to deal with someone than to *scold harshly, censure abusively*, or *berate* him or her publicly.

vivacious If a committee is formed on short notice, having a *vivacious* member is vital. A person *lively in temper or conduct* is advantageous to have on it, provided he or she is not too officious.

vivid She described the scene in such *vivid* detail that several people were vicariously "there." Her depiction was clearly *producing distinct mental images.*

vivify The contented, quiet crowd, resting on the grassy slope while watching a baseball game, was suddenly *vivified* when the sprinkling system came on unexpectedly. The water *animated* the people, *endued them with life, imparted vitality to* them as they scattered.

vixen She was a true *vixen*, i.e., a *shrewish ill-tempered woman.*

vociferous The crowd became *vociferous* over the referee's bad call against the home team. The reaction was *marked by vehement insistent outcry.*

vogue Body piercing, tattoos, and wearing baseball caps backward, were in *vogue* for a while. Each was *one that was in fashion at the time.*

void His prolix answer to the question was *void* of pith. His answer was *vain, useless,* and *containing nothing.*

ETYMOLOGY	OLD MEANING
WORD	**NEW MEANING**

L volo | to wish, want; be willing; to will
volition | **a choice or decision made; the power of choosing; the exercise of the will**

L volubilis | spinning, revolving; fickle; fluent (in speech)
voluble | **characterized by ready speech; glib; fluent**

L voluptas | pleasure, delight, enjoyment
voluptuous | **full of delight; luxurious, sensuous**

L vorare | to swallow, devour
voracious | **having a huge appetite; excessively eager**

L votum | vow, prayer; wish, longing
votary | **devoted admirer; worshiper; staunch advocate**

L vocare | to call, summon; to call, name
vouch | **to prove, substantiate; verify; give evidence**

ME vouchen + sauf | to vouch + safe
vouchsafe | **to grant as a privilege or special favor; allow, permit**

L votum | vow, prayer; wish, longing
vow | **solemn promise or binding assertion**

Fr voyeur | *Lit.,* one who sees
voyeur | **a peeping tom; an unduly prying observer**

L vulgus | mass of the people; mob, crowd; rabble, herd
vulgar | **vernacular; plebeian; coarse; gross; common ostentatious, pretentious, vain**

L vulnus | wound, injury; damage
vulnerable | **open to attack or damage; assailable**

of imitative origin woff | to yelp
waffle | **talk foolishly; to equivocate**

ONF waif | lost, unclaimed
waif | **a stray person, *esp.,* a homeless child**

SAMPLE SENTENCES

volition The highly voracious trencherman, of his own *volition,* passed the potatoes to the one next to him before helping himself, saying, "After you." The eager eater, by the *exercise of* his *choice*, allowed the other guest to help herself first.

voluble Two *voluble* people in the audience can annoy those around them. People who are *characterized by quick and ready speech* disrupt other people's attention.

voluptuous The interior designer gave the room an exotic and *voluptuous* aura. She made it one *full of delight, luxurious,* and of a somewhat *sensuous* quality.

voracious After the game, the *voracious* players of the winning team poured into the diner. They were *having huge appetites* and *excessively eager* to eat.

votary The nominee was happy to see thousands of *votaries* cheering him. They were the *devoted admirers* and *staunch advocates* whose support candidates cherish.

vouch The chauffeur, gatekeeper, gardener, butler, maid, and cook, can all *vouch* for his whereabouts at the time of the murder. Each can *substantiate* or *verify* it.

vouchsafe The police agreed to *vouchsafe* safety for the gunman in exchange for his surrender and his willingness to testify about the mob. The police decided to *grant* this deal *as a privilege or special favor* when he had no other choice.

vow A group of resolute freshmen made a *vow* never to lose to a rival team. Their *solemn promise*, or *binding assertion,* held up. They were known since as The *Vow* Boys.

voyeur A crepitation in the bushes led to the arrest of a *voyeur*. At the police station he was booked as a *peeping tom*, or an *unduly prying observer*.

vulgar Poorly educated people communicate with each other using *vulgar* speech, that is, in *vernacular* or *plebeian* terms. Also, a person can make a *vulgar* display of wealth or power; he or she can be *ostentatious, pretentious*, or *vain* about it.

vulnerable A person walking alone in a large city is *vulnerable* to pickpockets or gangs, that is, *assailable* or *open to attack*. Also, one who accuses is *vulnerable* to recriminations.

waffle If a person does not wish to commit himself too soon, he will *waffle* in his answers to questions. He will either *talk foolishly* or *equivocate*.

waif The kindly couple took home a *waif,* cleaned him up, fed him, even bought him some new clothes, before reporting him as a *homeless child*.

ETYMOLOGY	OLD MEANING
WORD	**NEW MEANING**

ONF waif
waive
lost, unclaimed
relinquish voluntarily; forgo; postpone

OE wan
wan
dark, livid; wanting, deficient
sickly, pallid; lacking vitality; languid

Ger wandern + lust
wanderlust
to wander + desire
strong longing for wandering

L vanus
wane
empty, idle, useless; vain; unreliable
to dwindle; dim; flow out, ebb; abate, decline

OE wan + teon
wanton
deficient + to tow
inhumane; unrestrained; brutally insolent

L vereri
wary
to fear, be afraid; to revere, respect
cautious in detecting and escaping danger

ME wey + faren
wayfarer
way + to go
a traveler esp. on foot; a transient patron

ME awayward
wayward
turned away
ungovernable; opposite to what is desired

OE wel
weal
well
a sound, healthy, or prosperous state

L volvere
welter
to roll, roll along
turmoil; a chaotic mass or jumble

OHG wenten
wend
to turn
to direct one's course; proceed on (one's way)

ME wight
whit
creature, thing, bit
the smallest part or particle imaginable; bit

L vannus
winnow
winnowing fan
remove; to separate good and bad elements (often used with *out*)

SAMPLE SENTENCES

waive He decided to *waive* his final year of eligibility in college in order to turn pro. It was his decision to *forgo* his final year, to *voluntarily relinquish* it.

wan She appeared *wan* in the locker room after the match. The coaches suggested that she see a doctor because of her *sickly* and *pallid* appearance.

wanderlust After weeks of tedious and quotidian travail, it is natural to have a case of *wanderlust*. A *strong longing for wandering* naturally follows such an ordeal.

wane Her interest in horses began to *wane* at seventeen, when she got a car, a job, and a boyfriend. Her equine interests started to *dwindle*, or, *decline*.

wanton Episodes of *wanton* destruction or killing are more frightening than planned vandalism or premeditated murder cases. Such *inhumane* acts and *unrestrained* brutality are vagaries of twisted minds.

wary Just as animals are *wary* of the presence of predators, people must be *cautious in detecting and escaping danger* in the vicissitudes of life.

wayfarer A steady, regular patron of a country inn does not know if the stranger is a *wayfarer* or a newcomer who plans to stay. He might be a *transient patron*.

wayward The astute twin went off to Penn State, but the *wayward* one was bound for the state pen. He was *ungovernable* and *opposite to what is desired.*

weal Many politicians claim to represent the will of the people, which in itself is a vague concept. The perspicacious one will promote the *weal* of the people, that is, the *sound, healthy, or prosperous state* of the people.

welter Just before going on vacation, the beleaguered accountant was faced with a last-minute *welter* of paperwork that needed attention. It was a *chaotic mass or jumble.*

wend Having descried an old friend at the reunion, he tried to *wend* his way through the crowd toward him. It was not easy to *direct his course* through the happy throng.

whit He did not care a *whit* about the vapid discussion between two voluble passengers just behind him. He was not one *bit* interested, not the *smallest part imaginable.*

winnow It should not be difficult to *winnow* out the bad elements from the good ones, provided they are not inextricably bound. Ordinarily one should be able to *remove* them, or *separate good and bad elements.*

ETYMOLOGY	OLD MEANING
WORD	**NEW MEANING**
OE wynn	joy
winsome	**pleasing, engaging because of childlike charm; cheerful**
OE witan	to know
wiseacre	**a pretender to knowledge or cleverness; smart aleck**
L vae	woe!, alas!
woeful	**grievous; bringing misfortune; bad or serious**
ME wonen	to dwell, be used to
wont	**habitual way of doing; use; habit**
OE wrath	angry
wrath	**strong vengeful anger or indignation**
OE writhan	to twist
wrest	**to gain with difficulty by or as if by force**
Gk rhoikos	crooked
wry	**cleverly humorous, often ironically or grimly**
ME yoman	young man, attendant
yeoman	**of laborious effort and great usefulness**
E *dial* yokel	green woodpecker
yokel	**naïve or gullible inhabitant of a rural area or small town**
Gk zelos	emulation, jealousy
zealot	**a fanatical partisan; vigorous supporter**

SAMPLE SENTENCES

winsome Her *winsome* nature caused her great uncle, a nabob, to will everything to her instead of to his fraternity. Her *pleasing, cheerful,* and *engaging childlike* charm convinced him to change his will.

wiseacre The levity of the *wiseacre* was not appreciated by the other members of the jury. The *pretender to cleverness* was ill-suited to consider a murder case.

woeful Some freshmen arrive on campus with *woeful* lack of preparation for college-level work. More must be done to ameliorate this *bad or serious* situation.

wont He took a crepuscular post-prandial stroll, as was his *wont.* It was his daily *habit* or *custom.*

wrath People try not to incur the *wrath* of the neighborhood virago. No one wants to arouse her *strong vengeful anger* or *indignation.*

wrest He tried *with difficulty to gain control* of the hose *by force,* but his efforts were in vain.

wry Some lost hikers, out of food, were pondering their fate of no dinner, when one of them suggested, with a *wry* smile, calling room service. It was a *grimly humorous* remark.

yeoman One of the hikers single-handedly caught several fish, cleaned them, built a fire, and cooked them—a real *yeoman* job. His feat of providing the desideratum was *of laborious effort and great usefulness.*

yokel The suave salesman tried to convince a local *yokel* to buy a complete cosmetics line to sell to friends and neighbors. Fortunately, his city cousin recognized a "pyramid scheme" and saved the *naïve and gullible inhabitant of a small town* from disaster.

zealot There is an enormous difference between an insouciant observer and a *zealot* at a football game or political rally. The former is light-hearted and unconcerned, while the latter is a *fanatical partisan,* or *vigorous supporter.*

QUIZ

Match the following words with their meanings:

(1) vernal   [   ] alertly watchful, *esp.* to avoid danger

(2) verve   [   ] trace of something lost; tiny remaining amount

(3) vet   [   ] to irritate, annoy, harass; to baffle, puzzle

(4) versatile   [   ] by way of; by means of

(5) viable   [   ] imagined through the experience of another

(6) vicissitude   [   ] spirit, enthusiasm, vivacity; energy

(7) veto   [   ] to subject to expert appraisal or correction

(8) vertiginous   [   ] changing readily; turning with ease from one thing to another

(9) vicarious   [   ] relating to spring; fresh or new

(10) vestige   [   ] a shift of luck, vagary of chance; difficulty

(11) vigilant   [   ] capable of existence and development as an independent unit

(12) vex   [   ] to refuse to admit, approve, or assent to

(13) via   [   ] dizzy; tending to cause dizziness

(1) vile   [   ] energetic, vigorous; masculine; forceful

(2) vilify   [   ] to confirm; justify; defend

(3) virago   [   ] a savant; one skilled in fine arts, esp. music

(4) virtual   [   ] instinctive; emotionally elemental; earthy

(5) virulent   [   ] morally despicable; obnoxious; repulsive

(6) vindicate   [   ] to contemn; express low opinion of; disparage

(7) virtuoso   [   ] a shrewish ill-tempered woman

(8) vis-à-vis   [   ] disposed to seek revenge; vengeful; spiteful

(9) virile   [   ] able to overcome bodily defenses; objectionably harsh

(10) vilipend   [   ] to slander, defame, malign

(11) vixen   [   ] a loud overbearing woman; termagant

(12) visceral   [   ] being such in effect but not actual

(13) vindictive   [   ] face to face with; in relation to; as compared with

(1) vital   [ ] caustic; virulent of feeling or speech
(2) visualize   [ ] to make defective; make faulty by adding
                               something bad
(3) visage   [ ] the cultivation or culture of grapes
(4) vitriolic   [ ] producing distinct mental images; acting
                               clearly and vigorously
(5) vivacious   [ ] containing nothing; vain, useless; null
(6) vitiate   [ ] endue with life, animate; impart vitality to
(7) vogue   [ ] the face or countenance of a person
(8) vociferous   [ ] of the utmost importance; essential
(9) vituperate   [ ] to see or form a mental image of
(10) void   [ ] lively in temper or conduct
(11) viticulture   [ ] popularity; that which is in fashion at the time
(12) vivify   [ ] to censure abusively; berate; scold harshly
(13) vivid   [ ] marked by vehement insistent outcry

(1) voluble   [ ] having a huge appetite; excessively eager
(2) votary   [ ] a peeping tom; an unduly prying observer
(3) vouch   [ ] to talk foolishly; to equivocate
(4) volition   [ ] a solemn promise or binding assertion
(5) voluptuous   [ ] vernacular; plebeian; coarse; ostentatious;
                               common; vain
(6) waif   [ ] devoted admirer; worshiper; staunch
                               advocate
(7) vouchsafe   [ ] to prove, substantiate; verify; give evidence
(8) voracious   [ ] full of delight; luxurious, sensuous
(9) voyeur   [ ] a traveler esp. on foot; a transient patron
(10) vow   [ ] a choice; power of choosing; exercise of the will
(11) vulgar   [ ] characterized by ready speech; glib; fluent
(12) waffle   [ ] to grant as a privilege or special favor;
                               allow, permit

(13) wayfarer   [ ] a stray person, esp. a homeless child
  (1) vulnerable   [ ] inhumane; unrestrained; brutally insolent
  (2) waive   [ ] to dwindle; to dim; flow out, ebb; abate,
                             decline
  (3) wanderlust   [ ] a sound, healthy, or prosperous state
  (4) wan   [ ] ungovernable; opposite to what is desired
  (5) wend   [ ] remove; to separate good from bad elements
  (6) weal   [ ] turmoil; a chaotic mass or jumble
  (7) wanton   [ ] cautious in detecting and escaping danger
  (8) wane   [ ] to gain with difficulty by force or as if by force
  (9) welter   [ ] strong longing for wandering
  (10) wayward   [ ] open to attack or damage; assailable
  (11) winnow   [ ] to direct one's course; proceed on (one's way)
  (12) wary   [ ] sickly, pallid; lacking vitality; languid
  (13) wrest   [ ] relinquish voluntarily; forgo; postpone

  (1) winsome   [ ] grievous; bringing misfortune; bad or serious
  (2) wont   [ ] the smallest part or particle imaginable; bit
  (3) wiseacre   [ ] naïve or gullible inhabitant of a rural area
or small town
  (4) wry   [ ] of laborious effort and great usefulness
  (5) wrath   [ ] habitual way of doing; use; habit
  (6) yokel   [ ] a fanatical partisan; vigorous supporter
  (7) woeful   [ ] cleverly humorous, often ironically or grimly
  (8) whit   [ ] strong vengeful anger or indignation
  (9) zealot   [ ] a pretender to knowledge or cleverness;
                             smart aleck
  (10) yeoman   [ ] pleasing; engaging because of childlike
                             charm; cheerful

QUIZ

1. On a long airplane ride one would prefer to sit next to a:
(a) virago   (b) wiseacre   (c) virtuoso   (d) zealot

2. The owner of a viticulture product hopes that the judges have come to:
(a) vilipend   (b) vet   (c) waive   (d) waffle

3. A vixen is probably:
(a) versatile   (b) voluptuous   (c) winsome   (d) vitriolic

4. Which kind of qualities do the hikers want in their leader?
(a) yeoman   (b) voracious   (c) voluble   (d) vociferous

5. A large department store seeks to hire a purchasing agent who knows how to:
(a) vex   (b) vituperate   (c) winnow   (d) vilify

6. The person most likely to have binoculars in an upstairs dormitory room is a:
(a) yokel   (b) voyeur   (c) waif   (d) wayfarer

7. Most people would prefer a neighbor who is:
(a) vile   (b) vindictive   (c) vivacious   (d) wanton

8. The person for whom the police would vouchsafe his safety for information is likely:
(a) wry   (b) wayward   (c) wan   (d) visceral

9. The team wants a coach known for his:
(a) visage   (b) vicissitudes   (c) verve   (d) wanderlust

10. A votary is usually:
(a) virulent   (b) vigilant   (c) wary   (d) virile

REVIEW QUIZ

Match these words with their meanings:

(1) problematic   [   ] factual; dull, unimaginative; suitable for the everyday world

(2) reconcile   [   ] make a return for, repay; get even, avenge

(3) provincial   [   ] complex; worldly-wise; finely aware; experienced

(4) transcend   [   ] to confirm; justify; defend

(5) prosaic   [   ] negligent, careless; inattentive, lax

(6) requite   [   ] restore to friendship; settle, resolve

(7) vindicate   [   ] to seize and hold without right or by force

(8) sophisticated   [   ] puzzling; not definite or settled; doubtful

(9) usurp   [   ] rise above or go beyond the limits of

(10) remiss   [   ] limited in outlook; lacking polish of the city; unsophisticated

(1) subtle   [   ] having false look of truth; having deceptive attractiveness

(2) savoir-faire   [   ] cutting wit or irony often used to expose vice

(3) seminal   [   ] elusive; hard to distinguish; crafty; operating insidiously

(4) tacit   [   ] of individual bias or personal views

(5) raison d'être   [   ] practice of producing fantastic imagery in the arts

(6) specious   [   ] contributing the seeds of later development; creative, original

(7) sine qua non   [   ] reason or justification for existence

(8) subjective   [   ] expressed or implied without words or speech

(9) satire   [   ] knowledge of just what to do (socially)

(10) surrealism   [   ] an absolutely essential thing

(1) salient   [   ] transcending experience but not knowledge

(2) vagary   [   ] rebirth, revival (of an activity)

(3) tenable   [   ] capable of existence and development as an independent unit

(4) vis-à-vis   [   ] last in a series; eventual; utmost

(5) synthesis   [   ] erratic, unpredictable manifestation or action; caprice

(6) transcendent   [   ] standing out conspicuously; striking

(7) transcendental   [   ] face to face with; in relation to; as compared with

(8) renaissance   [   ] combination of parts so as to form a whole

(9) viable   [   ] maintainable; defensible, reasonable

(10) ultimate   [   ] exceeding usual limits; beyond comprehension

PRONUNCIATION GUIDE

aborigine	a bor IJ eh nee
acquiesce	a kwee ess
aegis	ee juss
antuthesis	an TI the suss
apogee	apo JEE
ascetic	a SET ik
bailiwick	bale ee wik
baroque	ba ROKE
beleaguered	be LEE gord
blasé	blah ZAY
cabal	kuh bal
cachet	ka SHAY
cacophony	kak uh fun ee
caprice	ka PREES
captious	kapshus
cavil	kavel
charlatan	sharl a tun
chimerical	k-eye MER e kel
clandestine	klan DEST in
comity	kah met ee
comptroller	kun TRO ler
concierge	cone syerzh
connoisseur	kahn uh ser
contemn	kon TEM
coup	koo
coup de grace	koo de GRAHSS
coup d' état	koo day TAH
crème de la crème	krem de la krem
debut	day byoo
deign	dane
déjà vu	day zhah VUE (for the *ue* sound, shape lips for saying oo and try to say ee)
demur	duh mer
dénouement	day noo maw(n)
de rigueur	duh ree grrr
descant	des cant
desuetude	des wi tood
dichotomous	die kaht uh muss

dilettante	dill uh tahnt
disheveled	dish ev uhld
disparate	dis par ut
distrait	di stray
doughty	dawt ee
éclat	ay klah
élan	ay lahn
eleemosynary	el ee mahs n airy
ennui	awn wee
entrepreneur	awn truh preh neur (for the *eu* sound, shape lips for saying *o* and try to say *ee*)
epitome	ee pit uh mee
euphemism	you fuh miz um
facetious	fuh see shus
faux pas	fo pah
fief	feef
flaccid	flak sud
flagrant	flay grunt
gauche	go-sh
genre	zhawn ruh
gnome	nome
habitué	huh bich uh way
hegemony	hi jem uh nee
hors d'oeuvre	or derv
hyperbole	high purr buh lee
idyll	eyed (u)l
imbroglio	im brol yo
inchoate	in ko ut *or* in kuh wait
indict	in dite
ingenue	an zhuh new
insouciant	in soo see unt
inveigle	in vay gul
irrefragable	ir ref ruh guh bul
jihad	ji hod
joie de vivre	zhwad uh veev r(uh)
junta	hoon tah
lachrymose	lak ruhm ose
liaison	lee uh zon
lieu	loo
machiavellian	mak ee uh vel ee un
machinate	mak uh nate
maître d'	may truh dee

maladroit	mal uh droit
malaise	muh laze
mélange	may law(n)zh
minutia	muh n(y)oo sh(ee) uh
moiety	moy ut ee
naïve	nah eve
noetic	no et ik
obloquy	ahb luh kwee
onomatopoeia	ahn uh nat uh pee(y)uh
panache	puh nahsh
panegyric	pan uh jir ik
paradigm	par uh dime
patent	payt nt
patois	pah twah
pedagogy	ped uh gojee
per se	purr say
plethora	pleth uh ruh
poignant	poy nyant
potpourri	po poor ee
pourboire	poorb wahr
prima facie	pry muh fay shuh
prix fixe	pree feeks
prosaic	pro zay ik
puerile	pyoo er ul
pulchritude	pul kruh t(y)ood
Pyrrhic	pir ik
queue	kyoo
raison d'être	ray zo(n) detr(uh)
rapport	ruh por
recherché	ruh share shay
redoubtable	ri dout uh bul
repartee	rep ahr tay *or* rep er tee
repertoire	rep ur twar
requite	ri kwite
respite	res put
riposte	ri post
risqué	ri skay
sang-froid	saw(n) frwah
savoir-faire	sav wahr fair
schism	siz um *or* skiz um
sciolism	s-eye uh liz um
séance	say awn(t)s
segue	seg way *or* say gway

sine qua non	sin i kwa nahn
sobriquet	so bri kay
soi-disant	swahd ee zaw(n)
soigné	swan yay
soirée	swah ray
sommelier	sum ul yay
sous-chef	soo shef
subpoena	suh pee nah
surfeit	ser fet
sycophant	sik uh funt
tenebrous	ten uh bruss
tergiversate	ter jiv er sate
touché	too shay
variegated	vair ee uh gated
velleity	ve lee uht ee
viv-à-vis	veez uh vee
wanderlust	vahn der lust (the German W has the English V sound)
wont	wawnt *or* wont
zealot	zel ut